Pay for Performance

Evaluating Performance Appraisal and Merit Pay

George T. Milkovich and Alexandra K. Wigdor, Editors,
with Renae F. Broderick and Anne S. Mavor

Committee on Performance Appraisal for Merit Pay
Commission on Behavioral and Social Sciences and Education
National Research Council

NATIONAL ACADEMY PRESS
Washington, D.C. 1991

Pay for performance

itution Avenue, N.W.   ●   Washington, D.C. 20418

is report was approved by the Governing Board
or the National Research Council, whose members are drawn from the councils of the National
Academy of Sciences, the National Academy of Engineering, and the Institute of Medicine. The
members of the committee responsible for the report were chosen for their special competences
and with regard for appropriate balance.

This report has been reviewed by a group other than the authors according to procedures
approved by a Report Review Committee consisting of members of the National Academy of
Sciences, the National Academy of Engineering, and the Institute of Medicine.

This project was supported by the U.S. Office of Personnel Management.

Library of Congress Cataloging-in-Publication Data

Pay for performance : evaluating performance appraisal and merit pay /
    George T. Milkovich and Alexandra K. Wigdor, editors, with Renae
    F. Broderick and Anne S. Mavor ; Committee on Performance Appraisal
    for Merit Pay, Commission on Behavioral and Social Sciences and
    Education, National Research Council.
       p.   cm.
    Includes bibliographical references (p.   ) and index.
    ISBN 0-309-04427-8
    1. Compensation management—United States. 2. Merit pay—United
States. 3. Employees—United States—Rating of. 4. United States—
Officials and employees—Salaries, etc. 5. United States—
Officials and employees—Rating of. I. Milkovich, George T.
II. Wigdor, Alexandra K. III. National Research Council (U.S.).
Committee on Performance Appraisal for Merit Pay.
HF5549.5.C67P38   1991
658.3'125—dc20

90-25995
CIP

Printed in the United States of America

First Printing, January 1991
Second Printing, December 1991

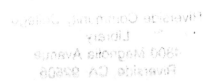

COMMITTEE ON PERFORMANCE APPRAISAL FOR MERIT PAY

Contents

The National Academy of Sciences is a private, nonprofit, self-perpetuating society of distinguished scholars engaged in scientific and engineering research, dedicated to the furtherance of science and technology and to their use for the general welfare. Upon the authority of the charter granted to it by the Congress in 1863, the Academy has a mandate that requires it to advise the federal government on scientific and technical matters. Dr. Frank Press is president of the National Academy of Sciences.

The National Academy of Engineering was established in 1964, under the charter of the National Academy of Sciences, as a parallel organization of outstanding engineers. It is autonomous in its administration and in the selection of its members, sharing with the National Academy of Sciences the responsibility for advising the federal government. The National Academy of Engineering also sponsors engineering programs aimed at meeting national needs, encourages education and research, and recognizes the superior achievements of engineers. Dr. Robert M. White is president of the National Academy of Engineering.

The Institute of Medicine was established in 1970 by the National Academy of Sciences to secure the services of eminent members of appropriate professions in the examination of policy matters pertaining to the health of the public. The Institute acts under the responsibility given to the National Academy of Sciences by its congressional charter to be an adviser to the federal government and, upon its own initiative, to identify issues of medical care, research, and education. Dr. Samuel O. Thier is president of the Institute of Medicine.

The National Research Council was organized by the National Academy of Sciences in 1916 to associate the broad community of science and technology with the Academy's purposes of furthering knowledge and advising the federal government. Functioning in accordance with general policies determined by the Academy, the Council has become the principal operating agency of both the National Academy of Sciences and the National Academy of Engineering in providing services to the government, the public, and the scientific and engineering communities. The Council is administered jointly by both Academies and the Institute of Medicine. Dr. Frank Press and Dr. Robert M. White are chairman and vice chairman, respectively, of the National Research Council.

Preface

This report is the work of the Committee on Performance Appraisal for Merit Pay, which was established late in 1989 at the request of the Office of Personnel Management. The report analyzes contemporary research on the assessment of job performance and on the effectiveness of performance-based pay systems. It also describes in broad outline the systems adopted by private-sector firms to link pay to performance.

The immediate impetus for the study that produced this report was the schedule for congressional hearings on the reauthorization of the federal Performance Management and Recognition System in the spring of 1991. The director of the Office of Personnel Management was anxious to bring to the policy deliberations whatever knowledge and insight can be gleaned from scientific research and, where research is silent, from the more pragmatic realms of everyday practice in private-sector firms. In preparation for what will be the third major examination of human resource management in the civil service since 1976, she turned to the National Academy of Sciences/National Research Council to provide the needed synthesis of research and practice.

A committee of 12 experts was appointed to conduct the study, and their work was supported by a three-member research staff. As is true of all study committees of the National Research Council, care was taken to ensure that the committee not only met rigorous standards in terms of expertise, but was also balanced with respect to questions of compensation policy, workplace arrangements, and fairness or equity concerns. Each committee and staff member brought a special area of competence to our work—knowledge of private-sector compensation systems, research on performance appraisal, the scholar's understanding of how organizations work, the manager's experience

viii   *PAY FOR PERFORMANCE*

of human resource management in a multinational corporation. Several members offered expertise on the federal bureaucracy, from either personal experience or scholarly interest; likewise a good number had long experience in and intimate knowledge of private-sector firms.

Each member of the committee and staff took an active role, both because there was a very large territory to cover in a short time and because the topic turned out to be extremely compelling. Our habit was to devote a portion of each committee meeting to the discussion of background papers produced by committee and staff members so that we all became conversant with new bodies of research, different research methods, and novel perspectives on performance appraisal and pay-for-performance plans. Many were involved in drafting portions of the final report, all were avid readers and commenters, and as a result this report is a consensus document in the best sense.

In the course of its work, the committee benefited from the contributions of many individuals and organizations. John Bernardin, professor of research at Florida Atlantic University, got us off to a good start by sharing up-to-date and comprehensive bibliographies on performance appraisal and merit pay compiled for a book in progress. Two federal managers' associations made membership surveys on the Performance Management and Recognition System available to us. Representatives of five Fortune 100 companies conferred with the committee on their merit systems. Our thanks go as well to Andrew Klein and Robert Ochsner of Hay Management Consultants and Howard Risher of the Wyatt Company for sharing information and ideas.

We are particularly grateful to the members of a liaison group made up of federal personnel managers that was established to ensure that the committee had access to those who really know and understand the workings of federal personnel and compensation systems. Its members were Donna Beecher, Office of Personnel Management; Frank Cipolla, U.S. Department of Defense; Kathleen H. Connelly, U.S. Department of Agriculture; Agnes D'Alessandro, Department of Defense Dependent Schools; Herbert R. Doggette, Jr., Social Security Administration; Barbara L. Fiss, Office of Personnel Management; Larry K. Goodwin, U.S. Department of Labor; Elizabeth Stroud, National Institute of Science and Technology; Dona Wolf (ex officio), Office of Personnel Management; and Brigitte W. Schay (ex officio), Office of Personnel Management.

Our acknowledgments would not be complete without special thanks to the National Research Council staff members who worked with the committee: Anne Mavor, associate study director, who made valuable contributions throughout the project; Renae Broderick, whose prodigious writing efforts helped us cover more territory than seemed possible; Carolyn Sax, who provided administrative support and kept smiling right down to the end; and our always gracious editor, Christine McShane.

GEORGE T. MILKOVICH, Chair
ALEXANDRA K. WIGDOR, Study Director
Committee on Performance Appraisal for Merit Pay

Pay for Performance

Executive Summary

THE CHARGE

This report reviews the research on performance appraisal and on its use in linking pay to performance. It was written to assist federal policy makers as they undertake a revision of the federal government's system of performance appraisal and merit pay for mid-level managers, called the Performance Management and Recognition System. Specifically, the Committee on Performance Appraisal for Merit Pay was asked by the Office of Personnel Management to review current research on performance appraisal and merit pay and to supplement the research findings with an examination of the practices of private-sector employers. Our investigation expanded beyond a restricted examination of merit pay plans to include pay-for-performance plans more generally, as well as the organizational and institutional conditions under which such plans are believed to operate best.

THE NATURE OF THE EVIDENCE

It is important to note that this study draws on diverse bodies of evidence and information, from research as well as private-sector practice. Because the issues of interest intersect different theories, disciplines, and levels of analysis, it was necessary for us to compare, contrast, and synthesize very different kinds of evidence, which do not address precisely the same issues or even apply the same standards of proof. For that reason, not all the evidence meets the same rigorous standards of scientific proof; we have been careful to identify the type of evidence and the level of confidence we feel it merits.

1

On balance, we believe that a careful piecing together of the many fragmentary kinds of evidence and experiential data gives federal policy makers the best available scientific understanding of performance appraisal as a basis for making personnel decisions and of the effectiveness of using pay to improve performance.

PERFORMANCE APPRAISAL

Performance appraisal has two ostensible goals: to create a measure that accurately assesses the level of a person's performance in a job, and to create an evaluation system that will advance one or more operational functions in an organization. These two goals are represented in the literature by two distinct, yet overlapping, approaches to theory and research. The measurement tradition emphasizes standardization, objective measurement, and psychometric properties. The applied tradition emphasizes the organizational context and the usefulness of performance appraisal for promoting communication, clarifying organizational goals, informing pay-based decisions, and motivating employees.

The Measurement Tradition: Findings

Prior to 1980, most research on performance appraisal was generated from the field of psychometrics. Performance appraisals were viewed in much the same way as tests: they were evaluated against criteria for validity and reliability and freedom from bias; a primary goal of the research was to reduce rating errors. On the basis of evidence in the measurement tradition, the committee presents five major findings:

- Organizations cannot use job analysis and the specification of performance standards to replace managerial judgment; at best such procedures can inform managers and help focus the appraisal process.
- The evidence supports the premise that supervisors are capable of forming reasonably reliable estimates of their employees' overall performance levels. Consistency among raters, however, is not proof of the accuracy of performance appraisal procedures; it can cloak systematic error or systematic bias in valuing performance.
- The accretion of evidence from many types of studies suggests that supervisors, when using appraisal instruments based on well-chosen and clearly defined performance dimensions, can make modestly valid evaluations of employee performance within the terms of psychometric analysis.
- A wide variety of rating scale types (traits, behaviors) and formats (behaviorally anchored, graphic), with varying levels of specificity, exist. Recent reviews of the relevant research suggest that scale types and formats have relatively little impact on psychometric quality, as long as the dimensions to be rated are well chosen and the scale anchors are clearly defined.

- The weight of evidence suggests that the reliability of ratings drops if there are fewer than 3, or more than 9, rating categories. Recent work indicates that there is little to be gained from having more than 5 response categories.

The Applied Tradition: Findings

Researchers in the applied tradition concentrate on the appraisal system and how it functions to serve organizational ends. On the basis of the evidence in the applied tradition, the committee presents two major findings:

- There is some evidence that performance appraisals can motivate employees when the supervisor is trusted and perceived as knowledgable by the employee.
- There is evidence from both laboratory and field studies to support the assumption that the intended use of performance ratings influences results. The most consistent finding is that ratings used to make decisions on pay and promotion are more lenient than ratings used for research purposes or for feedback.

Conclusions

The search for a high degree of precision in measurement does not appear to be economically viable in most applied settings; many believe that there is little to be gained from such a level of precision.

- The committee concludes that federal policy makers would not be well served by a commitment of vast human and financial resources to job analyses and the development of performance appraisal instruments and systems that can meet the strictest challenges of measurement science.
- The committee further concludes that, for most personnel management decisions, including annual pay decisions, the goal of a performance appraisal system should be to support and encourage informed managerial judgment, and not to aspire to the degree of standardization, precision, and empirical support that would be required of, for example, selection tests.

PERFORMANCE-BASED PAY SYSTEMS

The label *pay for performance* covers a broad spectrum of compensation systems that can be clustered under two general categories: merit pay plans and variable pay plans, which include both individual and group incentive plans. Although we set out to examine merit pay plans, we found virtually no research on the effects of merit pay systems, and so extended the scope of our review to include pay-for-performance and compensation research generally. We also realized that the effects of performance-based pay plans on individual and organizational performance cannot be easily disentangled from the broader context of an organization's structures, management strategies, and personnel systems. We present below our major finding and conclusion:

Finding

- The evidence on the effects of pay for performance, pieced together from research, theory, clinical studies, and surveys of practice, suggests that, in certain circumstances, variable pay plans produce positive effects on individual job performance. The evidence is insufficient, however, to determine conclusively whether merit pay can enhance individual performance or to allow us to make comparative statements about merit and variable pay plans.

Conclusion

- On the basis of analogy from the research and theory on variable pay plans, the committee concludes that merit pay can have positive effects on individual job performance. These effects may be attenuated by the facts that, in many merit plans, increases are not always clearly linked to employee performance, agreement on the evaluation of performance does not always exist, and increases are not always viewed as meaningful. However, we believe the direction of effects is nonetheless toward enhanced performance.

THE IMPORTANCE OF ORGANIZATIONAL CONTEXT

Our reviews of performance appraisal and merit pay research and practice indicate that their success or failure is substantially influenced by the organizational context in which they are embedded. Research on performance appraisal now encompasses a broader set of organizational factors; research on pay now stresses the importance of the firm's personnel system, its structure and managerial styles, and its strategic goals. Both researchers and managers acknowledge the influence of environmental conditions on organizational decisions about adopting and implementing performance appraisal, merit pay, and variable pay plans.

Three kinds of contextual factors are important. First, the strongest evidence on context has to do with the fit between a firm's appraisal and pay systems and the nature of the work it does. A firm's technologies and their pace of change influence the way the firm defines its jobs and people's performance in them. Second, there is a growing body of case studies that suggest the need for congruence between an organization's structure and culture and its appraisal and pay policies. Third, factors external to the firm, such as the economic climate, the presence of unions, and legal or political forces exerted by external constituencies can affect the success of its evaluation and pay systems.

IMPLICATIONS FOR FEDERAL POLICY

What the committee has learned in its wide-ranging study of performance appraisal and pay for performance in the private sector does not provide a blueprint for linking pay to performance in the federal sector, or even any specific remedy for what ails the federal system. The study does, however, offer some key considerations for the director of the Office of Personnel Management and other federal policy makers as they rethink the Personnel Management and Recognition System.

• Although performance appraisal ratings can influence many personnel decisions, and thus care in developing and using performance appraisal systems is warranted, there is no obvious technical solution to the performance management problems facing the federal government. The pursuit of further psychometric sophistication in the federal performance appraisal system is unlikely to contribute to enhanced individual or organizational performance.

• Where performance appraisal is viewed as most successful in the private sector, it is firmly embedded in a context that provides incentives to managers to use the ratings as the organization intends. These incentives include managerial flexibility or discretion in rewarding top performers and in dismissing those who continually perform below standards. When performance ratings are used to distribute pay, as in a merit plan, the size of the merit pay offered allows managers to differentiate outstanding performers from good and poor performers—providing them with incentives to differentiate.

• In order to motivate employees and provide incentives for them to perform, a merit plan (or any pay-for-performance plan) must communicate performance goals that employees understand and consider "doable," link pay and performance consistently, and provide payouts that employees see as meaningful. Although we cannot generalize about which pay-for-performance plans work best—especially for the federal government, with its considerable organizational and work force diversity—we do suggest that federal policy makers consider decentralizing the design and implementation of many personnel programs, including appraisal and merit pay programs, and supporting careful, controlled pilot studies of a variety of pay-for-performance systems in a variety of agencies.

• Although ensuring fair and equitable treatment for all employees is an important objective in any personnel system, the heavily legalistic environment surrounding the federal civil service has led to dependence on formal procedures that ultimately provide powerful disincentives for managers to use the system as the organization intends. Such safeguards are meant to ensure equity, but it is not clear that their proliferation provides federal employees with a greater sense of equity than their private-sector counterparts. Effective reform may well need to be part of a more fundamental rethinking of past notions of political neutrality, merit, and their protection in the civil service.

- Our entire review has stressed the importance of viewing performance appraisal and merit pay as embedded within broader pay, personnel, management, and organizational contexts. The larger changes suggested by an analysis of context can be costly, but we suggest that making programmatic changes to the Performance Management and Recognition System in isolation is unlikely to enhance employee acceptance of the system or improve individual and organizational effectiveness and, in the long run, may prove no less costly.

The final chapter of the report summarizes in greater detail the committee's findings and conclusions.

1

Introduction

At the request of the Office of Personnel Management (OPM), the Committee on Performance Appraisal for Merit Pay was established in the National Research Council, the working arm of the National Academy of Sciences, to assist federal policy makers as they undertake a revision of the federal government's system of performance appraisal for merit pay. Specifically, the committee was asked to review current scientific knowledge about performance appraisal and the use of performance appraisal in merit pay allocations, especially for managers and professionals. We were also asked to examine performance appraisal and pay-for-performance practices of private-sector employers and, if possible, to recommend models that federal policy makers might consider in revising the merit pay plans currently in place.

The committee's investigation, begun in January 1990, has of necessity been fast-paced; the legislative mandate for the federal government's current merit pay program, called the Performance Management and Recognition System (PMRS), is coming to an end, and widespread dissatisfaction with the system has brought about the third major examination of merit pay procedures in the federal government since 1978. There is renewed public debate over such issues as the pay gap between federal employees and their private-sector equivalents, the waning prestige of federal employment, employees' dissatisfaction over merit pay, training and development opportunities, performance appraisal, and union opposition to merit pay (Perry and Porter, 1982; Merit Systems Protection Board, 1988; Havemann, 1990).

During this time, too, private-sector compensation systems have been the topic of a great deal of attention. In particular, adoption of "pay-for-performance plans" has been highly publicized as a means for improving U.S. labor productivity. Public policy analysts have been exploring the impact that pay-for-performance plans might have on labor productivity in preparation for recommendations about national tax incentives for these plans (Blinder, 1990). Their interest was sparked by theoretical arguments that certain types of pay-for-performance plans (particularly profit sharing) might stabilize national employment without inflation (Weitzman, 1984). Many employers, having already trimmed their work forces, are exploring the potential of these plans for making their remaining work forces more productive while continuing labor cost control (TPF&C/Towers Perrin, 1990; Wallace, 1990). Consultants, academics, and employee advocate groups (including unions) are also beginning to seriously discuss the effects of pay-for-performance plans—and to explicate the potential downsides, in particular the high costs of organizational changes required for effective plan implementation, and the equity problems associated with asking employees to place a larger part of their pay at risk when they have little control over many factors influencing organizational outcomes. In other words, it is a time of reassessment in the private as well as the public sector.

Amidst widespread dissatisfaction with PMRS and the current celebration of pay-for-performance plans in the private sector, the question presents itself: Are there things to be learned from private-sector organizations that can improve human resource management in the federal bureaucracy? The government has many sources of advice on these issues, from blue ribbon groups like the Volker Commission, to federal employee associations, to a variety of consulting firms. Our task was to supply one perspective to the coming policy deliberations—that is, to bring together the best scientific evidence and knowledge derived from practice on performance appraisal and on linking pay to performance.

PAY FOR PERFORMANCE: A FIELD GUIDE

The Performance Management and Recognition System, like its predecessor the Merit Pay System, is a system of merit pay. This represents one genre in a broad spectrum of pay plans that bear the label *pay for performance*.

There is an important difference in the use of the terms *merit pay* and *pay for performance* by the government and the private sector that should be noted. In government parlance, *merit pay* and *pay for performance* tend to be used synonymously. In the private sector, it has become common in recent years to distinguish between the two. The term *pay for performance* is closely associated with the drive to make U.S. business more competitive; private-sector analysts use it to designate systems in which a sizable portion of a worker's annual compensation is partly or wholly dependent on the overall success of the firm, rather than on individual performance. Variable pay plans include profit-sharing and gainsharing plans of all descriptions.

In this report, we have chosen to use *pay for performance* generically to denote any compensation system that links pay and performance. Subsumed under that rubric are two distinct types of compensation systems: merit pay and variable pay.

Merit Pay

In merit pay plans, the locus of attention is individual performance. As one element in a meritocratic personnel system, merit pay plans link pay level or annual pay increases, at least in part, to how well the incumbent has performed on the job. Just as ability or skill is intended to rule employee selection in such systems, so the quality of each employee's job performance should, according to merit principles, be recognized through the pay system.

The most recent survey data indicates that 94 to 95 percent of private-sector companies have merit pay programs to provide individual pay increases to their eligible ("exempt") employees, and 71 percent of companies have merit pay programs for their nonunion hourly employees. Performance appraisal is at the heart of merit pay plans. Although there are numerous variations in systems labeled as merit plans, some sort of rating of each employee's performance precedes compensation decisions. In some firms, the rating of performance is informal, with very little committed to paper; some firms undertake detailed job analyses, which provide the underpinnings of the appraisal system; a majority of firms appear to base the performance appraisal on a set of goals established by the supervisor or negotiated by the supervisor and the employee.

The committee's review of private-sector compensation surveys suggests that the dominant model of merit pay plan can be characterized roughly by the characteristics listed below. They are discussed in more detail in the chapters of the report:

1. The plan is tied to a management-by-objectives system of performance appraisal for exempt employees and a work standards or graphic rating scale performance appraisal for salaried nonexempt employees.

2. The typical appraisal summary format has four to five levels of performance.

3. Pay increases are administered via a matrix (merit grid) that uses both an employee's performance level and position in the pay grade to determine a prespecified percentage increase (or increase range) in base salary. The other components of the merit grid are the organization's pay increase budget and the time between pay increases.

4. Merit increases usually are permanent increases, which are added into an individual employee's salary and are funded from a central compensation group. These funds are allocated to divisions or units as a percentage of payroll. Because merit pay increases are added to base pay and compounded into the earning stream, they can result in significant changes in pay levels over time.

5. In contrast to federal practice, most companies do not communicate their pay structure or average pay increase percentages to their employees. Many communicate all increases given to an individual employee as merit-related. (This is in contrast to communicating increases as general, seniority, and merit combined.)

6. The merit plan tends not to be accompanied by formal "due process" mechanisms for appealing unfavorable appraisals (unless an employee is covered by a collective bargaining contract), but it may be accompanied by informal protections.

7. It is characterized by limited training of the managers who administer the plan and virtually no training of employees covered by the plan in the performance appraisal process.

8. It is associated with relatively modest annual increases that are added into base salary. The Hay Company reported an average increase in 1989 of approximately 5 percent with a range of 2 to 12 percent.

Variable Pay

Variable pay plans fall into two categories, individual incentive plans and group plans. Piece work and sales commissions are the best known of the individual incentive plans. In recent years, a variety of group incentive plans have come into vogue. These pay plans are specifically designed to influence aggregate organization measures. They typically tie a significant portion of annual pay to organization-wide productivity or financial outcomes. For example, profit-sharing plans or equity plans link individual employee's pay to the overall fortunes of the firm as measured by some indicator of its financial health. Hence, one important distinction between merit pay plans and group incentive plans is that the latter base compensation decisions in whole or in part on organizational performance rather than individual performance. In addition, the portion of pay associated with the variable plans is usually a one-time payment, not an increase to base pay.

Variable pay plans have taken on an importance in our report that they would otherwise not have had, given our mandate to look at performance appraisal and merit pay, because virtually all of the research on the effectiveness of pay-for-performance plans deals with these compensation plans. The enormous difficulty of trying to link individual performance in most jobs to productivity (the grand exception being manufacturing piece work and sales) may have turned the attention of social scientists to system-level indicators of effectiveness, and hence to the variable pay incentive plans.

Advocates of variable pay plans argue that their implementation can help to revitalize organizations and control labor costs. They believe that the link between pay and organization outcomes is likely to motivate employees to work more creatively, smarter, harder, and as teams to achieve these outcomes. If the outcomes are achieved, they fund sizable payouts; if they are not, employee pay in addition to base would be small or nonexistent. In either case, the ratio of labor costs to total costs stays about the same, making the organization more competitive.

The actual impact these variable pay plans can have on an organization's productivity and financial competitiveness is just beginning to be seriously examined. But it is a fact that, by design, these plans either require system changes—such as redefinition of jobs, creation of teams, and changes in work methods and standards as is typical in gainsharing programs—or provide powerful monetary incentives to employees to experiment with changes in their own jobs (individual bonus and profit-sharing plans.) There is disagreement about whether it is the broader system changes (Deming, 1986; Beer et al., 1990), or the presence of the variable pay plans themselves (Schuster, 1984a) that are most critical to improvements in organizational effectiveness. No one denies, however, that broader system or context changes will influence the impact of a variable pay plan on an organization's performance.

The potential of variable pay plans to control labor costs and improve an organization's effectiveness has received the most attention in the press. Since such plans pay out only when they are funded by improvements in system measures, making a larger portion of a lower-level employee's pay dependent on them shifts management risks to those who have little say in management decisions. The potential abuse of employee equity with these plans is thus high.

ISSUES

With this background in mind, the committee has interpreted its charge from OPM as requiring the investigation of whether and under what conditions performance appraisal and merit pay can assist the federal government in regulating labor costs, managing performance, and fostering employee equity. We interpreted the managing of performance to include improvements in organization effectiveness, thus requiring some examination of variable pay plans and comparisons of their intended effects with those of merit pay plans. We broadly defined employee equity to include, not only employee perceptions of the legitimacy and fairness of performance appraisal and merit plans, but also incentives for managers to administer these plans equitably. By defining expectations for performance appraisal and merit pay plans in this way, our investigation was of necessity expanded beyond a restricted examination of the plans themselves to include an exploration of organizational and institutional conditions under which the plans are believed to operate best.

We ask the reader to keep in mind several caveats in reviewing this report. Most important is that there is no commonly accepted theory of pay for performance or performance appraisal. Therefore, we have to consider the proposition that pay-for-performance plans affect performance, given certain conditions, via the examination of research designed to answer somewhat different questions—primarily related to alternative theories of motivation, such as goal setting, expectancy, equity, and agency theories. Given the diverse and fragmentary nature of the available evidence, we rely on the convergence of interdisciplinary findings and professional expertise to offer insights—not proofs—to federal personnel managers.

We also lay no claim to making a comprehensive survey of all performance appraisal, merit pay, and variable pay plan methods and designs used in the private and public sectors today. We focused on predominant private-sector trends and examined only five "model" private-sector organizations more intensively.

Our committee's charge did not include an examination of the "total quality" or "organization revitalization" movements often associated with the implementation of variable pay plans; consequently, we draw no conclusions about them. Our review in this area was conducted to contrast the intended effects of these plans with those of performance appraisal and merit pay.

PLAN OF THE REPORT

We have organized our investigation of the issues in the following way. In Chapter 2 we begin by describing the history of merit principles in the federal government, the Civil Service Reform Act of 1978, and government workers' reactions to the act and its implementation. In Chapter 3 we summarize the nature of the evidence we examined and the implications of our decision to use convergent findings to generate the report's conclusions. In Chapter 4 we turn to a review of the psychometric properties and usability of performance appraisal instruments. In Chapter 5 we review the evidence from economics, sociology, psychology, and practice in the private sector on whether performance appraisal and pay-for-performance plans can affect labor costs, performance, and equity and what determinants or conditions are likely to influence these effects. In Chapter 6 we summarize trends in the design, administration, and use of performance appraisal and pay-for-performance plans—with a focus on the practices of five organizations that have a long history of satisfactory performance appraisal and merit pay programs. Our review then moves in Chapter 7 to a brief examination of the broader organizational and institutional context in which these plans are embedded to highlight other influential factors in both private- and public-sector organizations. In the final chapter we present our findings and conclusions for federal policy makers.

2
The History of
Civil Service Reform

For nearly 50 years, the federal government has operated with some performance appraisal procedures whose purposes have been to strengthen the link between pay and performance. Since 1978, specific pay-for-performance programs have been in place for mid- and upper-level federal managers. There is general agreement that these programs have not attained the desired objectives; their troubled history has included a series of adjustments and changes, differing levels of financial support, and little evidence of success. The ability to demonstrate a link between performance and pay—to both the employee and the public—remains problematic for the federal government.

As we approach the year 2000, the questions surrounding pay for performance in the public sector have assumed a new importance—indeed, a central position—in new proposals for federal civil service reform. Many of the questions raised in the debate about the 1978 reforms are being raised again. Why is this so? What accounts for the intransigence of problems surrounding effective pay-for-performance systems in the federal government? Is there evidence to support the validity of the effort, despite its problems?

In the federal government, the answers to these questions are made more difficult by the nature of the federal personnel system, by the intermingling of issues of political responsiveness with issues of effective management, and by the need to marshal very scarce resources for a policy activity that never ranks very high on the national agenda. It is our intent in this chapter to provide the historical and contextual information necessary to understand these constraints and their implications for performance-based pay schemes in the federal government.

THE CONTEXT AND THEORY OF CIVIL SERVICE REFORM

The Civil Service Reform Act of 1978 and its outcomes can be best understood within the context of the historic and institutional influences that led to its creation. Two aspects of this context are discussed here: (1) the historical evolution of merit principles in the federal sector and (2) the evolution of federal management strategy.

Evolution of the Federal Merit System

The passage of the Pendleton Act in 1883 marked the origin of the merit system and the classified civil service in the federal government. This landmark legislation was intended to create a system that not only protected federal employment and employees from the excesses of partisan politics, but also provided the federal government with a competent and politically neutral work force. The Pendleton Act contained three fundamental merit principles: fair and open competition for federal jobs, admission to the competitive service only on the basis of neutral examination, and protection of those in the service from political influence and coercion (Ingraham and Rosenbloom, 1990). At the time the Pendleton Act was passed, the spoils system had thoroughly politicized the federal service. The electoral success of candidates supported by civil service leagues in the 1882 congressional elections put civil service reform on the national agenda. Public attention to the problem was galvanized by the assassination of President Garfield by a demented campaign worker who sought federal office.

Despite the clarity of the problem and fairly widespread consensus on the need for action, the reality of the Pendleton Act was modest: only 10 percent of the federal work force at that time was covered by the initial legislation. Congress granted the President authority to add federal employees to the merit system as he saw fit. Van Riper (1958) notes that the act permitted ". . . an orderly retreat of parties from their prerogatives of plunder. . . ."

The Pendleton Act created decentralized Boards of Examiners to administer entrance examinations. Unlike the British system, which had served as the ideal for many reformers, the U.S. system did not rely on elite formal academic training. Rather, it emphasized common sense, practical information, and general skills. Neutrality was a primary value in the merit system. One observer wrote that ". . . the civil service was like a hammer or a saw; it would do nothing at all by itself, but it would serve any purpose, wise or unwise, good or bad, to which any user put it" (Kaufman, 1954).

The fledgling merit system, intended to remove politics from the federal service, developed and grew as politics allowed. Its history is not, therefore, one of coherent development; it reflects shifting and changing political priorities and cycles. Both Congress and the President retained a keen interest in patronage issues long after passage of the Pendleton Act. President McKinley, for example, included 1,700 new positions in the classified service, but exempted 9,000 that had previously been covered (Skrowonek, 1982). Congress excluded entire agencies from the classified service. In the New Deal years, Franklin D. Roosevelt successfully urged that the new agencies created be staffed by persons with policy expertise congruent with the President's interests, rather than the "neutral competents" produced by the civil service examination system. When Roosevelt assumed the presidency in 1932, about 80 percent of federal employees were in the competitive civil service. By 1936, that proportion was about 60 percent (U.S. Civil Service Commission, 1974).

Of equal significance, new provisions and procedures were layered on incrementally as the system grew. Until the time of the New Deal, most of the new provisions, with their emphasis on economy, efficiency, and standardization, reflected the scientific management principles in vogue in the business and public administration communities. One such effort was the creation, in 1912, of the skeleton of a performance appraisal system. In that year, the Civil Service Commission (CSC) was directed by Congress to establish a uniform efficiency rating system for all federal agencies. The commission established a Division of Efficiency to carry out this task (U.S. Civil Service Commission, 1974).

The passage of the Classification Act in 1923 represented a more ambitious attempt to bring scientific management principles to the federal merit system. In words that have a familiar ring, the Joint Commission on Reclassification of Salaries had concluded in 1920 that the United States government, the largest employer in the world, needed a "modern classification of positions to serve as a basis for just standardization of compensation" (quoted in Gerber, 1988). The Classification Act established in law the principle of nationally uniform compensation levels, providing for the standard classification of duties and responsibilities by occupations and positions with salary levels assigned to the resulting positions.

In addition, the Classification Act legalized the principle of rank in position. Unlike the more common European practice of rank in person, the U.S. system provided that wages and/or salary for each position were to be determined solely by the position description and the qualifications for it, not by the personal qualifications of the person who would occupy the position. Finally, the Classification Act of 1923 led to the creation of a standard rating scale, which required supervisors to rate employees for each "service rendered." This was the first government-wide effort to describe job requirements and employee performance.

The Classification Act came under almost immediate attack. Evaluations in 1929 and 1935 found major problems with the classification system that it established. Primary criticisms focused on the extremely narrow and complex nature of the classification process. The 1935 inquiry noted, for example, that "what seem to be the most trifling differences in function or difficulty are formally recognized and duly defined . . ." (Wilmerding, 1935). Nonetheless, the Classification Act was not reformed until 1949, following the release of the first Hoover Commission report. That report had been blunt about the state of the federal merit system:

Probably no problem in the management of the Government is more important than that of obtaining a capable and conscientious body of public servants. Unfortunately, personnel practices in the federal government give little room for optimism that these needs are being met.

Although not universally considered an improvement (see Gerber, 1988), the Classification Act of 1949 simplified the classification system by reducing the number of pay categories from five to two: the 18-grade General Schedule for white-collar employees and another schedule for blue-collar employees. It created the "supergrade" system (GS 16–18), which was in many ways the predecessor of the Senior Executive Service (a version of which had been recommended by the first Hoover Commission). The 1949 act also marked an early point on what has come to be a centralization-decentralization cycle in federal personnel policy, when it delegated some classification authority back to the agencies (Ingraham and Rosenbloom, 1990). Classification of managerial jobs in the federal merit system has not been reformed since the passage of the 1949 act.

There have been other initiatives related to performance appraisal, however, that are worth noting in this brief overview. The Ramspeck Act created efficiency rating boards of review in 1940. The uniform efficiency rating system that resulted was in place until 1950, when it was replaced by the provisions of the Performance Rating Act of 1950. The Performance Rating Act required agencies to establish a performance appraisal system with the prior approval of the CSC. This system established three summary rating levels: "Outstanding," "Satisfactory," and "Unsatisfactory." Employees were permitted to appeal ratings to a statutory board of three members consisting of representatives from the agency, one selected by employees, and a chairperson from the CSC. The act required a 90-day written warning of an unsatisfactory rating and opportunity for employees to improve.

Financial incentives to accompany performance were introduced by the Incentive Awards Act of 1954, which authorized recognition and cash payments for superior accomplishment, suggestions, inventions, or other personal efforts. The intent of the Incentive Awards Act was reinforced by passage of the Salary Reform Act of 1962. This act established an "acceptable level of competence" determination for granting General Schedule within-grade increases. Within-grade increases could be withheld when performance dropped below an acceptable level, but the agency was obliged to prove that performance was not acceptable. Employees were permitted to appeal to both the agency and, if denied at the agency level, to the Civil Service Commission. The Salary Reform

Act also authorized an additional step increase or quality step increase (QSI) for "high-quality performance." This system guided performance management in the federal government until the passage of Civil Service Reform Act in 1978.

These incremental changes and 100 years' accretion of laws and procedures have resulted in an enormously complex federal merit system. Entrance to the system can now be through "competitive," "noncompetitive," or "excepted" authority. Veterans have preference in hiring and, until 1953, did not have to pass an examination to be considered for employment. There are direct hiring authorities for hard-to-hire and specialized occupations, for outstanding scholars, for returned Peace Corps Volunteers, for Vietnam-era veterans, and many others. Examinations are not required in these cases. There is extensive use of temporary and part-time hiring; there are 35 different ways to hire temporary employees alone (for additional discussion, see Ingraham and Rosenbloom, 1990).

At the time the Civil Service Reform Act of 1978 was passed, over 6,000 pages of civil service law, procedure, and regulation governed the federal merit system. There were at least 30 different pay systems in place; there were over 900 occupations in the federal civil service. This complexity was one of the problems addressed by civil service reform; the history and development of the complexity profoundly influenced the reform's potential for success. It is significant that the 1978 act *did not* for the most part address basic entrance procedures, the classification system, or the basic federal compensation systems. In many respects, it reformed at the fringes of the system.

Federal Management Strategies and Civil Service Reform

Federal management strategies provide another set of influences that were important to the context and development of civil service reform. At least since 1937, when the Brownlow Commission issued its report on the Executive Office of the President, appropriate theories and structures for federal management have been debated by academic analysts and elected officials. The remarkable growth of government in Franklin Roosevelt's first term created a management problem unknown to previous presidents. The steady expansion of the civil service system in the years prior to the New Deal had created a large permanent bureaucracy founded on the neutral competence model. President Roosevelt wished, however, to have bureaucracies and bureaucrats more responsive to his policy agenda.

The Brownlow recommendations, while continuing to argue for neutral competence, firmly articulated the concept of the President as manager of the executive branch. The Federal Reorganization Act of 1939 was the cornerstone for the development of that presidential capacity. An emphasis on structural change, such as that found in President Carter's Reorganization Plan No. 2, has been a consistent emphasis of most presidential management initiatives since that time.

The evolution of those management efforts has been characterized by a shift from the basic question "How should government be managed?" to a new query: "*Who* should manage government?" The answer from the White House has been consistent and predictable: the President (and therefore *not* the Congress) is responsible for the coordination and direction of the executive branch. This view has grown more explicit in the past 25 years. Particularly since the Nixon presidency, it has been an aggressively pursued ideal.

There have been three basic components to the presidential control strategies that have emerged: structural change, governmental reorganization, and larger numbers of political appointees to direct the career bureaucracy (see Ingraham, 1987; Pfiffner, 1988). President Nixon essentially created the model for future presidents by combining all of these strategies into an overall vision of presidential management. The "administrative presidency" that he attempted to create was cut short by Watergate; the lessons from it, however, were quickly adopted by the presidents who followed. (For a complete discussion of the Nixon strategy, see Nathan, 1983.)

President Carter, for example, agreed with the intent of the administrative presidency—better management and coordination and greater accountability of the career bureaucracy to elected officials. Carter, in fact, used the Schedule C political appointment authority more heavily than had any president since its creation in 1956 (Ingraham, 1987). The Civil Service Reform Act of 1978 was one part of this larger strategy. Carter's primary interest was in improving the managerial and technical competence of the presidential office; Alan Campbell, Carter's director of the Office of Personnel Management, observed in a 10-year retrospective on the design of the Civil Service Reform Act that its structural changes were intended to work ". . . no matter who was in office" (Campbell, 1988). In retrospect, however, many observers feel that the emergence of the administrative presidency has politicized the bureaucracy and placed the ideal of a politically neutral and protected civil service under stress. This in turn has implications for compensation policy and the efficacy of performance appraisal.

THE CIVIL SERVICE REFORM ACT OF 1978

Civil service reform was central to President Carter's election campaign and he selected an adviser to spearhead the effort shortly after his announcement to seek the office. One of Carter's first acts as President was to create the President's Personnel Management Project (PMP) to assist him and his staff in the design of the promised reform.

The structure of the PMP was purposefully comprehensive: there were nine task forces, an assistant secretary's advisory group, several other more informal advisory groups, and a number of public hearings. From these activities, the

PMP produced a two-volume report of problem analysis and recommendations. The report contained well over 100 specific recommendations for reform; it was released in December 1977. From that report, members of the Inter-Agency Advisory Group drafted the legislation (for a complete discussion of the design, see Ingraham, 1989).

President Carter first introduced the broad outlines of the Civil Service Reform Act in his State of the Union message on January 19, 1978. At that time, he called the reforms "absolutely vital." It was the first time that a U.S. president had included civil service reform among his major legislative proposals. President Carter's ultimate objective, he said, was to create ". . . a government that is efficient, open and truly worthy . . . of understanding and respect."

Carter's reforms came in two parts. Reorganization Plan No. 2 preceded the actual reform legislation: it abolished the Civil Service Commission and replaced it with the Office of Personnel Management, the Merit Systems Protection Board (including the Office of Special Counsel), and the Federal Labor Relations Authority. The Office of Personnel Management would oversee the human resource management activities of the federal government. Those responsibilities would include implementation of the other reforms. The Merit Systems Protection Board would serve as guardian of the merit system and merit principles and as an appeals body for personnel actions brought by federal employees. During congressional consideration of Reorganization Plan No. 2, Carter administration officials argued that the board and the special counsel would protect the merit system from any abuse resulting from reform provisions regarding pay for performance, discipline, or the senior civil service (Vaughn, 1989).

The Civil Service Reform Act itself contained a number of provisions intended to improve the performance of the federal civil service. Major provisions included the creation of the Senior Executive Service, a rank-in-person system for top executives, performance appraisals for all employees, merit pay for middle managers, delegations of specified personnel management authorities to the line agencies, formalization of the federal labor management relations program, and modifications in procedures for dealing with poor performers.

The Senior Executive Service

The Senior Executive Service (SES) was conceived by the designers of the reform as the centerpiece of the Civil Service Reform Act. The Senior Executive Service was a multipurpose reform. Its members were to be the federal government's managerial elite. They were to participate in policy-making activities as well as the management activities reserved for the traditional career civil service. The structure of the SES, and the removal of some civil service protections from its members, also ensured that the link between political executives and senior career managers would be strengthened. The inclusion of some political appointees in the Senior Executive Service itself further emphasized the objective of political responsiveness of the reform. This emphasis on responsiveness to political direction can be read, in the context of pay for performance, as an effort to more closely link individual managerial activity to organizational objectives.

Performance appraisal and pay for performance were important parts of the concept of a Senior Executive Service. The act required the establishment of a performance appraisal system designed to permit the accurate evaluation of performance in any SES position. Performance criteria were to be position-specific and were to identify critical elements of the position. Performance appraisals were intended to encourage excellence in performance by senior executives. They were to provide a basis for performance awards and for promotions and other executive development opportunities, as well as for retention decisions.

SES performance appraisals were to be based on both individual and agency performance, and were to include such factors as improvements in efficiency, productivity, quality of service, cost efficiency, timeliness of performance, and the achievement of equal employment opportunity requirements. SES performance appraisals were required on an annual basis, with performance described according to one of several standard summary ratings. Final appraisals could be made only upon review by an agency-level Performance Review Board, which was required by the act.

The SES pay system included strong pay-for-performance elements. It did not provide for any type of annual pay increases, except the general "comparability" increases. Instead, incentives were offered in the form of awards and bonuses. Thus, the only way for an SES employee to move up in pay is to receive a change in rank to a higher level. The act created two levels of SES awards: Meritorious Executive and Distinguished Executive. Subject to the congressionally mandated limitations, the President would designate career appointees to either of these two ranks. A designation as a Meritorious Executive carried with it a cash award of $10,000; receipt of a Distinguished Executive award provided the recipient with a lump sum award of $20,000. A minimum of a fully successful rating (equivalent to a satisfactory rating) was required for nomination to one of the ranks.

To provide incentives for excellent performance, Congress also created a bonus system for SES incumbents. Fully satisfactory performance was established as a baseline for eligibility for bonuses. The number of bonuses awarded within any agency was limited to less than 50 percent of the SES positions allocated to the agency. The act further stipulated that individual awards could not exceed 20 percent of the career appointee's rate of basic pay.

Performance Appraisal

The general logic of the SES performance appraisal provisions was applied to non-SES employees as well. But while the primary emphasis of the SES system appeared to be on linking individual performance to organizational objectives, the program for mid-level managers (GS 13–15 supervisors and management officials) emphasized the link between individual performance and pay. Under the performance appraisal provisions of the Civil Service Reform Act, each agency was required to develop performance appraisal systems that "(1) provide for periodic appraisals of job performance of employees; (2) encourage employee participation in establishing performance standards; and (3) use the results of performance appraisals as a basis for training, rewarding, reassigning, promoting, reducing in grade, retaining and removing employees." These systems were required to meet criteria prescribed in OPM regulations and were required to be implemented by October 1, 1981, three years after the act was passed. The designers of the act believed that this time lag would permit the SES reforms to become institutionalized before other pay-for-performance reforms were implemented.

The OPM regulations were intended to develop job-related and objective performance appraisal systems consistent with the dictates of the statute. The regulations required that performance standards and critical elements be consistent with the duties and responsibilities covered in an employee's position description. OPM guidance suggested that performance standards be based on a job analysis to identify critical elements of a position, and that each agency develop a method for evaluating its system to ensure its validity.

This identification of critical elements of a job was a key component of the performance appraisal reforms. A critical element was defined by OPM as "any requirement of the job which is sufficiently important that inadequate performance of it outweighs acceptable or better performance in other aspects of the job." Employees who failed to perform at a satisfactory level on a critical element were to be subject to performance-based actions, including dismissal if performance did not improve.

Merit Pay

The Civil Service Reform Act also created a new pay-for-performance system for middle managers, GS 13–15. The merit pay provisions represented a break from the long tradition of essentially automatic salary increases based on length of service. Borrowing from private-sector practices, Title V of the Civil Service Reform Act contained provisions intended to motivate mid-level managers to perform at higher levels by tying performance to financial incentives.

The Merit Pay System (MPS), which became mandatory on October 1,

1981, altered the pattern of annual incremental adjustments to salary. Under MPS, employees received only half of the comparability adjustment automatically. The nonautomatic portion of the comparability adjustment, plus the within-grade and quality step increase monies were pooled and distributed according to performance ratings (U.S. Office of Personnel Management, 1981). A crucial point is that the legislation provided that the Merit Pay System would be revenue neutral, so that if some employees benefited, others would of necessity be less well off than they would have been under the General Schedule.

Federal Employee Expectations About the Reform

It is difficult to identify the attitudes of federal employees toward performance appraisal, pay for performance, and other reform provisions prior to the Civil Service Reform Act because of the lack of baseline data. One survey, conducted by Lynn and Vaden, questioned a random sample of about 2,000 federal employees about their attitudes toward the reform in general. Lynn and Vaden (1979) reported fairly high levels of skepticism and distrust about the reforms, including frequent references to them as a "return to the spoils system."

The most comprehensive source of data about employee attitudes prior to reform is the Federal Employee Attitude Survey, Phase I (FEAS I), conducted by OPM. This survey, which preceded implementation of the act but followed its passage, yielded about 14,500 responses. A second survey, which used the same questionnaire, was administered to GS 13–15 employees at four Navy research and development laboratories. The Navy survey produced 2,068 valid responses. Data from these surveys are reproduced in Tables 2-1 and 2-2.

Based on the Federal Employee Attitude Survey, Nigro (1982) reported that employee responses revealed a widespread lack of satisfaction with the pre-1978 performance appraisal system. Nigro argued that this created a favorable climate for the performance appraisal reforms and that a system that promoted the developmental aspects of performance appraisal stood a good chance of success. He found that employees considered performance appraisals consequential, but that there were problems with the critical link between performance and reward. He concluded that there was potentially large support for the merit pay provisions of the Civil Service Reform Act. Significantly, Nigro also noted that trust in the organization was relatively low and could create serious problems if implementation was conducted in a top-down fashion. From the same data, Bann and Johnson (1984:79) concluded that ". . . there was neither a wholesale rejection of the old system, nor unqualified support. . . . [T]hose most dissatisfied with the old system of performance appraisal . . . were also unhappy with their jobs and with the organization in general. . . . Those who were relatively content with the old performance appraisal system also placed more trust in the organization and demonstrated greater satisfaction with their jobs."

It is also important to note, though with less empirical foundation, that the political rhetoric surrounding the Civil Service Reform Act influenced expectations and created both positive and negative perspectives on its likely outcomes. The positive expectations are reflected in the objectives for performance appraisal and merit pay contained in OPM's evaluation plan:

Performance Appraisal

Short-Term Objectives:

1. Increase employees' understanding of performance standards.
2. Ensure effective appraisal of performance.
3. Ensure equitable appraisal of performance.
4. Link performance to personnel actions through the performance appraisal process.

Long-Term Objectives:

1. Increase the effectiveness of employees and supervisors.
2. Improve the quality of federal working life.
3. Contribute to agency productivity.

Merit Pay

Short-Term Objectives:

1. Relate pay to performance.
2. Provide flexibility in recognizing and rewarding good performance with cash awards.

Long-Term Objectives:

1. Motivate merit pay employees by making pay increases contingent on performance; clarifying job expectations, i.e., defining goals and objectives, increasing competition for recognition and rewards.
2. Improve the productivity, timeliness, and quality of work in the federal government through better management and more effective programs.

The negative expectations resulted from the punitive tone—the "bureaucrat bashing," as it came to be known—that accompanied descriptions of the need for reform. New whistleblower protections were said to be necessary to ferret out waste and fraud; greater managerial flexibilities were needed to eliminate deadwood; performance appraisal and pay for performance were necessary because federal employees were not productive and did not measure up to their private-sector counterparts (see Ingraham and Barrilleaux, 1983). This, coupled with the characterization of the federal bureaucracy as the "giant Washington

TABLE 2-1 Opinions of Federal Workers Concerning Established Performance Appraisal Systems and Pay-Performance Linkages (1979)

	Response (%)					
	OPM Survey Respondents			Navy R&D Laboratories Respondents		
Item	D	DK	A	D	DK	A
Performance appraisals do influence personnel actions taken in this organization.	22	17	62	28	24	48
This organization considers performance appraisal to be an important part of a supervisor's duties.	18	21	61	25	29	45
My job performance is carefully evaluated by my supervisor.	22	19	59	23	23	53
The standards used to evaluate my performance have been fair and objective.	17	26	57	15	32	52
My performance rating presents a fair and accurate picture of my actual job performance.	26	23	51	30	27	44
In the past I have been aware of what standards have been used to evaluate my performance.	23	16	61	27	20	54

Did your last performance appraisal
help you to:

	NH	SH	H	NH	SH	H
a. Assess you strengths and weaknesses?	44	33	23	47	33	19
b. Establish a plan for training and development?	60	25	15	60	27	13
c. Determine your contribution to the organization?	42	30	27	47	29	24
d. Improve your performance?	46	31	23	51	31	18

	NI	SI	I	NI	SI	I
How important is the quality of your performance in determining your pay?*	15	23	62	16	29	53
How important should the quality of your job performance be in determining your pay?*	0	4	95	0	3	97

*GS 13+ only.

D = Disagree; DK = Don't Know; A = Agree; NH = Not Helpful; SH = Somewhat Helpful; H = Helpful; NI = Not Important; SI = Somewhat Important; I = Important

TABLE 2-2 Federal Employee Trust and Confidence in Their Organizations, Supervisors, and Coworkers

	Response (%)					
	OPM Survey Respondents			Navy R&D Laboratories Respondents		
Item	D	DK	A	D	DK	A
When changes are made in this organization, the employees usually lose out in the end.	46	19	36	38	25	38
Employees here feel you can't trust this organization.	41	16	42	36	21	44
My supervisor deals with subordinates well.	24	15	61	23	16	62
I have confidence and trust in my coworkers.	10	9	82	7	8	85

D = Disagree; DK = Don't Know; A = Agree

Due to rounding, row percentages may not add up to 100 percent.

marshmallow" during the presidential campaign created a negative aura around the reforms for many federal employees.

Finally, it is significant that employee expectations about the reform were strongly influenced by the federal pay situation. For senior career managers, the link of federal employees' pay to that of members of Congress created a situation in which they had "topped out," that is, reached the top statutory pay level. Many career executives had been at this level for several years prior to the passage of the act. Absent fundamental pay reform, the pay-for-performance provisions in the SES were the *only* means available for escaping the pay cap. In this regard, both the stakes and the expectations were very high.

The Record

The record of the Civil Service Reform Act has been turbulent. The orderly implementation of the act envisioned by the Carter administration was interrupted by the election of Ronald Reagan in 1980. President Reagan was not a supporter of the civil service; cutting back the size and cost of government was high on the Reagan policy agenda. OPM's human resource function was redefined; most planning, evaluation, and research activities were eliminated; the organization was downsized and restructured. Because political control of key components of executive branch agencies was considered critical to policy success, a specifically political role emerged for OPM.

Donald Devine, the director of OPM for the first Reagan term, explicitly espoused the Weberian view of organizations; under his direction, OPM emerged as a political management arm of the White House, rather than an agency concerned with broader human resource management issues (Newland, 1983). The organization was not so overtly political in the second Reagan term, and serious efforts were made to address some of the most pressing federal personnel and management problems. Nonetheless, many of the reforms created by the Civil Service Reform Act had been deferred, eliminated, or redefined. Many observers have noted that the reforms were simply overwhelmed by the dramatically changed political environment in which federal agencies existed in the 1980s.

Pay for performance and performance appraisal were also affected by the turbulence of implementation. The experience of the Senior Executive Service is notable in a number of respects. Because it was the first to be implemented, the SES performance appraisal and bonus system was carefully watched by most federal employees. It did not serve as a positive model.

The first SES payouts occurred in the year following passage of the reform. The first agency to complete the process paid out the full amount allowable under the law; not only was the number who received bonuses considered excessive in the view of Congress and some other external observers, the proportion of Performance Review Board members who themselves received a bonus was much too high. As a result, six months into the implementation of the SES system, Congress altered the provisions of the act. Under the new provisions, the percentage of SES positions in the agency eligible for a bonus was reduced from 50 to 25 percent. OPM, using its rulemaking authority in an effort to demonstrate its good faith to Congress, further lowered that percentage to 20 percent of the total approved positions.

This dramatic change in the SES pay-for-performance system had an immediate and negative impact. Members of the SES, who had viewed the bonus system as an escape from the federal pay cap, were disillusioned with the new system. The formation of the Senior Executive Association to lobby Congress for the interests of the SES was one indicator of the disenchantment and dissatisfaction with the reform very early in the implementation process.

The Merit Pay System

If pay for performance was less than triumphant in the Senior Executive Service, how successful was the Merit Pay System (MPS) in rejuvenating the mid-level managerial work force? Its clearest shortcoming was its failure to establish a demonstrable relationship between pay and performance. This failure is attributable to a variety of causes. One of the chief ones was a lack of adequate funding for merit pay. Agencies were required by law to spend no more on the Merit Pay System than they had under the previous General Schedule system. This problem was exacerbated by implementation difficulties. For example, a dispute between OPM and the General Accounting Office concerning the permissible size of payout led, in September 1981 (one month before payout), to a determination that the OPM formula for calculating the merit pay fund was not in conformance with the statute. The ruling resulted in a modified payout that provided only small differentials among the mid-level managers covered, again undercutting pay-for-performance principles and diminishing the incentives for supervisors to differentiate among employees.

Because the Merit Pay System was not perceived as fair in some fundamental ways, it failed to establish credible links between pay and performance. Managers who performed satisfactorily often found themselves receiving lesser rewards than their nonmanagerial counterparts at grades 13–15, whose pay was set under the General Schedule. The perceptions of employees that nonperformance factors (e.g., the composition of the pay pool) affected payout and that ratings were arbitrarily modified also diminished the effectiveness of the pay-for-performance aspects of the system. Employees in most agencies perceived no greater likelihood that their performance would be recognized with a cash award after the establishment of the Merit Pay System than had previously been the case (U.S. General Accounting Office, 1984).

The reported successes of the Merit Pay System in motivating employees emanated primarily from the performance appraisal requirements of the Civil Service Reform Act. Gaertner and Gaertner (1984) reported that developmental appraisals—those that focused on planning for the coming year and clarifying expectations—were more effective than appraisals that focused only on past performance. However, developmental appraisal strategies were seldom used, and the pay administration role for appraisals tended to undermine this function. In fact, one study reported a significant drop in the organizational commitment of employees who received satisfactory, but not outstanding, ratings (Pearce and Porter, 1986).

The Performance Management and Recognition System

Although the Merit Pay System did not take effect for most federal managers until 1981, it very quickly became apparent that it performed poorly when judged by the objectives established for it. Relief was sought in legislation, introduced in 1984, that proposed the Performance Management and Recognition System (PMRS). PMRS was enacted on November 8, 1984, but the first payout was made retroactive to the fiscal 1984 performance cycle. Retroactive application created a number of short-term implementation problems (U.S. General Accounting Office, 1987).

The drafters of the legislation sought to retain pay-for-performance principles but to eliminate the dysfunctions of the original system. Under PMRS, employees are rated at one of five summary rating levels: two levels below fully successful, fully successful, and two levels above fully successful. The system has three monetary components: (1) employees who are rated fully successful or better are assured of receiving the full general pay or comparability increase. (2) They are also eligible for merit increases, which are equivalent to within-grade increases. The size of the merit increase depends on an employee's position in the pay range and performance rating. (3) In addition to these monies, employees rated fully successful or above also qualify for performance awards or bonuses. Beginning in fiscal 1986, performance awards of no less than 2 percent and no more than 10 percent became mandatory for employees rated two levels above fully successful. Moreover, an agency may give a performance award of up to 20 percent of base salary for unusually outstanding performance. An upper limit of 1.5 percent-of-payroll for all performance awards was placed on agency payout under the system.

PMRS also created Performance Standards Review Boards, modeled after the Performance Review Boards in the Senior Executive Service, to review performance standards within an agency to ensure their validity and to perform other oversight functions. At least half of each board is required to be made up of employees eligible for merit pay. Although the number and functioning of these boards was left to agency discretion, they are required to report annually to the agency head.

Although the evidence is thin, there are some indications that PMRS has functioned better than the Merit Pay System. The Merit Systems Protection Board (MSPB) conducted surveys of employee attitudes at three-year intervals beginning in 1983. The report of the most recent survey (Merit Systems Protection Board, 1990) says that, in 1986 and 1989, 32 and 36 percent, respectively, of the federal employees surveyed believed they would receive more pay for performing better. This represents a substantial increase over the 17 percent of employees surveyed in 1983 who perceived a link between pay and performance and provides an interesting comparison to the Wyatt Company's 1989 report on employee attitudes in private-sector firms that about 28 percent of those surveyed saw a link between their pay and their job performance.

It nevertheless remains true that the conceptual support of pay for performance remains far stronger among federal employees—the report of the 1989 MSPB survey says that 72 percent of respondents endorse the proposition—than their support of existing pay-for-performance systems. Only 42 percent indicated that they would choose to be under a pay-for-performance system if given the choice; about the same proportion of respondents indicated that they would not so choose, many of them citing the shortcomings of the present system as the grounds for their disinclination. The most commonly registered reservations involved (1) the ability and freedom of managers to make meaningful distinctions among levels of performance and (2) the availability of enough money to reward the best performers. The monetary concern coincides with a more general dissatisfaction with pay expressed by 60 percent of respondents to the 1989 MSPB survey.

It is not clear that PMRS has provided the hoped-for motivational stimuli. It is unlikely that pay-for-performance devices such as merit increases, bonuses, and awards would produce performance effects in the context of a deep, generalized dissatisfaction with pay levels of the kind reported in each of the three MSPB surveys. In addition, even though most merit system employees have received performance awards (U.S. Office of Personnel Management, 1989), the General Accounting Office found that 50 percent of the employees surveyed in the first year of PMRS felt the size of the awards was inadequate. Insofar as performance may be affected by the communication of performance standards, the Performance Management and Recognition System appears to be functioning well. Nine out of ten respondents to the 1989 survey said that they understand the performance standards for their jobs.

A somewhat more negative picture of PMRS emerges from informal surveys of their membership conducted recently by two federal managers' associations. Most of the managers responding to the surveys indicated support for the concept of basing pay on performance. Only 3 percent, however, felt that PMRS should be maintained in its current form and approximately 40 percent said that PMRS should be completely abolished. More than 75 percent of the managers indicated that they believed that their ratings were influenced by officials above their supervisors, that their performance evaluations were of little guidance for development purposes, and that insufficient funds have resulted in meaningless performance awards. Given that the current system is viewed as so unfair and ineffective, there is a concern over whether any new pay-for-performance system could function effectively.

The evaluations of PMRS to date have been silent with respect to the influence of PMRS on agency effectiveness. The Merit Systems Protection Board has identified a tentative relationship between turnover and performance ratings that suggests that poor performers are more likely than good performers to leave federal service (Merit Systems Protection Board, 1988). However, no such relationship was found between turnover and performance ratings in an earlier study by the General Services Administration (Perry and Petrakis, 1987).

IMPLICATIONS

This brief account of civil service reform is a record of modest changes and frequently conflicting objectives, accompanied perhaps by unrealistic expectations about the effects of the reforms on the performance and productivity of federal personnel. Neither the Merit Pay System nor the Performance Management and Recognition System has been able to counteract what, since at least the early 1980s, has come to be called the "quiet crisis" in the federal government. That crisis, according to the National Commission on the Public Service and others, is marked by below-market public-sector salaries, an inability to recruit new employees for many federal occupations, an inability to retain seasoned federal managers, and a perceived decline in the overall quality of the federal work force (National Commission on the Public Service, 1990).

The uncompetitiveness of the Civil Service is particularly noticeable in certain fields, for example, law and the scientific and engineering professions. A recent National Research Council report noted that recruitment of scientific and engineering personnel was a problem for the National Institutes of Health, the Environmental Protection Agency, the National Institute of Standards and Technology, the Department of Health and Human Services, the Social Security Administration, and the National Science Foundation, among many others (National Research Council, 1990). However, the overall problem of recruiting and retaining a well-qualified work force is being felt throughout the federal government.

While there is no reason to believe that the present malaise cannot be reversed, there are important tensions between the potential benefits of pay for performance and the reality of the federal personnel and compensation systems. We describe these tensions below.

1. The tension between the principle of neutral competence and pay for performance. We have described the centrality of the principle of neutral competence to the modern civil service. In turning away from the spoils system, the founders of the merit system in the late nineteenth century envisioned federal employees as dispassionate servants to the body politic who, to function properly, needed to be shielded from invidious political influences. Many of the most characteristic elements of the merit system—entry by competitive examination, retention rights, limitations on partisan activities—derive from this vision of neutral competence. Efforts to ensure that political neutrality could be maintained for the career service, however, have created an extremely complex system of constraints that have come to place severe limits on the discretion of career managers, in addition to controlling partisanship. Two outcomes of a merit system built on the concept of neutral competence are directly related to the potential success of pay for performance. First, the managerial constraints and legalistic environment that have come to characterize federal management are antithetical to the managerial discretion necessary for effective pay-for-performance processes (National Academy of Public Administration, 1983). Second, merit pay carries far more meaning in the context of the civil service than in the private sector. The objective of any merit pay system is to relate pay to individual or group contributions to organizational purposes. But in the public sector, the possible impact of political influence on ratings of individual performance will inevitably be of concern. Moreover, the definition of organizational purpose will always be complicated in the public sector because of the frequent turnover of the political leadership. These considerations at the very least raise questions about the transferability of private-sector practice.

Perhaps the fundamental problem is with the concept of neutral competence itself. It has not been articulated in a way that distinguishes sufficiently between politics and policy. The elaboration of merit protections during the twentieth century has tended to make the bureaucracy unresponsive to presidential leadership. Hence the recent spiral of presidential efforts to better manage and control executive branch employees, which has raised the flag of partisan intrusion to new levels.

Two conditions appear to be necessary if pay for performance is to be compatible with a merit system based on the ideal of neutral competence. First, a fundamental rethinking of the concept of neutral competence is needed that will offer a more appropriate balance between merit protections and the effective implementation of the administration's policy. Second, a much broader view and acceptance of career managerial discretion is critical. Managers must have the authority and the support to manage employees effectively if the necessary conditions for pay for performance are to be present.

2. *The tension between the promise of pay for performance and the reality of the federal record.* As the following chapters demonstrate, there is an association between levels of organizational trust and shared values on one hand and perceptions of the fairness and effectiveness of pay-for-performance systems on the other. Of course, in both the public and private sectors, there will always be some dissatisfaction with merit pay because not everybody gains from such a system. Nonetheless, in the federal government, the absence of organizational trust and shared values and objectives may be an obstacle to effective pay for performance. Expectations have been high for previous reforms; in most cases, the reality has not approached the expectations. At the same time, increased efforts at political control and rhetoric that has devalued the public service have created high levels of dissatisfaction and demoralization among members of the career civil service. In such a setting, common goals and objectives, consensus, and trust may be difficult to achieve.

3. *The tension between inadequate resources and pay for performance.* If pay for performance is to contribute to perceptions of equity in compensation systems, the base from which it builds should be perceived as equitable and fair. At the present time, there is nearly unanimous agreement that federal pay is not competitive with private-sector pay in many regions. Every major survey of federal employees in the last 10 years has documented dissatisfaction with pay. Simply put, at the present time, base federal pay levels are *not* perceived to be equitable.

Moreover, revenue-neutral provisions for merit pay programs have resulted in small or modest bonuses. The General Accounting Office and the Merit Systems Protection Board report that employees do not perceive the link between performance and reward to be strong—or even present in some cases (U.S. General Accounting Office, 1988; Merit Systems Protection Board, 1990). In this context, the utility of pay-for-performance plans in contributing to equitable compensation systems appears to be very limited.

Our purpose in this chapter was to provide a general flavor of the complexities of the federal sector and to introduce some of the more salient issues to be considered as policy makers turn to the redesign of the merit pay system in the federal government. We turn now to an examination of the scientific and clinical evidence on performance appraisal and pay for performance and an assessment of the implications of this evidence for a merit pay system for federal managers.

3

The Nature of the Evidence

We have been asked to assess the role of performance appraisals and pay-for-performance systems in promoting excellence at work and to identify promising models for potential application to the federal work force. A number of major evidentiary obstacles impede scientific study of these issues, for reasons that go well beyond the scholar's perennial lament that more data are needed. As this chapter articulates, there are some conceptual and methodological mine fields implicit in this charge. At the same time, there are a number of strengths in this literature in terms of methodological rigor and relevance to organizational practices. These strengths and limitations need to be made explicit so that readers of this report can accurately gauge the existing scientific evidence bearing on performance appraisal and pay-for-performance systems.

This chapter does not aim to provide a comprehensive introduction to methodology in the social and behavioral sciences. Rather, it briefly reviews some of the evidentiary issues that arose in pursuing the committee's charge and summarizes the different kinds of research methods and data that have been brought to bear on performance appraisal and pay-for-performance plans. The diverse and fragmentary nature of the research evidence available to us turned out to have important implications for how we carried out the study and formulated our conclusions.

THE DIVERSITY OF RELEVANT THEORIES AND METHODS

Understanding how organizations appraise performance and the extent to which they allocate rewards on the basis of performance involves processes operating at numerous levels. The issues involved range from the intrapsychic (e.g., memory and attention allocation) to the interpersonal (e.g., affect, group dynamics) to the organizational, interorganizational, and even societal level (e.g., organizational structure, the role of money, legal constraints on performance appraisal and pay systems). Accordingly, the kinds of research relevant to our charge also run the gamut: research on the nature of jobs and job performance; investigations into the accuracy and context of human judgment; analyses of the impact of pay on motivation and behaviors; research on how organizational structure and environment influence personnel practices; studies of the effects of performance appraisal and pay systems on organizational functioning; proprietary surveys on attitude and climate undertaken by specific companies; and everything in between.

Because the issues of interest to the committee lie at the interstices between different theories, disciplines, audiences, and levels of analysis, there is not a single predominant type of research evidence for us to evaluate. Rather, we are faced with the task of trying to compare, contrast, and synthesize very different kinds of evidence relevant to the charge.

THE EVIDENCE

All the different kinds of evidence do not address the same issues or even employ the same standards of proof. Each type has its strengths and its limitations, and each brand of research implies its own definition of what kinds of evidence are most relevant and useful. In this section, we briefly summarize the quality of existing evidence and discuss a number of challenges faced by the committee in reviewing, synthesizing, and drawing inferences from such diverse strands of research.

One of the clear areas of strength is the research on performance appraisal. There is an enormous literature, stretching back well over half a century, on the assessment of work performance. Although the particular topics that have captured the attention of researchers have changed from time to time, the sheer accumulation of empirical work, laboratory studies, surveys of practice, and analytical models provides a rich backdrop for contemporary thinking about the use of performance appraisal. An additional, although sometimes unrecognized, virtue of the work on performance appraisal in recent decades derives from the pressures of litigation under Title VII of the Civil Rights Act of 1964. Performance appraisal systems have had to be defended in high-stakes situations, a fact that has made researchers in the field more cognizant of actual practice and the problems of evaluating performance in applied settings.

Pay for performance is a much younger research field. Although there is a good deal of suggestive theory, there is not an equivalent cumulation of empirical research. The field is, however, energetic and protean. Pay-for-performance compensation strategies have begun to draw the attention of students of economics, finance, accounting, sociology, psychology, management, and organizational science, as well as compensation consultants. The topic is fundamentally interdisciplinary, and that quality provides its own richness in terms of the variety of viewpoints and methods that are being brought to bear. This is an important strength—if also a complication—for it gives us a variety of clues to the hypothesized links between pay and performance.

In addition to the pertinent scholarly theory and research, there is also an extensive body of clinical knowledge and experience with organizations that is by no means irrelevant to our task. Hence, we have looked for points of convergence between the findings of detached scholarly studies and the intimate understandings of clinicians and practitioners. Furthermore, although we lack the wealth of empirical data that would permit us to make precise predictions about the effects of performance-based pay, we are not wholly ignorant about its effects. Our review of existing theory, diverse types of research, and clinical experience suggests that there are certain preconditions that appear to be necessary (though not sufficient) for pay for performance to do more good than harm: for instance, ample performance-based rewards available to be distributed; participants who are knowledgeable about the linkage between their actions and rewards received; credible indices of performance; and incentives for those doing the performance appraisal to do it well versus incentives for them to *not* differentiate among subordinates. To the extent that some of these necessary preconditions may not be satisfied in many government contexts (see Chapters 2 and 7), there is reason to question whether the prerequisites for beneficial effects are satisfied.

EVIDENTIARY CHALLENGES

The evidence relating to performance appraisal and to pay-for-performance compensation systems is discussed in detail in Chapters 4 through 7. On a more general plane, however, there are a number of issues and evidentiary challenges that merit the reader's attention, ranging from how to gauge the effectiveness of performance-based pay to questions of causality.

Criteria for Gauging the Effectiveness of Personnel Practices

The Office of Personnel Management wishes to identify performance appraisal and pay systems that "work." However, there are so many conceivable definitions of what works—so many different ways of conceptualizing, measuring, and judging the effectiveness of a given performance appraisal and pay system—that it is difficult to render scientific assessments in this domain with confidence. In the course of the committee's review of the evidence, it became clear that there are at least four types of benefits that the theoretical and empirical literatures have posited in discussing performance-based pay systems: (1)

positive effects on the behaviors of individual employees (including decisions to join an organization, attend, perform, and remain attached); (2) increasing organization-level effectiveness (including cost-effectiveness); (3) facilitating socialization and communication (by transmitting expectations, goals, and role requirements); and (4) ensuring that the way the organization compensates, manages, and treats its employees is perceived as legitimate by important internal and external constituencies.

This is clearly a diverse set of criteria for gauging the effectiveness of an organization's performance appraisal and pay system. Agreeing on the relevant one(s) is hardly straightforward, especially because the criteria that may be important to scientists or academicians interested in performance appraisal and pay systems may not correspond to the ones of interest to managers and policy makers.

Moreover, the diverse criteria make radically different evidentiary demands. Marshaling evidence for the effectiveness of a performance appraisal system in facilitating socialization and communication, for example, would be fairly straightforward: careful surveys of supervisor and employee attitudes would satisfy most observers. The criterion of enhanced effectiveness at the organizational level, however, is largely (although not entirely) beyond the reach of social science analysis at present. Psychologists do not yet know much about the links between individual performance and group performance; neither psychology nor economics offers much empirical evidence of the effects of improved performance on productivity, although both disciplines have produced some interesting theory (see Hartigan and Wigdor, 1989). Accordingly, our conclusions about the organization-level effects of performance appraisal and pay-for-performance systems are necessarily guarded, based as they are on analogy to other compensation systems rather than direct evidence.

Validity and Reliability

Even if the relevant dimensions or criteria of effectiveness can be specified, however, they remain to be *measured*. In assessing the value of social science evidence, researchers emphasize two factors: validity and reliability.

Put simply, validity concerns the relevance or appropriateness of the measurement. The concept of validity is often expressed in terms of whether one is measuring what one intends to measure (e.g., Nunnally, 1967). Recent definitions focus on the appropriateness and meaningfulness of the inferences drawn from measurement data, such as test scores or performance ratings (American Educational Research Association et al., 1985). Reliability concerns the extent to which the measurement is consistent or dependable—that is, whether repeating a measurement in the absence of significant changes would yield the same measurement outcome. Both validity and reliability point to a process of gathering evidence. More extensive discussion of issues of validity and reliability is provided in Chapter 4.

Clearly, validity and reliability are interrelated: a valid measure of Brand X word-processing skill, for instance, presumes a reliable one (e.g., computers free of malfunctions and operating with the same software). The point to be made here is that there are often trade-offs between the reliability and validity of evidence concerning the issues at hand. Laboratory experiments looking at performance appraisals or the impact of contingent rewards on behavior are often able to control for confounding factors and measure the relevant variables much more reliably than can be accomplished in field studies of real organizational settings. For example, participants in lab studies exposed to identical stimuli, such as film clips of a person performing a task adroitly and then inadequately, provide highly consistent evaluations of the good and poor behaviors. However, it is difficult to gauge the external validity (or generalizability) of the appraisal tools from evidence gathered in laboratory settings—that is, whether they would be as accurate when used to evaluate job performance in operational settings.

It is equally difficult to know what inferences to draw from the limited number of field-based and statistically controlled studies examining the consequences of tying rewards to performance. For instance, there is an increasing literature in economics assessing the effects of performance-based rewards on organizational performance among top managers and executives. There is also some empirical work looking at related issues in professional sports, and there are studies showing that salespeople tend to sell more when at least some of their compensation is based on commission. Needless to say, generalizing from this evidence to many of the managerial jobs that are the focus of our work is tenuous. To put the matter simply: work settings in which there are no problems finding valid and reliable measures of performance are likely not to be very interesting for our purposes. In these settings, pay is almost invariably based on performance. Examples would include door-to-door sales, piece-rate sewing of garments, and prize fights. However, few jobs within federal government agencies permit such concrete measurement, thereby making validity and reliability concerns much more salient (and much more matters of perception than of statistical reality).

Sources and Quality of Available Data

Knowing what one wants to measure and measuring it well are only part of the challenge. One's measures are only as good as the sample from which they are drawn. A perfectly valid and reliable public opinion survey administered to a random sample of adults entering and leaving the Veterans Administration, for instance, may be of limited value in predicting or understanding the attitudes of the U.S. population as a whole.

Studying organizational phenomena presents a number of challenges regarding data quality. Organizations often regard their performance appraisal and compensation policies as privileged information and are reluctant or unwilling to divulge information about them to researchers. Consequently, a considerable amount of information regarding prevailing practices in the performance appraisal and pay-for-performance area derives from three sources: surveys conducted by business associations, consulting organizations, and the like (e.g., the Wyatt Company and HayGroup surveys discussed extensively in Chapter 6); case studies of individual companies by researchers; and knowledge obtained by organizational consultants.

This state of affairs raises several possible problems in interpreting the available evidence. First, organizations that have been or are willing to share information on their practices with researchers need not be representative of any clearly defined population of interest. For instance, it seems likely that there is more information available about the personnel policies of an organization if it is in the public sector, publicly traded, or otherwise highly visible; has been taken to court; regards itself as a leader in the personnel field; belongs to industry or professional associations; or is large (and therefore more able to absorb the costs of complying with requests for information).

Statisticians refer to this problem as *sample selection bias*, whereby some observations are systematically excluded from the sample available for analysis. Sample biases can take two forms: the sample may be biased with respect to the dependent variables or outcomes of interest (typically referred to as censoring bias) and/or with regard to the independent variables or explanatory factors presumed to be at work (typically referred to as truncation bias). Both types of sample selection bias may be at work in our case, confounding the inferences we wish to draw. We are interested in understanding the factors that determine why organizations appraise performance and allocate pay differently and what consequences those differences have. It seems likely that the available data underrepresent organizations that appraise performance informally, that do not pay for performance, and that are performing poorly. (There are a number of justifications for this assumption. Poorly performing organizations are unlikely to respond to requests for information for many reasons, not the least of which is organizational mortality: when an organization is performing poorly enough, it ceases to exist, thereby precluding study. Moreover, we assume that organizations with elaborate performance appraisal and pay-for-performance systems are more likely to advertise the fact, perceiving their activities to be more legitimate and businesslike. As we note below, personnel professionals reporting on the organizations in which they work are also likely to have reasons to be partisan.) The extant data are also likely to overrepresent organizations of particular types, thereby resulting in truncation bias when it comes to examining the role of some explanatory factor (such as organizational size) in influencing how performance is appraised and pay is allocated and with what effects. After all, if only large organizations were to permit researchers to study them, what could be said scientifically about small organizations?

It is important to emphasize that the mere fact that a sample is nonrandom in some respects does not make it unrepresentative or useless. The extent of bias depends on the population to which researchers wish to make generalizations. Results from the above-mentioned hypothetical survey outside the Veterans Administration may be perfectly appropriate for making generalizations to some populations.

In our case, much of the relevant organizational evidence bearing on performance-based pay comes from private-sector corporations. Leaving aside all the complications of measurement, causal inference, and the like discussed throughout this chapter, even if we could make perfectly valid and precise inferences about corporations, we would still face the difficult issue of whether those conclusions can safely be generalized to workers in federal agencies. (That question, of course, is hardly idiosyncratic to the work of this committee; after all, scientific debates occur constantly about the relevance of specific evidence from animal studies for human health and behavior.)

In addition, as we noted earlier, much of the data derive from clinical knowledge and experience. Although this sort of data can be informative, it is important to acknowledge the potential limits of clinical expertise. The opinions of managers about their companies or the assessments of paid consultants about organizations for whom they have consulted can be illuminating, but the potential for bias and conflict of interest must also be recognized. Furthermore, relying on the "excellent company" method to make inferences about the effectiveness of organizational practices is perilous. The mere observation that many organizations with a reputation for success appraise performance or allocate pay in a particular way does not constitute scientific evidence or a basis for prescription—any more than would the fact that most successful companies have male chief executive officers justify the recommendation that women should not be promoted at the top.

Two other related concerns should be noted about the sources and quality of available data bearing on performance-based pay. First, experimental control or random assignment of subjects to treatments is often difficult or impossible to obtain in studying organizational phenomena. Firms typically do not design or alter their appraisal or pay systems randomly over time, but rather in response to real or perceived dilemmas.

Second, it has been well documented that organizational intervention as such has effects on the behavior of organizational members. Physical scientists have documented that even physical phenomena are altered by the very process of scientific observation and measurement. However, in the organizational world, this problem, frequently called the Hawthorne effect, is much more severe and more difficult to disentangle. The mere entry of researchers or consultants into an enterprise or a change by the organization in its personnel system can be enough to occasion large attitudinal and behavioral changes. The reactivity of organizations to policy changes and to external scrutiny further obscures inferences about the consequences of performance appraisal and pay systems for organizational effectiveness.

Determinants Versus Consequences

We have quite a bit of data describing organizational and industrial variations in performance appraisal and pay systems, and there are numerous respected consulting firms and other organizations (e.g., The Conference Board) in the business of tabulating and disseminating such data by size of firm, type of business, and so on. Yet one cannot infer from such evidence alone that, say, a given compensation plan is appropriate for other organizations of that size, technology, or industry, unless one is prepared to assume that "what is should be," and that the prevalence of a particular practice among organizations of a given type suggests some adaptive value of that practice. A considerable body of recent research suggests that inertia is a powerful force in organizations; many contemporary structures and practices appear to be residues or carryovers from the circumstances that prevailed when a particular organization was founded, rather than arrangements well suited to its contemporary environment (see Hannan and Freeman, 1984).

Attributing Causality

Much of the evidence concerning differences in performance appraisal systems, pay systems, the relationship between them, and their link to performance, which we summarize in this report, is based on studies that are cross-sectional or nearly cross-sectional (i.e., very short time series). This evidence is thus of limited power in making statements about causal relationships. Yet even if these difficulties could be surmounted and a causal link established between performance-based pay and some dimension of organizational performance, tricky issues remain that cloud the interpretation of the findings and their practical relevance.

First, inferences about the effects of performance-based pay plans on organization- or individual-level outcomes are only as valid as the statistical model used to look at the question. Any judgment about performance is always a judgment about performance *compared with something*. In statistical studies, that something is specified by control variables. If important control variables are omitted, or if the effects of the variables of interest are confounded with included or omitted control variables, then it can be perilous to make inferences about how some factor affects performance.

Another reason why empirical evidence regarding the effects of pay for performance can be misleading concerns *unobserved heterogeneity*. Even in studying biochemical processes, variations across individuals and environments can make a big difference. In trying to assess statistically the impact of linking pay to performance, the accuracy of one's conclusions depends critically on how accurately the relevant heterogeneity has been taken account of. We have some theory and past research to guide us in specifying what the relevant dimensions of heterogeneity might be, but we actually know relatively little. The effect of pay for performance is likely to vary considerably across individuals (e.g., as a function of wealth, age, values, and the like), jobs, organizational context, dimensions of performance, time periods, and locales. Failure to capture this heterogeneity can produce misleading inferences.

One other difficulty in formulating policy or managerial prescriptions is that we might be able to document felicitous effects of performance-based pay systems without necessarily understanding why those effects obtain, and therefore how likely they are to persist. In particular, a number of different streams of research suggest that *how* organizations do things often matters at least as much as what they do (see Chapter 7). The literature on procedural justice, for instance, indicates that procedures for allocating rewards matter a great deal, quite apart from the actual magnitude of rewards allocated. Similarly, surveys of worker satisfaction and commitment, as well as field research on gain-sharing, employee stock ownership plans, and the like routinely report that such factors as the extent of communication, participation, openness, flexibility, and "humaneness" surrounding employment and reward systems make a strong independent contribution to workers' subjective well-being, attachment, and (in some cases) work product (e.g., Halaby, 1986; Rosen, 1986). A common theme running through the presentations made by industry representatives to our committee was that their companies take the *process* very seriously.

These process effects are likely to be particularly elusive to researchers. Moreover, given the importance of belief systems, organizations may be extremely reluctant to permit their practices to be studied explicitly, since it may be preferable to have current practices taken for granted than to run the risk of uncovering evidence that those practices are dubious. The point here is that the ideology of pay for performance, based on fair and accurate performance appraisals, serves important functions. Accordingly, it may be no less difficult for managers and workers than for researchers and policy makers to separate the facts from beliefs about this topic.

IMPLICATIONS

In reviewing these various issues, we do not wish to overstate the complexities involved in weighing the evidence on performance appraisal and pay for performance. The issues raised in this chapter are generic to studies of social and organizational phenomena. Indeed, in some respects, there is a larger and higher-quality body of research bearing on these concerns than is often the case in studying applied social science concerns. We have surveyed the nature of the evidence simply to underscore the need for caution (and additional research) in drawing policy inferences from the scientific evidence and prevailing practice and to explain the general approach we take throughout this report in weighing the evidence and drawing conclusions from it.

In carrying out the study we built upon our own diversity, which went well beyond simple differences in disciplinary training or occupation, to encompass fundamental differences in approach to issues in human motivation and behavior, the nature of organizations, and the relevant questions to be asked about performance appraisal and pay for performance. Some of us viewed the problem at the individual level of analysis; others were concerned with organizational effectiveness and change. Some employed criteria of individual or organizational performance, while others interpreted the issues in terms of procedural justice or the role of performance appraisal and pay for performance in legitimizing organizations.

We have been catholic in pulling together evidence and information that might bear on the effectiveness of performance appraisal and performance-based compensation systems, taking account of theory, empirical research, and clinical studies not only from many disciplines but also from any research topics that seemed relevant. We have supplemented formal evidence with as much information about current practices in private-sector firms as we could reasonably gather in the limited time available for the study.

For example, our findings about performance appraisal and pay for performance rely on and exploit existing knowledge about organizations available from related areas. We know a great deal about how organizations vary along a number of other dimensions of their personnel systems, as well as some of the consequences of those differences. For instance, we know what types tend to pay higher wages, to promote more from within, to provide on-the-job training, to emphasize seniority more in pay and promotion decisions, and so on. We also know that personnel practices tend to be part of a larger system governing employment. Accordingly, it would be surprising if the insights we have gleaned from this other research were irrelevant to understanding the determinants and consequences of performance appraisal and performance-based pay systems.

Not all of this evidence will meet rigorous standards of scientific proof. We have been careful throughout the text to identify the type of evidence and the level of confidence we feel that it merits. But the fact is that managers in the private and public sector routinely have to make choices about management practice in the absence of definitive evidence. Federal leaders are currently working on compensation policy and will soon revise the Performance Management and Recognition System. In the end, we judged it better to paint as rich a picture as possible. We felt that a careful weaving together of the many kinds of evidence and experiential data would provide useful insights into general tendencies or likelihoods, if not precise predictions about specific outcomes. In the language of statistical inference, we have aimed to draw rather broad confidence intervals around what is likely to happen in any given organizational setting, rather than seeking to offer point estimates. Stated more colloquially, answering a policy maker's query with "it depends" can nonetheless be useful, if one can articulate the factors on which it depends.

Finally, although we are confident that federal policy makers can benefit from a careful assessment of the scientific and impressionistic evidence on performance appraisal and pay for performance, we are also mindful of the broader political and normative concerns impinging on personnel management in the context of the federal civil service. By their very nature, governmental institutions rely significantly on public trust. Such institutions are predicted by organizational theorists to adopt elaborate evaluation rituals because of a need for perceived legitimacy in the eyes of constituencies (Meyer and Rowan, 1977). Indeed, government bureaus have long sought to bolster their public image by emulating what is thought to be state-of-the-art practice in the private sector. DiPrete (1989:81) suggests that even more than 100 years ago, "a principal argument for the merit system was that it would put the personnel affairs of government on a more businesslike footing" by emulating prevailing corporate practice.

We recognize that current efforts to reform federal personnel policies involve an effort to increase the perceived legitimacy of the federal government. It may be public *perceptions* of how performance is appraised and pay administered within the civil service that matter more than anything else. We also recognize that the legitimation aspects of performance appraisal and pay for performance may to some extent work at cross-purposes with other functions of those practices—for instance, practices that adhere to some idealized business model might provide the greatest legitimacy to a given agency but not necessarily do the best job of communicating its organizational goals or motivating its employees. The fact that personnel systems have important symbolic purposes, which may in some cases be in conflict with other important objectives, prompts us to be cautious about making suggestions for radical changes in prevailing practice within the federal civil service.

4
Performance Appraisal:
Definition, Measurement, and Application

INTRODUCTION

The science of performance appraisal is directed toward two fundamental goals: to create a measure that accurately assesses the level of an individual's job performance and to create an evaluation system that will advance one or more operational functions in an organization. Although all performance appraisal systems encompass both goals, they are reflected differently in two major research orientations, one that grows out of the measurement tradition, the other from human resources management and other fields that focus on the organizational purposes of performance appraisal.

Within the measurement tradition, emanating from psychometrics and testing, researchers have worked and continue to work on the premise that accurate measurement is a precondition for understanding and accurate evaluation. Psychologists have striven to develop definitive measures of job performance, on the theory that accurate job analysis and measurement instruments would provide both employer and employee with a better understanding of what is expected and a knowledge of whether the employee's performance has been effective. By and large, researchers in measurement have made the assumption that if the tools and procedures are accurate (e.g., valid and reliable), then the functional goals of organizations using tests or performance appraisals will be met. Much has been learned, but as this summary of the field makes explicit, there is still a long way to go.

In a somewhat different vein, scholars in the more applied fields—human resources management, organizational sociology, and more recently applied psychology, have focused their efforts on usability and acceptability of performance appraisal tools and procedures. They have concerned themselves less with questions of validity and reliability than with the workability of the performance appraisal system within the organization, its ability to communicate organizational standards to employees, to reward good performers, and to identify employees who require training and other development activities. For example, the scholarship in the management literature looks at the use of performance appraisal systems to reinforce organizational and employee belief systems. The implicit assumption of many applied researchers is that if the tools and procedures are acceptable and useful, they are also likely to be sufficiently accurate from a measurement standpoint.

From a historical perspective, until the last decade research on performance appraisal was largely dominated by the measurement tradition. Performance appraisals were viewed in much the same way as tests; that is to say, they were evaluated against criteria of validity, reliability, and freedom from bias. The emphasis throughout was on reducing rating errors, which was assumed to improve the accuracy of measurement. The research addressed two issues almost exclusively—the nature and quality of the scales to be used to assess performance and rater training. The question of which performance dimensions to evaluate tended to be taken as a given.

Although, strictly speaking, we do not disagree with the test analogy for performance appraisals, it can be misleading. Performance appraisals are different from the typical standardized test in that the "test" in this case is a combination of the scale and the person who completes the rating. And, contrary to standardized test administration, the context in which the appraisal process takes place is difficult if not impossible to standardize. These complexities were often overlooked in the performance appraisal literature in the psychometric tradition. The research on scales has tended to treat all variation attributable to raters as error variance. The classic training research can be seen as attempting to develop and evaluate ways of standardizing the person component of the appraisal process.

In the late 1970s there was a shift in emphasis away from the psychometric properties of scales. The shift was initially articulated by Landy and Farr (1980) and was extended by Ilgen and Feldman (1983) and DeNisi et al. (1984). They expounded the thesis that the search for rating error had reached the point of diminishing returns for improving the quality of performance appraisals, and that it was time for the field to concentrate more on what the rater brings to performance appraisal—more specifically, how the rater processes information about the employee and how this mental processing influences the accuracy of the appraisal. The thrust of the research was still on accuracy, but now the focus was on the accuracy of judgment rather than rating errors and the classical psychometric indices of quality.

Just as there was dissatisfaction with progress in performance appraisal research at the end of the 1970s, recent literature suggests dissatisfaction with the approaches of the 1980s. But this time the shift promises to be more fundamental. The most recent research (Ilgen et al., 1989; Murphy and Cleveland, 1991) appears to reject the goal of precision measurement as impractical. From this point of view, prior research has either ignored or underestimated the powerful impact of organizational context and people's perceptions of it. The context position is that, although rating scale formats, training, and other technical qualities of performance appraisals do influence the qualities of ratings, the quality of performance appraisals is also strongly affected by the context in which they are used. It is argued that research on performance appraisals now needs to turn to learning more about the conditions that encourage raters to use the performance appraisal systems in the way that they were intended to be used. At this juncture, therefore, it appears that the measurement and management traditions in performance appraisal have reached a rapprochement.

How do these varied bodies of research contribute to an understanding of performance appraisal technology and application? Can jobs be accurately described? Can valid and reliable measures of performance be developed? Does the research offer evidence that performance appraisal instruments and procedures have a positive effect on individual and organizational effectiveness? Is there evidence that performance appraisal systems contribute to communication of organizational goals and performance expectations as management theory would lead us to believe? What does the recent focus on the interactions between appraisal systems and organizational context suggest about the probable accuracy of appraisals when actually used to make decisions about individual employees? These questions and their treatment in the psychological research and human resources management literature form the major themes of this chapter.

In the following pages we present the results of research in the areas of psychometrics, applied psychology, and human resources management on performance description, performance measurement, and performance assessment for purposes of enhancing individual employee performance. The first section deals with measurement issues. The discussion proceeds from a general description of the research on job performance and its measurement to a description of the factors that can influence the quality of the performance assessment. Research relating to managerial-level jobs is presented as available, but most of the work in job performance description and measurement has involved non-managerial jobs.[1] The second section deals with research on the more applied

---

[1] The reason for this imbalance in the research literature is obvious: managerial jobs are difficult to define and assess at a specific level—not only are they fragmented, diverse, and amorphous, but many of the factors leading to successful outcomes in such jobs are not directly measurable. Moreover, in

issues, such as the effects of rater training and the contextual sources of rating distortion.

PERFORMANCE APPRAISAL AND
THE MEASUREMENT TRADITION

The Domain of Job Performance

The definition and measurement of job performance has been a central theme in psychological and organizational research. Definitions have ranged from general to specific and from quantitative to qualitative. Some researchers have concentrated their efforts on defining job performance in terms of outcomes; others have examined job behaviors; still others have studied personal traits such as conscientiousness or leadership orientation as correlates of successful performance. The more general, qualitative descriptions tend to be used for jobs that are complex and multifaceted like those at managerial levels, while quantitative descriptions are used frequently to describe highly proceduralized jobs for which employee actions can be measured and the resulting outcomes often quantified. The principal purpose of this research has been to enhance employee performance (via better selection, placement, and retention decisions), under the assumption that cumulative individual performance will influence organizational performance.

When considering measures of individual job performance, there is a tendency in the literature to characterize some measures as objective and others as subjective. We believe this to be a false distinction that may create too much confidence in the former and an unjustified suspicion about the latter. Measurement of performance in all jobs, no matter how structured and routinized they are, depends on external judgment about what the important dimensions of the job are and where the individual's performance falls on each dimension. Our discussion in this chapter avoids the artificial distinctions of objective and subjective and instead focuses on the role of human judgment in the performance appraisal process.

Initially, applied psychologists were optimistic about their ability to identify and measure job performance. Job analyses were used as the basis for constructing selection tests, for developing training programs, and for determining the strengths and weaknesses of employees. However, many of the results were disappointing and, as experience was gained, researchers began to realize that describing the constituent dimensions of a job and understanding its performance requirements was not a straightforward task. Today it is recognized

---

practice, most managerial appraisals involve some form of management by objective. This approach represents an attempt to finesse the problem of evaluating performance by defining good performance a priori—instead, the employee participates in establishing the performance objectives that are used to evaluate the performance.

that job performance is made up of complex sets of interacting factors, some of them attributable to the job, some to the worker, and some to the environment. Thus, in even the simplest of jobs many elements of "job performance" are not easily isolated or directly observable. It is also clear to social scientists that the definition of what constitutes skill or successful work behavior is contingent and subject to frequent redefinition. In any appraisal system, the performance factors rated depend on the approach taken to job analysis, i.e., worker attributes or job tasks. There is evidence that different expert analysts and different analytic methods will result in different judgments about job skills (England and Dunn, 1988).

Furthermore, the evaluation of job performance is subject to social and organizational influences. In elucidation of this point, Spenner (1990) has identified several theoretical propositions concerning the social definition of skill or of what is considered effective job behavior. For example, scholars in the constructionist school argue that what is defined as skilled behavior is influenced by interested parties, such as managers, unions, and professions. Ultimately, what constitutes good and poor performance depends on organizational context. The armed forces, for example, place a great deal of importance on performance factors like "military bearing." Identical task performance by an auto mechanic would be valued differently and therefore evaluated differently by the military than by a typical car dealership. In order to capture some of this complexity, Landy and Farr (1983) propose that descriptions of the performance construct for purposes of appraisal should include job behavior, situational factors that influence or interact with behavior, and job outcomes.

Dimensions of Job Performance

Applied psychologists have used job analysis as a primary means for understanding the dimensions of job performance (McCormick, 1976, 1979). There have been a number of approaches to job analysis over the years, including the job element method (Clark and Primoff, 1979), the critical incident method (Flanagan, 1954; Latham et al., 1979), the U.S. Air Force task inventory approach (Christal, 1974), and those methods that rely on structured questionnaires such as the Position Analysis Questionnaire (McCormick et al., 1972; Cornelius et al., 1979) and the Executive Position Description Questionnaire developed by Hemphill (1959) to describe managerial-level jobs in large organizations. All of these methods share certain assumptions about good job analysis practices and all are based on a variety of empirical sources of information, including surveys of task performance, systematic observations, interviews with incumbents and their supervisors, review of job-related documentation, and self-report diaries. The results are usually detailed descriptions of job tasks, personal attributes and behaviors, or both.

One of the more traditional methods used to describe job performance is the critical incident technique (Flanagan, 1954). This method involves obtaining reports from qualified observers of exceptionally good and poor behavior used to accomplish critical parts of a job. The resulting examples of effective and ineffective behavior are used as the basis for developing behaviorally based scales for performance appraisal purposes. Throughout the 1950s and 1960s, Flanagan and his colleagues applied the critical incident technique to the description of several managerial and professional jobs (e.g., military officers, air traffic controllers, foremen, and research scientists). The procedure for developing critical incident measures is systematic and extremely time-consuming. In the case of the military officers, over 3,000 incident descriptions were collected and analyzed. Descriptions usually include the context, the behaviors judged as effective or ineffective, and possibly some description of the favorable or unfavorable outcomes.

There is general agreement in the literature that the critical incident technique has proven useful in identifying a large range of critical job behaviors. The major reservations of measurement experts concern the omission of important behaviors and lack of precision in working incidents, which interferes with their usefulness as guides for interpreting the degree of effectiveness in job performance.

Moreover, there is some research evidence—and this is pertinent to our study of performance appraisal—suggesting that descriptions of task behavior resulting from task or critical incident analyses do not match the way supervisors organize information about the performance of their subordinates (Lay and Jackson, 1969; Sticker et al., 1974; Borman, 1983, 1987). In one of a few studies of supervisors' "folk theories" of job performance, Borman (1987) found that the dimensions that defined supervisors' conceptions of performance included: (1) initiative and hard work, (2) maturity and responsibility, (3) organization, (4) technical proficiency, (5) assertive leadership, and (6) supportive leadership. These dimensions are based more on global traits and broadly defined task areas than they are on tightly defined task behaviors. Borman's findings are supported by several recent cognitive models of the performance appraiser (Feldman, 1981; Ilgen and Feldman, 1983; Nathan and Lord, 1983; De Nisi et al., 1984).

If, as these researchers suggest, supervisors use trait-based cognitive models to form impressions of their employees, the contribution of job analysis to the accuracy of appraisal systems is in some sense called into question. The suggestion is that supervisors translate observed behaviors into judgments about general traits or characteristics, and it is these judgments that are stored in memory. Asking them via an appraisal form to rate job behaviors does not mean that they are reporting what they saw. Rather, they may be reconstructing a behavioral portrait of the employee's performance based on their judgment of the employee's perseverance, maturity, or competence. At the very least, this research makes clearer the complexity of the connections between job requirements, employee job behaviors, and supervisor evaluations of job performance.

The Joint-Service Job Performance Measurement (JPM) Project undertaken by the Department of Defense is among the most ambitious efforts at systematic job analysis to date (Green et al., 1991). This is a large-scale, decade long research effort to develop measures of job proficiency for purposes of validating the entrance test used by all four services to screen recruits into the enlisted ranks. By the time the project is completed in 1992, over $30 million will have been expended to develop an array of job performance measures—including hands-on job-sample tests, written job knowledge tests, simulations, and, of particular interest here, performance appraisals—and to administer the measures to some 9,000 troops in 27 enlisted occupations.

Each of the services already had an ongoing occupational task inventory system that reported the percentage of job incumbents who perform each task, the average time spent on the task, and incumbents' perceptions of task importance and task difficulty. The services also had in hand soldier's manuals for each occupation that specify the content of the job. From this foundation of what might be called archival data, the services proceeded to a more comprehensive job analysis, calling on both scientists and subject matter experts (typically master sergeants who supervise or train others to do the job) to refine and narrow down the task domain according to such considerations as frequency of performance, difficulty, and importance to the job. Subject matter experts were used for such things as ranking the core tasks in terms of their criticality in a specific combat scenario, clustering tasks based on similarity of principles or procedures, or assigning difficulty ratings to each task based on estimates of how typical soldiers might perform the task. Project scientists used all of this information to construct a purposive sample of 30 tasks to represent the job. From this sample the various performance measures were developed.

The JPM project is particularly interesting for the variety of performance measures that were developed. In addition to hands-on performance tests (by far the most technically difficult and expensive sort of measure to develop and administer) and written job-knowledge tests, the services developed a wide array of performance appraisal instruments. These included supervisor, peer, and self ratings, ratings of very global performance factors as well as job-specific ratings, behaviorally anchored rating scales, ratings with numerical tags, and ratings with qualitative tags. Although the data analysis is still under way, the JPM project can be expected to contribute significantly to our understanding of job performance measurement and of the relationships among the various measures of that performance.

For our purposes, it is instructive to note how the particular conception of job performance adopted by the project influenced everything else, from job analysis to instrument development, to interpretation of the data. First, it was decided to focus on proficiency (*can* do) and not on the personal attributes that determine whether a person *will* do the job. Second, tasks were chosen as the central unit of analysis, rather than worker attributes or skill requirements. It follows logically that the performance measures were job-specific and that the measurement focus was on concrete, observable behaviors. All of these decisions made sense. The jobs studied are entry-level jobs assigned to enlisted personnel—jet engine mechanic, infantryman, administrative clerk, radio operator—relatively simple and amenable to measurement at the task level. Moreover, the enviable trove of task information virtually dictated the economic wisdom of that approach. And finally, the objectives of the research were well satisfied by the design decisions. During the 1980s the military was faced each year with the task of trying to choose from close to a million 18- to 24-year-olds, most with relatively little training or job experience, in order to fill perhaps 300,000 openings spread across hundreds of military occupations. It was important to be able to demonstrate that the enlistment test is a reasonably accurate predictor of which applicants are likely to be successful in a broad sample of military jobs (earlier research focused on success in training, not job performance). For classification purposes, it was important to understand the relationship between the aptitude subtests and performance in various categories of jobs.

In other words, the picture of job performance that emerged from the JPM research was suited to the organizational objectives and to the nature of the jobs studied. The same job analysis design would not necessarily work in another context, as the following discussion of managerial performance demonstrates.

Descriptions of Managerial Performance

Most of the research describing managerial behavior was conducted between the early 1950s and the mid-1970s. The principal job analysis methods used (in addition to critical incident techniques) were interviews, task analyses, review of written job descriptions, observations, self-report diaries, activity sampling, and questionnaires. Hemphill's (1959) Executive Position Description Questionnaire was one of the earliest uses of an extensive questionnaire to define managerial performance. The results, based on responses from managers, led to the identification of the following nine job factors.

FACTOR A: Providing a Staff Service in Nonoperational Areas. Renders various staff services to supervisors: gathering information, interviewing, selecting employees, briefing superiors, checking statements, verifying facts, and making recommendations.

FACTOR B: Supervision of Work. Plans, organizes, and controls the work of others; concerned with the efficient use of equipment, the motivation of subordinates, efficiency of operation, and maintenance of the work force.

FACTOR C: Business Control. Concerned with cost reduction, maintenance of proper inventories, preparation of budgets, justification of capital expenditures, determination of goals, definition of supervisor responsibilities, payment of salaries, enforcement of regulations.

FACTOR D: Technical Concerns With Products and Markets. Concerned with development of new business, activities of competitors, contacts with customers, assisting sales personnel.

FACTOR E: Human, Community, and Social Affairs. Concerned with company goodwill in the community, participation in community affairs, speaking before the public.

FACTOR F: Long-range Planning. Broad concerns oriented toward the future; does not get involved in routine and tends to be free of direct supervision.

FACTOR G: Exercise of Broad Power and Authority. Makes recommendations on very important matters; keeps informed about the company's performances; interprets policy; has a high status.

FACTOR H: Business Reputation. Concerned with product quality and/or public relations.

FACTOR I: Personal Demands. Senses obligation to conduct oneself according to the stereotype of the conservative business manager.

FACTOR J: Preservation of Assets. Concerned about capital expenditures, taxes, preservation of assets, loss of company money.

An analysis of these factors suggests relatively little focus on product quality. Rather, most factors dealt with creating internal services and controls for efficiency and developing external images to promote acceptability of the company in the community.

More recently, Flanders and Utterback (1985) reported on the development and use of the Management Excellence Inventory (MEI) by the Office of Personnel Management (OPM). The MEI is based on a model describing management functions and the skills needed to perform each function. Analyses conducted at three levels of management suggested that different skills and knowledge are needed to be successful at different levels. Lower-level managers needed technical competence and interpersonal communication skills; middle-level managers needed less technical competence but substantial skill in areas such as communication, leadership, flexibility, concern with goal achievement, and risk-taking; and top-level managers needed all the skills of a middle-level manager plus sensitivity to the environment, a long-term view, and a strategic view. A review of these skill areas indicates that all are general, some are task-oriented, and some, such as flexibility and leadership, are personal traits.

The finding that managers at different levels have different skill requirements is also reflected in the research of Katz (1974), Mintzberg (1975), and Kraut et al. (1989). In essence, the work describing managerial jobs has concentrated on behaviors, skills, or traits in general terms. These researchers suggest that assessment of effective managerial performance in terms of specific behaviors is particularly difficult because many of the behaviors related to successful job performance are not directly observable and represent an interaction of skills and traits. Traits are widely used across organizations and are easily accepted by managers because they have face validity. However, they are relatively unattractive to measurement experts because they are not particularly sensitive to the characteristics of specific jobs and they are difficult to observe, measure, and verify. In many settings, outcomes have been accepted as legitimate measures. However, as measures of individual performance they are problematical because they are the measures most likely to be affected by conditions not under the control of the manager.

Implications

In sum, virtually all of the analysis of managerial performance has been at a global level; little attention has been given to the sort of detailed, task-centered definition that characterized the military JPM research. (One exception is the work of Gomez-Mejia et al. [1982], which involved the use of several job analysis methods to develop detailed descriptions of managerial tasks.) This focus on global dimensions conveys a message from the research community about the nature of managerial performance and the infeasibility of capturing its essence through easily quantified lists of tasks, duties, and standards. Reliance on global measures means that evaluation of a manager's performance is, of necessity, based on a substantial degree of judgment. Attempts to remove subjectivity from the appraisal process by developing comprehensive lists of tasks or job elements or behavioral standards are unlikely to produce a valid representation of the manager's job performance and may focus raters' attention on trivial criteria.

In a private-sector organization with a measurable bottom line, it is frequently easier to develop individual, quantitative work goals (such as sales volume or the number of units processed) than it is in a large bureaucracy like the federal government, where a bottom line tends to be difficult to define. However, the easy availability of quantitative goals in some private-sector jobs may actually *hinder* the valid measurement of the manager's effectiveness, especially when those goals focus on short-term results or solutions to immediate problems. There is evidence that the incorporation of objective, countable measures of performance into an overall performance appraisal can lead to an overemphasis on very concrete aspects of performance and an underemphasis on those less easily quantified or that yield concrete outcomes only in the long term (e.g., development of one's subordinates) (Landy and Farr, 1983).

It appears that managerial jobs fit less easily within the measurement tradition than simpler, more concrete jobs, if one interprets valid performance measurement to require job-related measures, and the preference for "objective" measures (as the Civil Service Reform Act appears to do). It remains to be seen whether any approaches to performance appraisal can be demonstrated to be reliable and valid in the psychometric sense and, if so, how global ratings compare with job-specific ratings.

Psychometric Properties of Appraisal Tools and Procedures

Approaches to Appraisal

As is true of standardized tests, performance evaluations can be either norm-referenced or criterion-referenced. In norm-referenced appraisals, employees are ranked relative to one another based on some trait, behavior, or output measure—this procedure does not necessarily involve the use of a performance appraisal scale. Typically, ranking is used when several employees are working on the same job. In criterion-referenced performance evaluations, the performance of each individual is judged against a standard defined by a rating scale. Our discussion in this section focuses on criterion-referenced appraisal because it is relevant to more jobs, particularly at the managerial level, and because it is the focus of the majority of the research.

In criterion-referenced performance appraisal the "measurement system" is a person-instrument couplet that cannot be separated. Unlike counters on machines, the scale does not measure performance; *people* measure performance using scales. Performance appraisal is a process in which humans judge other humans; the role of the rating scale is to make human judgment less susceptible to bias and error.

Can raters make accurate assessments using the appraisal instruments? In addressing this question, researchers have studied several types of rating error, each of which was believed to influence the accuracy of the resulting rating. Among the most commonly found types of errors and problems are (1) halo: raters giving similar ratings to an employee on several purportedly different independent rating dimensions (e.g., quality of work, leadership ability, and planning); (2) leniency: raters giving higher ratings than are warranted by the employee's performance; (3) restriction in range: raters giving similar ratings to all employees; and (4) unreliability: different raters rating the same ratee differently or the same rater giving different ratings from one time to the next.

Over the years, a variety of innovations in scale format have been introduced with the intention of reducing rater bias and error. Descriptions of various formats are presented below prefatory to the committee's review of research on the psychometric properties of performance appraisal systems.

Scale Formats

The earliest performance appraisal rating scales were graphic scales—they generally provided the rater with a continuum on which to rate a particular trait or behavior of the employee. Although these scales vary in the degree of explicitness, most provide only general guidance on the nature of the underlying dimension or on the definition of scale points along the continuum. Some scales present mere numerical anchors:

Leadership: 1   2   3   4

Others present adjectival descriptions at each anchor point:

Leadership:	1	2	3	4
	poor	satisfactory	exceeds expectations	outstanding

Raters are given the freedom to mark anywhere on the continuum—either at a defined scale point or somewhere between the points. Trait scales, which are constructed from employees' personal characteristics (such as integrity, intellectual ability, leadership orientation) are generally graphic scales. Many decades of research on ratings made with graphic scales found them fraught with measurement errors of unreliability, leniency, and range restriction, which many scholars attributed to the limited amount of definition and guidance they provided the rater.

In reaction to these perceived limitations of graphic scales, a second type of scale—behaviorally anchored rating scales (BARS)—was developed. The seminal work on BARS was done by Smith and Kendell (1963). Although BARS scales still present performance on a continuum, they provide specific behavioral anchors to help clarify the meaning of the performance dimensions and help calibrate the raters' definitions of what constitutes good and poor performance. Some proponents of behaviorally focused scales also claimed that they would eliminate unnecessary subjectivity (Latham and Wexley, 1977). The methodology used in BARS was designed by researchers to form a strong link between the critical behaviors in accomplishing a specific job and the instrument created to measure those behaviors. Scale development follows a series of detailed steps requiring careful job analysis and the identification of effective and ineffective examples of critical job behavior. The design process is iterative and there are often two or three groups of employees involved in review and evaluation. The final scales usually range from five to nine points and include behavioral examples around each point to assist raters in observing and evaluating employees' performance.

A third type of scale, the Mixed Standard Scale proposed by Blanz and Ghiselli (1972), was designed to be proactive in preventing rater biases. For each performance dimension of interest, three behavioral examples are developed that describe above-average, average, and below-average performance. However, raters are presented with a randomly ordered list of behavioral examples without reference to performance dimensions and are asked to indicate whether the ratee's performance is equal to, worse than, or better than the performance presented in the example. In this method, the graphic continuum and the definitions of the performance dimensions are eliminated from the rating form. The actual performance score is computed by someone other than the rater.

Forced-choice scales represent an even more extreme attempt to disguise the rating continuum from the rater. This method is based on the careful development of behavioral examples of the job that are assigned a preference value based on social desirability estimates made by job experts. Raters are presented with three or four equally desirable behaviors and asked to select the one that best describes the employee. The employee's final rating is calculated by someone other than the rater.

We turn now to a discussion of the validity, reliability, and other psychometric properties of performance appraisals, pointing out (as the literature allows) any evidence as to the relative merits of particular scale formats.

Validity

Validity is a technical term that has to do with the accuracy and relevance of measurements. Since the validity of performance appraisals is a critical issue to measurement specialists and a basic concern to practitioners who must withstand legal challenges to their performance appraisal tools and procedures, we are presenting the following discussion of validation strategies and how they apply to the examination of performance appraisal.

Cronbach (1990:150-151) describes validation as an "inquiry into the soundness of an interpretation." He sees the validation process as one of posing hypotheses, testing them, and supporting or revising the interpretation based on the findings. He makes the point that challenge to a proposition or hypothesis is as important as the collection of evidence supporting the interpretation. Within this framework, the researcher is continually recognizing rival hypotheses and testing them—the result is a greater understanding of the inferences that can be made about the characteristics of the individuals who take a test or who are measured on a performance appraisal scale.

If the discussion seems rarified thus far, a practical example drawn from one of the biggest success stories of the measurement tradition—testing to select aircraft crew members during World War II—may be of interest. In an article with the pithy title "Validity for What," Jenkins (1946) describes the development and use of a test to select pilots, navigators, and bombardiers. For each position, military psychologists found that those who scored well on the test were also the most successful in technical training, so the test was put into use to select aircrews. Several years into the war, uneasiness with the hit ratios on bombing runs led to Jenkins's follow-up study, which revealed that scores on the selection test, though they predicted success in bombardier training, were not correlated with success in hitting the target—and this, ultimately, was the performance of greatest interest.

At least three major validation strategies have been proposed in the area of testing—criterion-related, content, and construct validation. Although these strategies often have been treated as separate in the past, current thinking emphasizes that validation should integrate information from all approaches (Landy, 1986; Wainer and Braun, 1988; Cronbach, 1990). Content validation gives confidence in a test or measure by exploring the match between the content of the measure and the content of the job (e.g., a test of typing speed and accuracy for a clerk/typist job). Criterion-related validation demonstrates statistically the relationships between people's scores on a measurement instrument and their scores on the performance of interest (e.g., scores on an employment test and supervisor ratings of on-the-job performance; Scholastic Aptitude Test [SAT] scores and college grade-point average). This is an important way of providing scores with meaning. For example, if a company finds that job applicants who score 8 on an entry test usually get positive supervisor ratings or are likely to be the ones chosen for promotion at the end of a probationary period, whereas those who score 4 are far less likely to, the scores of 4 and 8 begin to take on some meaning. The search for construct validity is an attempt to get at the attribute that makes some individuals score 4 and others 8.

Cronbach (1990:179) views construct validation as a continuous process. He states: "An interpretation is to be supported by putting many pieces of evidence together. Positive results validate the measure and the construct simultaneously. Failure to confirm the claim leads to a search for a new measuring procedure or for a concept that fits the data better." In traditional analysis, two forms of evidence have been used to demonstrate construct validity. The first is convergent evidence, which shows that the measure in question is related to the other measures of the same construct. In psychological testing there are many tests or parts of tests that purport to measure the same construct. The second form of evidence is discriminant validity, which shows that a given measure of a construct has a weak relationship with measures of other constructs. Discriminant validity, according to Angoff (1988), is a stronger test of construct validity than is convergent validity because discriminant validity implies a challenge from rival hypotheses. Recently, psychometricians have expanded the view of construct validity to include evidence of content and criterion validity as well as other sources of evidence that serve to test hypotheses about the underlying nature of a construct. This expanded definition provides the opportunity for introducing a variety of forms of evidence to test validity.

Content Evidence   In performance appraisal, a determination of the content validity of the appraisal has been based on the type of analysis used in developing the appraisal instrument. If detailed job analyses or critical incident techniques were used and behaviorally based scales were developed, it has been generally assumed that the appraisal instruments have content validity. That is, the behaviors placed on the performance dimension scales look like they are representative of the behaviors involved in performing the job and they have been judged by the subject matter experts to be so. Several researchers have used this approach (e.g., Campbell et al., 1970; DeCotiis, 1977; Borman, 1978).

However, any simple reliance on content validity to justify a measurement system has long since been dismissed by measurement specialists. Even if the accomplishment of particular tasks is linked to effective job performance, a comprehensive enumeration of all job tasks and rating on each of them does not give any guidance on what is important to effective job performance and what is not. For example, at a nonmanagerial level, Bialek et al. (1977) reported that enlisted infantrymen spent less than half of their work time performing the technical tasks for which they had been trained; in many cases, only a small proportion of a soldier's time was devoted to accomplishing the tasks contained in the specific job description. These results are reinforced by the work of Campbell et al. (1970) and Christal (1974). What is needed is to go beyond the list of behaviors to a testable hypothesis about the behaviors that constitute effective task performance for a specific job construct.

Moreover, for some jobs, such as those involving managerial performance, the content validity approach is not particularly useful because a large portion of the employee's time is spent in behaviors that are either not observable or are not related to the accomplishment of a specific task. This is particularly true for managers who do many things that cannot be linked unambiguously to the accomplishment of specific tasks (Mintzberg, 1973, 1975). Thus it appears that a content approach is not likely to be sufficient for establishing measurement validity for any job, and for some jobs it will be of little value in making the link between job behaviors and effective performance.

Criterion Evidence   The criterion-related approach to validation is not as useful for evaluating performance appraisals as it is with selection tests used to predict later performance. The strength of the approach derives largely from showing a relationship (often expressed as a correlation coefficient) between the measure being validated and some independent, operational performance measure. The fact that course grades are moderately correlated with the SAT or American College Testing (ACT) examinations lends credibility to the claim that the tests measure verbal and quantitative abilities that are important to success in college. The crucial factor is the independence of the operational measure, and that is where difficulty arises. When the measure being studied is a behavioral one, it is difficult to find operational measures for comparison that have the essential independence.

So-called objective behavioral measures—attendance, tardiness, accidents, measures of output, or other indices that do not involve human judgment—appear to provide the best approximation of criteria for performance measures, but studies using such indices are rare. Heneman (1984) was able to locate only 23 studies with a total sample size of 3,178 workers, despite a literature search covering more than 50 years of published research. His meta-analysis assesses the relationship between supervisory ratings and a variety of unspecified "operational indicators" of job performance that do not derive from the rating process. Overall, the magnitude of the relationship between supervisor ratings and the results measures was, in the author's words, relatively weak (a mean correlation of .27, corrected for sampling error and attenuation, with a 90-percent confidence interval of −.07 to .61). The author concludes from this that supervisor ratings and results measures are clearly not interchangeable performance measures. Likewise, the overall results are not a terribly convincing demonstration of the criterion-related validity of performance appraisal, although that finding is hard to interpret since we know virtually nothing about the operational indicators used or, as the author points out, the many possible moderators of the relationship between the ratings and results measures. Furthermore, it is not clear from the article whether the objective measures and the performance ratings were used to evaluate the same performance dimension. Comparing ratings on one dimension with objective measures of another performance dimension tells us little about the relationship between the two measures.

John Hunter's (1983) meta-analysis takes a slightly different approach, looking at the relationships between tests of cognitive ability, tests of job knowledge, and two types of performance measures—job samples and supervisor ratings. He located 14 studies that included at least 3 of the 4 variables, 4 of them on military enlisted jobs (armor crewman, armor repairman, cook, and supply specialist), and 10 on civilian jobs such as cartographer, customs inspector, medical laboratory worker, and firefighter. The question that interested the author was whether supervisor ratings are determined entirely by job performance (the job sample measure) or whether the ratings are influenced by the employee's job knowledge. Hunter reaches the conclusion that job knowledge is twice as important as job performance in the determination of supervisor ratings. Thus his finding of a "moderately high" correlation between supervisor ratings and job performance (.35, corrected for unreliability) is "in large part due to the extent to which supervisors are sensitive to differences in job knowledge" (Hunter, 1983:265).

At least one old hand in the field interpreted Hunter's analysis as good news about performance appraisal. Guion (1983) commented that he had all but concluded that performance appraisal had only public relations value, but that the Hunter data showed to his satisfaction that ratings of performance are "valid, at least to a degree," because they are based to some degree on demonstrated ability to do the job (job sample measures) and on job knowledge. Guion offers a number of explanations for Hunter's finding that job knowledge is more highly correlated with supervisory ratings than are the performance measures. The nature of the performance measures may be part of the answer. Work samples are measures of maximum performance—what a person can do when being observed—rather than typical performance—what a person will do, day in and day out. It may well be that most supervisory ratings are more influenced by typical performance than the occasional best efforts. Or it may simply be that supervisors are more influenced by job knowledge because the direct contact of the supervisor with the employee to be rated is usually some sort of discussion, and discussion is likely to be more informative about job knowledge than actual performance. Whatever the exact cause, Guion suggests an important implication of Hunter's analysis that has special salience for this study: supervisor ratings, if they are more influenced by what employees have learned about their jobs than what they actually do on a day-to-day basis, may be more accurately viewed as trainability ratings than performance ratings.

The Army Selection and Classification Project (Project A) offers another study of the relationship between performance ratings and other measures of job proficiency, including hands-on performance, job knowledge tests, and training knowledge tests (*Personnel Psychology*, 1990). One of the purposes of this large-scale project was to develop a set of criteria for evaluating job performance in 19 entry-level army jobs. There were five performance factors identified for the criterion model: (1) core technical proficiency (tasks central to a particular job); (2) general soldiering proficiency (general military tasks); (3) effort and leadership; (4) personal discipline; and (5) physical fitness and military bearing. All types of proficiency measures, including performance ratings, were provided for each factor. The results, as reported by Campbell et al. (1990) show that overall performance ratings correlated .20 with a total hands-on score; when corrected for attenuation, the correlation increases to .36. This finding is consistent with the results presented in Hunter's meta-analysis (1983).

Convergent and Discriminant Evidence   Since other measures of the job performance construct have not been readily available in most settings, it has been necessary for researchers in performance appraisal to rely on agreement among raters or to develop special study designs that produce more than one measure of performance. Campbell and Fiske (1959) proposed the multimethod-multirater method for the purpose of determining the construct validity of trait ratings. Using this approach, two or more groups of raters are asked to rate the performance of the same employees using two rating methods. Examples of methods include BARS, graphic scales, trait scales, and global evaluation. Convergent validity is demonstrated by the agreement among raters across rating methods; discriminant validity is demonstrated by the degree to which the raters are able to distinguish among the performance dimensions.

Campbell et al. (1973) used the multimethod-multirater technique to compare the construct validity of behaviorally based rating scales with a rating of each behavioral example separated from its dimension (like a Mixed Standard Scale approach). In the summated rating method, raters provided one of four descriptors about the behavior ranging from "exhibiting almost never" to "almost always." The dimension score was the average of the item responses for that dimension. Both rating procedures were used for 537 managers of department stores within the same company. Ratings were provided by store managers and assistant store managers using each method. The behaviorally anchored scales were based on critical incidents collected and analyzed by study participants and researchers.

The results indicated significant convergent validity between rating methods and high discriminant validity between dimensions. That is, the raters agreed about ratees and about their perceptions of the dimensions as they were defined on the instruments. This suggests that the scales provided clear definitions of behaviors, which allowed the raters to discriminate among the behaviors with some degree of consistency. The behavioral rating scales were superior to the summated ratings in terms of halo (similarity of ratings across performance dimensions), leniency (inflated ratings), and discriminant validity. It is not surprising to find agreement between the rating methods, as they are based on the same dimension definitions and the raters were participants in the development of the rating instruments. It is worth noting that developing the behavioral scales was extremely time-consuming, but that the managers felt they gained a better understanding of critical job behaviors—those that could contribute to effective performance. This could be useful if the results were integrated into the management development process.

The weakness of this study is that it does not really compare substantially different methodologies. As Landy and Farr (1983) remarked with reference to a different set of studies, when a common procedure is used to develop the dimensions and/or examples, then the study is really only about different presentation modes—that is, the type of anchor.

Kavanagh et al. (1971) and Borman (1978) also used the multimethod-multirater method to examine convergent and discriminant validity. Kavanagh et al. (1971) compared ratings of managerial traits and job functions made by the superior and two subordinates of middle managers. The traits rated included intellectual capacities, concern for quality, and leadership, while job functions included factors like planning, investigating, coordinating, supervising, etc. The results showed agreement among raters about ratees (.44) but did not demonstrate the ability of the raters to discriminate among the rating dimensions. Raters were more consistent when evaluating personal traits than job functions and, according to Kavanagh et al. (1971), that finding suggests that ratings based on personality traits are more reliable than performance traits. However, they also show an increased level of halo over ratings based on job functions.

Borman (1978) examined the construct validity of BARS under highly controlled laboratory conditions for assessing the performance of managers and recruiting interviewers. Different groups of raters provided ratings for videotaped vignettes representing different levels of performance effectiveness on selected rating dimensions. Performance effectiveness on each dimension was established by a panel of experts. Convergent validity was determined by comparing the performance effectiveness rating of the experts with those of the raters viewing the taped performances—the resulting correlations was .69 for managers and .64 for recruiters. The discriminant validity, as measured by differences in raters' ratings of ratees across performance dimensions, was .58 for managers and .57 for recruiters. According to Borman, these correlations are higher than those generally found in applied settings. However, the results show that, if rating scales are carefully designed to match the characteristics of the job and if environmental conditions are controlled, highly reliable performance ratings can be provided.

Other Evidence of Construct Validity Under the expanded definition of validation strategies, there is an opportunity to incorporate information from all sources that might enhance our understanding of a construct. Three useful sources of research evidence that can contribute to knowledge about the validity of performance appraisal measures are (1) research studies reporting positive correlations of performance appraisal ratings with predictors of performance, (2) research studies suggesting that, for the most part, performance ratings do not correlate significantly with systematic sources of bias such as gender and age of either the rater or the ratee, and (3) research studies showing a positive relationship between performance appraisal feedback and worker productivity.

Validity studies that employ supervisory ratings as criteria for measuring the strength of predictors, such as cognitive or psychomotor ability tests, provide indirect evidence for the construct validity of performance ratings. There are literally thousands of validation studies in which supervisors provided performance ratings for use as criteria in measuring the predictive power of ability tests such as the General Aptitude Test Battery (GATB). The Standard Descriptive Rating Scale was specifically developed and used for most of the GATB criterion-related validity studies—raters participating in these studies were told that their ratings were for research purposes only. The results, based on 755 studies, showed that the average observed correlation between supervisor ratings and GATB test score was .26 (Hartigan and Wigdor, 1989).

Many of the advances in meta-analysis suggested by Schmidt and Hunter (1977) and Hunter and Hunter (1984) were developed to provide integrations of the vast literature on job performance prediction. Hunter (1983) in a detailed meta-analysis showed a corrected correlation of .27 between cognitive ability tests and supervisor ratings of employee job performance. Two additional meta-analyses compared supervisor ratings with other criteria used for test validation (Nathan and Alexander, 1988; and Schmitt et al., 1984). Nathan and Alexander (1988) found that for clerical jobs, ability test scores correlated with supervisor ratings .34, with rankings .51, and with work samples .54 (correlations were corrected for test unreliability, sample size, and range restriction). The results obtained by Schmitt et al. (1984) were similar: the average correlation between ability tests and supervisor ratings was .26 and between ability tests and work samples it was .40 (corrected for sampling error only). All of these studies demonstrate the existence of moderate correlations between employment test scores and supervisor ratings of employee job performance.

There are several studies that have examined the effects on performance appraisal ratings of the demographic characteristics of the ratee and the rater (e.g., race, gender, age). The hypothesis to be tested here is that these demographic characteristics do not influence performance appraisal ratings. On one hand, rejection of the hypothesis would mean that the validity of the performance ratings was weakened by the existence of these systematic sources of bias. On the other hand, if the hypothesis is not rejected, it can be assumed that the validity of the performance ratings is not being compromised by these sources of rating error.

There are meta-analyses of the research dealing with both race and gender effects. Kraiger and Ford's (1985) survey of 74 studies reported that the race of both the rater and the ratee had an influence on performance ratings; in 14 of the studies, both black and white raters were present. Over all studies supervisors gave higher ratings to same-race subordinates than to subordinates of a different race. The results showed that white raters rated the average white ratee higher than 64 percent of black ratees and black raters rated the average black ratee higher than 67 percent of white ratees. (The expected value, if there were no race effects, would be 50 percent in both cases.) In this analysis, ratee race accounted for 3.3 percent and 4.8 percent of the variance in ratings given by white and black raters, respectively. In a later study, the authors (Ford et al., 1986) attempted to assess the degree to which black-white differences on performance appraisal scores could be attributed to real performance differences or to rater bias. They looked at 53 studies that had at least one judgment-based and one independent measure (units produced, customer complaints) of performance. Among other things, they found that the size of the effects attributable to race were virtually identical for ratings and independent measures, which led the authors to conclude that the race effects found in judgment-based ratings cannot be attributed solely to rater bias—i.e., there were also real performance differences.

Carson et al. (1990) conducted a meta-analysis on 24 studies of gender effects in performance appraisal. In this review, gender effects were extremely small—the gender of both the ratee and the rater accounted for less than 1 percent of the variance in ratings. Although there was some evidence of a ratee-gender by rater-gender interaction (higher ratings for same gender versus mixed gender pairs), the interaction was not statistically significant. Murphy et al. (1986) reached similar conclusions in their review.

Age has also been shown to have a minimum effect on performance ratings. McEvoy and Cascio (1988) reported a meta-analysis of 96 studies relating ratee age to performance ratings. On average, the age of the ratee accounted for less than 1 percent of the variance in performance ratings. In addition, Landy and Farr (1983) suggest that if age effects exist at all, they are likely to be small.

Another source of indirect evidence for suggesting that under some conditions supervisors can make accurate performance ratings is the strength of the relationship between performance appraisal feedback and worker productivity— by inference, if feedback results in increased productivity, then the performance appraisal must be accurate. There are several studies that have shown that performance feedback does have a positive impact on worker productivity as measured in terms of production rates, error rates, and backlogs (Guzzo and Bondy, 1983; Guzzo et al., 1985; Kopelman, 1986). Landy et al. (1982) have shown that performance feedback has utility that far exceeds its cost, and that a valid feedback system can lead to substantial performance gains. They reviewed several studies showing that individual productivity increased as much as 30 percent as a function of feedback. In one of the studies (Hundal, 1969), a correlation of .52 (p < .01) was found between the level of feedback specificity and productivity. The subjects of Hundal's research were 18 industrial workers whose task was to grind metallic objects. This evidence is particularly interesting because it gets to the relevance of the appraisal, whereas much of the evidence of interrater reliability does not.

Interrater Reliability

There have been several studies suggesting that two or more supervisors in a similar situation evaluating the same subordinate are likely to give similar performance ratings (Bernardin, 1977; see Bernardin and Beatty, 1984 for a review of research on interrater reliability). For example, Bernardin et al. (1980) reported an interrater reliability coefficient of .73 among raters at the same level in the organization.

Other studies have examined the agreement among raters who occupy different positions in the organization. Although there is evidence that ratings obtained from different sources often differ in level—for example, self-ratings are usually higher than supervisory ratings (Meyer, 1980; Thornton, 1980)— there is substantial agreement among ratings from different sources with regard to the relative effectiveness of the performance of different ratees. Harris and Schaubroeck (1988), in a meta-analysis of research on rating sources, found an average correlation of .62 between peer and supervisory ratings (correlations between self-supervisor and self-peer ratings were .35 and .36, respectively).

One question of scale format that has received a good deal of attention in the reliability research concerns the number of scale points or anchors. According to Landy and Farr (1980), there is no gain in either scale or rater reliability when more than five rating categories are used. However, the reliability drops with the use of fewer than 3 or more than 9 rating categories. Recent work indicates that there is little to be gained from having more than 5 response categories.

Implications

There are substantial limitations in the kinds of evidence that can be brought to bear on the question of the validity of performance appraisal. The largest constraint is the lack of independent criteria for job performance that can be used to test the validity of various performance appraisal schemes. Given this constraint, most of the work has focused on (1) establishing content evidence through applying job analysis and critical incident techniques to the development of behaviorally based performance appraisal tools, (2) demonstrating interrater reliability, (3) examining the relationship between performance appraisal ratings, estimates of job knowledge, work samples, and performance predictors such as cognitive ability as a basis for establishing the construct validity of performance ratings, and (4) eliminating race, age, and gender as significant sources of rating bias. The results show that supervisors can give reliable ratings of employee performance under controlled conditions and with carefully developed rating scales. In addition, there is indirect evidence that supervisors can make moderately accurate performance ratings; this evidence comes from the studies in which supervisor ratings of job performance have been developed as criteria for testing the predictive power of ability tests and from a limited number of studies showing that age, race, and gender do not appear to have a significant influence on the performance rating process.

It should be noted that the distinction between validity and reliability tends to become hazy in the research on the construct validity of performance appraisals. Much of the evidence documents interrater reliabilities. While consistency of measurement is important, it does not establish the relevance of the measurement; after all, several raters may merely display the same kinds of bias. Nevertheless, the accretion of many types of evidence suggests that performance appraisals based on well-chosen and clearly defined performance dimensions can provide modestly valid ratings within the terms of psychometric analysis. Most of the research, however, has involved nonmanagerial jobs; the evidence for managerial jobs is sparse.

The consensus of several reviews is that variations in scale type and rating format have very little effect on the measurement properties of performance ratings as long as the dimensions to be rated and the scale anchors are clearly defined (Jacobs et al., 1980; Landy and Farr, 1983; Murphy and Constans, 1988).[2] In addition, there is evidence from research on the cognitive processes of raters suggesting that the distinction between behaviors and traits as bases for

---

[2] On a cautionary note, there are some important methodological weaknesses in the research comparing behaviorally anchored rating scales with other types of rating scales. In particular, the performance dimensions for the scales to be compared were generated by the same BARS methodology in some

rating is less critical than once thought. Whether rating traits or behaviors, raters appear to draw on trait-based cognitive models of each employee's performance. The result is that these general evaluations substantially affect raters' memory for and evaluation of actual work behaviors (Murphy et al., 1982; Ilgen and Feldman, 1983; Murphy and Jako, 1989; Murphy and Cleveland, 1991).

In litigation dealing with performance appraisal, the courts have shown a clear preference for job-specific dimensions. However, there is little research that directly addresses the comparative validity of ratings obtained on job-specific, general, or global dimensions. There is, however, a substantial body of research on halo error in ratings (see Cooper, 1981, for a review) that suggests that the generality or specificity of rating dimensions has little effect. This research shows that raters do not, for the most part, distinguish between conceptually distinct aspects of performance in rating their subordinates. That is, ratings tend to be organized around a global evaluative dimension (i.e., an overall evaluation of the individual's performance—see Murphy, 1982), and ratings of more specific aspects of performance provide relatively little information beyond the overall evaluation. This suggests that similar outcomes can be expected from rating scales that employ highly general or highly job-specific dimensions.

RESEARCH ON PERFORMANCE APPRAISAL APPLICATION

Chapter 6 provides a summary of private-sector practices in performance appraisal. Our purpose here is to present a general review of the research in industrial and organizational psychology and in management sciences that contributes to an understanding of how appraisal systems function in organizations. The principal issues include (1) the role of performance appraisal in motivating individual performance, (2) approaches to improving the quality of performance appraisal ratings, and (3) the types and sources of rating distortions (such as rating inflation) that can be anticipated in an organizational context. The discussion also includes the implications of links between performance appraisal and feedback and between performance appraisal and pay.

Performance Appraisal and Motivation

Information about one's performance is believed to influence work motivation in one of three ways. The first of these, formally expressed in contingency theory, is that it provides the basis for individuals to form beliefs about the causal connection between their performance and pay. Two contingency beliefs are important. The first of these is a belief about the degree of association

studies, so that what was really being tested was different presentation modes, not different scaling approaches (see Kingstrom and Bass, 1981; Landy and Farr, 1983).

between the person's own behavior and his or her performance. In Vroom's (1964) Expectancy X Valence model, these beliefs are labeled expectancies and described as subjective probabilities regarding the extent to which the person's actions relate to his or her performance. The second contingency is the belief about the degree of association between performance and pay. This belief is less about the person than it is about the extent to which the situation rewards or does not reward performance with pay, where performance is measured by whatever means is used in that setting. When these two contingencies are considered together, so goes the theory, it is possible for the person to establish beliefs about the degree of association between his or her actions and pay, with performance as the mediating link between the two.

The second mechanism through which performance information is believed to affect motivation at work is that of intrinsic motivation. All theories of intrinsic motivation related to task performance (e.g., Deci, 1975; Hackman and Oldham, 1976, 1980) argue that tasks, to be intrinsically motivating, must provide the necessary conditions for the person performing the task to feel a sense of accomplishment. To gain a sense of accomplishment, the person needs to have some basis for judging his or her own performance. Performance evaluations provide one source for knowing how well the job was done and for subsequently experiencing a sense of accomplishment. This sense of accomplishment may be a sufficient incentive for maintaining high performance during the time period following the receipt of the evaluation.

The third mechanism served by the performance evaluation is that of cueing the individual into the specific behaviors that are necessary to perform well. The receipt of a positive performance evaluation provides the person with information that suggests that whatever he or she did in the past on the job was the type of behavior that is valued and is likely to be valued in the future. As a result, the evaluation increases the probability that what was done in the past will be repeated in the future. Likewise, a negative evaluation suggests that the past actions were not appropriate. Thus, from a motivational standpoint, the performance evaluation provides cues about the direction in which future efforts should or should not be directed.

The motivational possibilities of performance appraisal are qualified by several factors. Although the performance rating/evaluation is treated as the performance of the employee, it remains a judgment of one or more people about the performance of another with all the potential limitations of any judgment. The employee is clearly aware of its character, and furthermore, it is only one source of evaluation of his or her performance. Greller and Herold (1975) asked employees from a number of organizations to rate five kinds of information about their own performance as sources of information about how well they were doing their job: performance appraisals, informal interactions with their supervisors, talking with coworkers, specific indicators provided by the job itself, and their own personal feelings. Of the five, performance appraisals were seen as the least likely to be useful for learning about performance. To the extent that many other sources are available for judging performance and the appraisal information is not seen as a very accurate source of information, appraisals are unlikely to play much of a role in encouraging desired employee behavior (Ilgen and Knowlton, 1981).

If employees are to be influenced by performance appraisals (i.e., attempts to modify their behavior in response to their performance appraisal), they must believe that the performance reported in the appraisal is a reasonable estimate of how they have performed during the time period covered by the appraisal. One key feature of accepting the appraisal is their belief in the credibility of the person or persons who completed the review with regard to their ability to accurately appraise the employee's performance. Ilgen et al. (1979), in a review of the performance feedback literature, concluded that two primary factors influencing beliefs about the credibility of the supervisor's judgments were expertise and trust. Perceived expertise was a function of the amount of knowledge that the appraisee believed the appraiser had about the appraisee's job and the extent to which the appraisee felt the appraiser was aware of the appraisee's work during the time period covered by the evaluation. Trust was a function of a number of conditions, most of which were related to the appraiser's freedom to be honest in the appraisal (Padgett, 1988) and the quality of the interpersonal relationship between the two parties.

A difficult motivational element related to acceptance of the performance appraisal message is the fact that the nature of the message itself affects its acceptance. There is clear evidence that individuals are very likely to accept positive information about themselves and to reject negative. This effect is often credited for the frequent finding that subordinates rate their own performance higher than do their supervisors (e.g., see Holzbach, 1978; Zammuto et al., 1981; and Shore and Thornton, 1986). Although this condition is not a surprising one, if the focus is on the nature of the response that employees will make to performance appraisal information, then the existence of the discrepancy means that the employee is faced with two primary methods of resolving the discrepancy: acting in line with the supervisor's rating or denying the validity of that rating. The fact that the latter alternative is very frequently chosen, especially when the criteria for good performance are not very concrete (as is often the case for managerial jobs), is one of the reasons that performance appraisals often fail to achieve their desired motivational effect.

Approaches to Increasing the Quality of Rating Data

Applied psychologists have identified a variety of factors that can influence how a supervisor rates a subordinate. Some of these factors are associated with the philosophy and climate of the organization and may influence the rater's willingness to provide an accurate rating. Other factors are related to the technical aspects of conducting a performance appraisal, such as the ability of the rater (1) to select and observe the critical job behaviors of subordinates, (2) to recall and record the observed behaviors, and (3) to interpret adequately the contribution of the behaviors to effective job performance. This section will discuss the research designed to reduce errors associated with the technical aspects of conducting a performance appraisal. Specific areas include rater training programs, behaviorally based rating scales, and variations in rating procedures.

Rater Training

The results of the effects of training on rating quality are mixed. A recent review by Feldman (1986) concluded that rater training has not been shown to be highly effective in increasing the validity and accuracy of ratings. Murphy et al. (1986) reviewed 15 studies (primarily laboratory studies) dealing with the effects of training on leniency and halo and found that average effects were small to moderate. In a more recent study, Murphy and Cleveland (1991) suggest that training is most appropriate when the underlying problem is a lack of knowledge or understanding. For example, training is more necessary if the performance appraisal system requires complicated procedures, calculations, or rating methods. However, these authors also suggested that the accuracy of overall or global ratings will not be influenced by training.

Taking the other position, Fay and Latham (1982) proposed that rater training is more important in reducing rating errors than is the type of rating scale used. They compared the rating responses of trained and untrained raters on three rating scales (one trait and two behaviorally based scales). The results showed significantly fewer rating errors for the trained raters and for the behaviorally based scales compared with the trait scales. The rating errors were one and one half to three times as large for the untrained group.

The training was a four-hour workshop consisting of (1) having trainees' rate behaviors presented on videotape and then identifying similar behaviors in the workplace, (2) a discussion of the types of rating errors made by trainees, (3) a group brainstorming on how to avoid errors. The workshop contained no examples of appropriate rating distributions or scale intercorrelations; the focus was on accurate observation and recording. Researchers have found that instructing raters to avoid giving similar ratings across rating dimensions or giving high ratings to several individuals may not be appropriate; some individuals do well in more than one area of performance and many individuals may perform a selected task effectively (Bernardin and Buckley, 1981; Latham, 1988). Thus, these instruction could result in inaccurate ratings.

Other researchers have shown that training in observation skills is beneficial (Thornton and Zorich, 1980) and that training can help raters develop a common frame of reference for evaluating ratee performance (Bernardin and Buckley,

1981; McIntyre et al., 1984). However, the training effects documented in these laboratory studies are typically not large, and it is not clear whether they persist over time.

Behaviorally Based Rating Scale Design

Another approach used by researchers to reduce rating errors has involved the use of rating scales that present the rater with a more accurate or complete representation of the behaviors to be observed and evaluated. Behaviorally based scales may serve as a memory or observation aid; if developed accurately, they can provide raters with a standard frame of reference. The strategy of using behaviorally based scales to improve observation might be especially helpful if combined with observation skill training. However, there is some evidence that these scales can unduly bias the observations and the recall processes of raters. That is, raters may attend only to the behaviors depicted on the scales to the exclusion of other, potentially important behaviors. Moreover, there is no compelling evidence that behaviorally based scales facilitate the performance appraisal process in a meaningful way, when these scales are compared with others developed with the same care and attention.

Rating Sequence

Supervisors rating many individuals on several performance dimensions could either complete ratings in a person-by-person sequence or in a dimension-by-dimension sequence (rate all employees on dimension I and then go on to dimension II, etc.). Presumably, a person-by-person procedure focuses the rater's attention on the strengths and weaknesses of the individual, while the dimension-by-dimension procedure focuses attention on the differences among individuals on each performance dimension. A review of this research by Landy and Farr (1983) indicates that identical ratings are obtained with either strategy.

Implications

Although the results are mixed, the most promising approach to increasing the quality of ratings appears to be a combination of factors including good scales, well-trained raters, and a context that supports and encourages the appraisal process. With respect to training, Latham (1988) and Fay and Latham (1982) found that training in the technical aspects of the performance appraisal process, if done properly, can lead to more accurate ratings. Their results suggest that if raters are trained to recognize effective and ineffective performance and are informed about pitfalls such as the influence of false first impressions, they can provide more reliable and accurate ratings than raters who have not received training.

The implication is that training in the use of performance appraisal technology can lead to both a more acceptable and a more effective system. However, training is only one among several factors with potential influences on the performance appraisal process. As mentioned earlier, the rater's approach to the process is affected by organizational goals, degree of managerial discretion, management philosophy, and external political and market forces, to name a few. Even if raters have been trained properly and have a good grasp of the rating process, they may distort their ratings on the basis of their perceptions of organizational factors. There is also evidence to suggest that the purpose of the rating may lead to rating distortion.

Context: Sources of Rating Distortion

It is widely assumed that the purpose of rating, or more specifically, the uses of rating data in an organization, affects the appraisal process and appraisal outcomes (Landy and Farr, 1980; Mohrman and Lawler, 1983; Murphy and Cleveland, 1991). That is, it is assumed that the same individual might receive different ratings and different feedback if a performance appraisal system is used to make administrative decisions (e.g., salary adjustment, promotion) than if it is used for employee development, systems documentation, or a number of other purposes. Furthermore, it is assumed that the rater will pay attention to different information about the ratee and will evaluate that information differently as a function of the purpose of the appraisal system.

One of the major barriers to testing the assumption stated above has been the complexity of actual appraisal systems. Cleveland et al. (1989) documented 20 separate uses for performance appraisal and showed that most organizations use appraisal for a large number of different purposes, some of which may be conflicting (e.g., salary administration versus employee development). Thus, it is often difficult to characterize the primary purpose or even the major purposes of appraisal in any given setting. Some authors have suggested separate appraisal systems for different purposes (Meyer et al., 1965), but Cleveland et al.'s (1989) survey suggests that this is rarely done.

Most studies of the effects of the purpose of rating involve comparisons between ratings that are used to make administrative decisions and ratings collected for research purposes only (a few studies have examined ratings collected for feedback purposes only). Many of these studies were carried out in the laboratory, although there have been some field studies, particularly in the area of teacher evaluations. The most common finding is that ratings used to make administrative decisions are higher or more lenient than ratings used for research or feedback (Taylor and Wherry, 1951; Heron, 1956; Sharon and Bartlett, 1969; Bernardin et al., 1980; Zedeck and Cascio, 1982; Williams et al., 1985; Reilly and Balzer, 1988). Other studies have failed to demonstrate the effects of rating purpose on rating results (Berkshire and Highland, 1953; Borreson, 1967; Murphy et al., 1984).

There is a broader literature that is mainly speculative or anecdotal dealing with the effects of rating purpose on rating outcomes. For example, in a series of interviews with executives, Longenecker et al. (1987) reported frank admissions of political dimensions of performance appraisal—i.e., the conscious manipulation of appraisals to achieve desired outcomes (see Longenecker, 1989; Longenecker and Gioia, 1988). Similarly, interviews conducted by Bjerke et al. (1987) showed clear evidence of conscious manipulation of ratings. This study was conducted in the Navy, and the majority of raters reported that they considered the outcomes of giving high or low ratings before filling out appraisal forms, and that they filled out forms in ways that would maximize the likelihood of outcomes they desired (e.g., promotion for a deserving subordinate) rather than reporting their true evaluations of each subordinate's present performance level.

One reason for the relative lack of field research on rating distortion is that, although thought to be widespread, rating distortion is a behavior that is officially subject to sanction. Longenecker (1989) and Murphy and Cleveland (1991) make the point that rating distortion is often necessary and beneficial; brutally frank ratings would probably do more harm than good. Nevertheless, organizations rarely admit that ratings should sometimes be distorted. As a result, it is difficult to secure cooperation from organizations in research projects that examine the incidence, causes, or effects of rating distortion.

Both Mohrman and Lawler (1983) and Murphy and Cleveland (1991) applied instrumentality models of motivation to explain rating distortion. These models suggest that raters will fill out appraisal forms in ways that maximize the rewards and minimize the punishment that they are likely to receive as a result of rating. Instrumentality theories suggest that the rater's choice to turn in distorted ratings will depend on: (a) the value he or she attaches to the outcomes of turning in distorted ratings and (b) the perceived likelihood that turning in distorted ratings will lead to those outcomes.

In the context of pay for performance, instrumentality theories suggest that the motivation to distort ratings may be strong. Turning in low ratings could have substantial negative consequences for subordinates (i.e., lower pay), which are very likely to lead to subsequent interpersonal difficulties between supervisors and subordinates and to lower levels of subordinate motivation. By turning in high ratings, supervisors may be able to avoid a number of otherwise difficult problems in their interactions with their subordinates.

Equity theory provides a second, related framework for explaining rating distortion. That is, raters might distort ratings to achieve or maintain equity within the work group. For example, an individual who received a low raise last year, perhaps because of a budgetary shortfall, might receive higher-than-deserved ratings this year in an attempt to restore equity. Similarly, raters might distort ratings to guarantee that salaries stay reasonably constant for individuals within the work group who perform similar jobs. In both cases, attaining or maintaining parity might be viewed as more important then rewarding present performance.

While these predictions of instrumentality theories are reasonable, empirical research on motivational factors in rating distortion is rare. For example, there is some disagreement about the extent to which negative reactions on the part of ratees will actually affect the rater's behavior (Napier and Latham, 1986). More fundamentally, little is known about the factors actually considered by raters when they decide how to complete their rating forms (Murphy and Cleveland, 1991).

FINDINGS

Job Analysis

1. Job analysis and the specification of critical elements and standards can inform but not replace the supervisor's judgment in the performance appraisal process.

Managerial Performance

1. Most of the research on managerial performance describes broad categories of managerial tasks such as leadership, communication, and planning.

2. Managerial performance does not lend itself to easily quantifiable job-specific measurement: many of the tasks performed by managers are amorphous and not directly observable. The bulk of the existing research on job performance and performance appraisal deals with jobs that are more concrete and with clearer outcome measures—research that is not directly relevant to managerial jobs.

Psychometric Properties

1. Within the framework of the psychometric tradition, research establishes that performance appraisals show a fairly high degree of reliability and moderate validities.

2. There is some evidence that performance appraisals can motivate employees and can improve the quality and quantity of their work when the supervisor is trusted and perceived as knowledgeable by the employee.

3. Real-world influences such as organizational culture, market forces, and rating purposes can work to distort performance appraisals.

4. The research does not provide clear guidance on which scale format to use or whether to rely on global or job-specific ratings, although a consensus seems to be building that scale type and scale format are matters of indifference,

all things being equal. For example, one line of research suggests that rating scale format and the number of rating categories are not critical as long as the dimensions to be rated and the scale anchors are clearly defined. Another line of research suggests that raters tend to rely on broad traits in making judgments about employee performance, making the old distinctions between trait scales and behavioral scales appear less important.

5.   Although behaviorally based scales have not been shown to be superior to other scales psychometrically, some researchers suggest that behaviorally anchored rating scales offer advantages in providing employees with feedback and in establishing the external and internal legitimacy of the performance appraisal system.

6.   There is some evidence that rater training in the technology of performance appraisal tools and procedures can lead to more accurate performance ratings.

In sum, the research examined here does not provide the policy maker with strong guidance on choosing a performance appraisal system. Instead, the literature presents the complexities and pitfalls of attempting to quantify and assess what employees, particularly managers and professionals, do that contributes to effective job performance. All of the appraisal systems that are behaviorally based require a significant amount of initial development effort and cost, are not easily generalizable across jobs, apparently offer little if any psychometric advantage, and require significant additional effort as jobs change. The primary value of behaviorally based appraisal is that it appears relevant to both the supervisor and the employee and it may provide an effective basis for corrective feedback.

GAPS IN EXISTING RESEARCH

A critical gap in the empirical research on performance appraisal relates to the influence of the rating context on the rating outcome. How does context affect the relationship between the supervisor and the employee and how does the nature of this relationship modify the supervisor's willingness to provide reliable ratings? Moreover, how specifically does the purpose of the rating change the rater's willingness to be accurate? Although the literature on performance appraisal discusses a variety of theoretical positions that bear on these questions, there is little convincing data on the extent or the causes of distortion in rating. As noted earlier, the existing theory suggests that pay-for-performance systems will be especially prone to distortion, particularly in contexts in which the base pay is regarded as unfairly low. However, it is unlikely that an adequate body of evidence *could* be assembled to document this phenomenon.

A second gap, already noted above, concerns managerial performance appraisal. The existing body of research deals with different (i.e., lower-level) jobs, and more important, different types of appraisal systems. The federal system has characteristics of both the traditional top-down system and management-by-objective systems (e.g., the use of elements, standards, and objectives that are defined by the supervisor represents a mix of concepts from both types of systems). It is not clear whether either the body of research at lower levels in the private sector or research on managerial appraisal and management-by-objective systems is fully relevant to the federal system.

A third gap has to do with the implications of the reliability, validity, and other psychometric properties of appraisal systems for the behavior of employees and the organization's effectiveness. With few exceptions, the research does not establish any performance effects of performance appraisal. The preponderance of evidence relates to the consistency of measurement, not the relevance. Research documenting the impact of appraisal systems on organizations and their members is sparse, fragmented, and often poorly done. Empirical evidence is needed to determine whether organizations or their members actually benefit in any substantial way when appraisals are done, other than to the extent that legitimacy is provided and belief systems reinforced.

5

Pay for Performance:
Perspectives and Research

The committee's charge from the Office of Personnel Management included an examination of research on the effects of performance appraisal and merit pay plans on organizations and their employees. We have extended the scope of our review to include research on the performance effects of pay-for-performance plans more generally (merit, individual, and group incentive pay plans) and other research on pay system fairness and costs. We did this for two reasons. First, we found virtually no research on merit pay that directly examined its effects. Second, the research on pay-for-performance plans makes it clear that their effects on individual and organization performance can not be easily disentangled from other aspects of pay systems, other pay system objectives, and the broader context of an organization's strategies, structures, management and personnel systems, and environment (Galbraith, 1977; Balkin and Gomez-Mejia, 1987a; Ehrenberg and Milkovich, 1987; Milkovich and Newman, 1990).

This chapter is organized around these points. The first section describes merit, individual, and group incentive pay-for-performance plans and classifies them in a matrix formed by two major dimensions of plan design. We next use this matrix to review research on the influence of different pay-for-performance plans on the pay system objectives that organizations typically report—improving the attraction/retention/performance of successful employees, fair treatment and equity, and cost regulation, with the trade-offs among other pay objectives it entails. When relevant, we describe the contextual conditions that appear to influence plan effects or are associated with unintended, negative consequences when pay-for-performance plans are used. We then summarize

77

our conclusions drawn from this research and discuss their implications for federal policy makers.

PAY-FOR-PERFORMANCE PLANS: A FIELD GUIDE

Although there is a startling array of pay-for-performance plan designs in use, they can be described and classified on some common design dimensions. In Figure 5-1 we have classified pay-for-performance plans in a two-dimensional matrix. The first dimension represents design variation in the level of performance measurement—individual or group—to which plan payouts are tied. The group level of measurement encompasses work group performance, facility (plant or department) performance, and organization performance. The second dimension represents design variation in the plan's contribution to growth in base pay: some plans add payouts to base salary; others do not.

The matrix cells in Figure 5-1 provide examples of pay-for-performance plans distinguished on both design dimensions. Merit plans are an example of pay-for-performance plans found in the first cell. They are tied to individual levels of performance measurement (typically performance appraisal ratings), and the payouts allocated under merit plans are commonly added into an individual employee's base salary. The performance appraisal ratings used with merit plans often combine both behavioral (for example, provided timely feedback to employees) and outcome (for example, reduced overhead 10 percent) measures of performance. Performance appraisal ratings are used along with the employee's pay grade, position in grade, and the company's increase budget to determine the payout each employee will receive. The average payout offered by a merit plan is typically smaller than that offered by other types of plans and is provided annually (HayGroup, Inc., 1989). (Merit pay increases do, however, compound from one year to the next—over time, outstanding performers will reach a significantly higher pay level than average performers.) Merit plans are used across the spectrum of employee groups, from hourly and clerical to high-level managers.

Examples of individual pay-for-performance plans in which payouts are not

| | | LEVEL OF PERFORMANCE | |
		Individual	Group
CONTRIBUTION TO BASE SALARY	Added to base	(a) Merit plans	(d) Small group incentives
	Not added to base	(b) Piece rates Commissions Bonuses	(c) Profit sharing Gainsharing Bonuses

FIGURE 5-1 Pay-for-performance plan classes.

added to base salaries—cell b—include piece rate and sales commission plans. Piece rate plans involve engineered standards of hourly or daily production. Workers receive a base wage for production that meets standard and incentive payments for production above standard. Piece rate plans are most commonly found in hourly, clerical, and technical jobs. Sales commission plans tie pay increases to specific individual contributions, such as satisfactory completion of a major project or meeting a quantitative sales or revenue target. These plans are most commonly found among sales employees. Payouts under individual incentive plans are typically larger than those found under merit plans (Hay-Group, Inc., 1989) and are often made more frequently (piece rate plans, for example, can pay out every week).

It is important to note that, although individual incentive plans can offer relatively large payouts that increase as an employee's performance increases, they also carry the risk of no payouts if performance thresholds are not reached. Thus, unless employers make market or cost-of-living adjustments to base salaries, individual incentives pose the risk of lower earnings for employees and the potential advantage of lower proportional labor costs for employers. The same is true of group incentive plans.

The matrix in Figure 5-1 helps to simplify and guide our discussion of research on pay-for-performance plans, but it is difficult to classify all plans neatly into one cell or another. Bonus plans—particularly those typical for managerial and professional employees—are a good example. These plans often combine both individual- and group-level measures of performance, with an emphasis on the latter. For example, a managerial bonus plan may combine measures of departmental productivity and cost control with individual behavioral measures, such as "develops employees." Like the other individual and group incentive plans, these bonus plans offer relatively large payments that are not added into base salaries (HayGroup, Inc., 1989), but they do not necessarily pay out more than once a year. We consider these types of bonus plans under research on group incentives.

Pay-for-performance plans tied to group levels of measurement can, in principle, also be divided into those that add payouts to base salaries and those that do not. However, few examples of group plans that add payouts into base salaries exist (cell d in Figure 5-1). More common are plans that tie payouts to work group, facility (such as a plant or department), or organization performance measures and do not add pay into base salaries (cell c). There are many variations on profit-sharing plans, but most link payouts to selected organization profit measures and often pay out quarterly. A cash profit-sharing plan, for example, might specify that each employee covered will receive a payout equal to 15 percent of salary if the company's profit targets are met. Gainsharing plans, like profit sharing, come in many forms, but all tie payouts to some measure of work group or facility performance, and most pay out more than once a year. Traditional gainsharing plans, such as Scanlon, Rucker, or

Improshare plans (named by or for their inventors), commonly provide a monthly bonus to workers of a production line or plant. The bonus is based on value added or cost savings, defined as the difference between current production or labor costs and the historical averages of these costs (as established by accounting data). Savings are split between employees and management; the employees' share of the savings is then typically allocated to each employee as some uniform percentage of base pay.

Our choice of matrix dimensions was deliberate; they distinguish the major differences between merit pay and other types of pay-for-performance plans, and they reflect distinctions made in the research we reviewed. We refer to the matrix throughout our review of research to help distinguish the four types of pay-for-performance plans and the research findings related to each.

PAY FOR PERFORMANCE: RESEARCH FINDINGS

Organization pay objectives include motivating employees to perform, as well as attracting and retaining them; the fair and equitable treatment of employees; and regulating labor costs. We are interested in research on how pay-for-performance plans influence an organization's ability to meet these objectives and in the conclusions we can draw—particularly regarding merit pay plans. Obviously, the pay objectives listed are related, and organizations will face trade-offs in trying to meet them, whether a particular pay-for-performance plan or no pay-for-performance plan is adopted. We deal with these trade-offs in a subsequent section.

Do pay-for-performance plans help sustain or improve individual and group or organization performance? Research examines this question most directly, and we review it first.

Motivating Employee Performance

The research most directly related to questions about the impact of pay-for-performance plans on individual and organization performance comes from theory and empirical study of work motivation. The social sciences have produced many theories to explain how making pay increases contingent on performance might motivate employees to expend more effort and to direct that effort toward achieving organizational performance goals. Expectancy theory (Vroom, 1964) has been the most extensively tested, and there appears to be a general consensus that it provides a convincing (if simplistic) psychological rationale for why pay-for-performance plans can enhance employee efforts, and an understanding of the general conditions under which the plans work best (Lawler, 1971; Campbell and Pritchard, 1976; Dyer and Schwab, 1982; Pinder, 1984; Kanfer, 1990). Expectancy theory predicts that employee motivation will be enhanced, and the likelihood of desired performance increased, under pay-for-performance plans when the following conditions are met:

(1) Employees understand the plan performance goals and view them as "doable" given their own abilities, skills, and the restrictions posed by task structure and other aspects of organization context;

(2) There is a clear link between performance and pay increases that is consistently communicated and followed through; and

(3) Employees value pay increases and view the pay increases associated with a plan as meaningful (that is, large enough to justify the effort required to achieve plan performance goals).

Goal-setting theory (Locke, 1968; Locke et al., 1970), also well tested, complements expectancy theory predictions about the links between pay and performance by further describing the conditions under which employees see plan performance goals as doable. According to Locke et al. (1981) the goal-setting process is most likely to improve employee performance when goals are specific, moderately challenging, and accepted by employees. In addition, feedback, supervisory support, and a pay-for-performance plan making pay increases—particularly "meaningful" increases—contingent on goal attainment appear to increase the likelihood that employees will achieve performance goals.

Taken together, expectancy and goal-setting theories predict that pay-for-performance plans can improve performance by directing employee efforts toward organizationally defined goals, and by increasing the likelihood that those goals will be achieved—given that conditions such as doable goals, specific goals, acceptable goals, meaningful increases, consistent communication and feedback are met.

Individual Incentive Plans

Among the pay-for-performance plans displayed in our matrix (Figure 5-1, cell b), individual incentive plans, such as piece rates, bonuses, and commissions, most closely approximate expectancy and goal-setting theory conditions. Individual incentive plans tie pay increases to individual level, quantitative performance measures. It is generally believed that employees view individual-level measures as more doable, because they are more likely to be under the individual's direct control. This is in contrast to group incentive plans (cells c and d in Figure 5-1), which are typically tied to measures of work group, facility, or organization performance. Similarly, quantitative measures are seen as more acceptable to employees because their achievement is less likely to be distorted and more directive because they dictate specific goals. This is in contrast to merit plans (cell a in Figure 5-1), which are typically tied to more qualitative, less specific measures of performance (see Lawler, 1971, 1973, for a more detailed analysis of these points). Individual incentive plans also typically offer larger, and thus potentially more meaningful, payouts than most merit pay plans.

Given that individual incentive plans meet several of the ideal motivational conditions prescribed by expectancy and goal-setting theories, it is not surprising that related empirical studies tend to focus on individual rather than merit or group incentive plans. In reviews of expectancy theory research, Campbell and Pritchard (1976), Dyer and Schwab (1982), and Ilgen (1990) all agree that these studies establish the positive effect of individual incentive plans on employee performance. The studies reviewed include both correlational field studies and experimental laboratory studies, with the correlational studies predominating. While these studies were primarily designed to test specific components of expectancy theory models, they all show simple correlations, ranging from .30 and .40, between expectancy theory conditions and individual performance measures; this means that, when these conditions are met, 9 to 16 percent of the variance in individual performance can be explained by differences in incentives.

Cumulative studies (primarily laboratory) also support goal-setting theory predictions that specific goals, goal acceptance, and so forth, will increase employee goal achievement—in some cases, by as much as 30 percent over baseline measures (Locke et al., 1981). A laboratory study by Pritchard and Curts (1973) also reported that individual pay incentives increased the probability of goal achievement, but only if the incentive amount was meaningful. In this study "meaningful" was three dollars versus fifty cents versus no payment for different levels of goal achievement on a simple sorting task. Only the three-dollar incentive had a significant effect on individual goal achievement. Similar findings have been reported by others (see Terborg and Miller, 1978).

There are also some early field studies of piece-rate-type individual incentive plans conducted in the wake of claims made by Frederick W. Taylor (1911), the prophet of "scientific management" and inventor of the time and motion study. The more methodologically sound studies generally compared the productivity of manufacturing workers paid by the hour and those paid on a piece rate plan, reporting that workers paid on piece rates were substantially more productive—between 12 and 30 percent more productive—as long as 12 weeks after piece rates were introduced (Burnett, 1925; Wyatt, 1934; Roethlisberger and Dickson, 1939).

Viewed as a whole, these studies establish that individual incentives can have positive effects on individual employee performance. But it is also important to understand the restricted organizational conditions under which these results are observed without accompanying unintended, negative consequences. Case studies suggest that individual incentive plans are most problem-free when the employees covered have relatively simple, structured jobs, when the performance goals are under the control of the employees, when performance goals are quantitative and relatively unambiguous, and when frequent, relatively large payments are offered for performance achievement.

There are a number of case studies that document the potentially negative, unintended consequences of using individual incentive plans outside these restricted conditions. Lawler (1973) summarizes the results of these case studies and their implications for organizations. He points out that individual incentive plans can lead employees to (1) neglect aspects of the job that are not covered in the plan performance goals; (2) encourage gaming or the reporting of invalid data on performance, especially when employees distrust management; and (3) clash with work group norms, resulting in negative social outcomes for good performers.

Babchuk and Goode (1951) reported an example of neglecting aspects of a job not covered by plan performance goals. Their case study of retail sales employees in a department store showed that when an individual incentive plan tying pay increases to sales volume was introduced, sales volume increased, but work on stock inventory and merchandise displays suffered. Employees were uncooperative, to the point of "stealing" sales from one another and hiding desirable items to sell during individual shifts. Whyte (1955) and Argyris (1964) provided examples of how individuals on piece rate incentives or bonus plans tied to budget outcomes distorted performance data. Whyte described how workers on piece rate plans engaged in games with the time study man who was trying to engineer a production standard; Argyris described how managers covered by bonus plans tied to budgets bargained with their supervisors to get a favorable budget standard. Many studies of individual incentive plans—from the Roethlisberger and Dickson field experiments to case studies like those of Whyte—have shown clashes between work group production norms and high production by individual workers, which led to negative social sanctions for the high performers (for example, social ostracism by the group).

These studies also suggested that development of restrictive social norms had some economic foundation: employees feared that high levels of production would lead to negative economic consequences such as job loss, lower incentive rates, or higher production standards. Restrictive norms were also more common when employee-management relations were poor, and employees generally distrusted managers.

These findings suggest the dangers of using individual incentive plans for employees in complex, interdependent jobs requiring work group cooperation; in instances in which employees generally distrust management; or in an economic environment that makes job loss or the manipulation of incentive performance standards likely. Indeed, a recent study by Brown (1990) reported that manufacturing organizations were less likely to use piece rate incentives for hourly workers when their jobs were more complex (a variety of duties) or when their assigned tasks emphasized quality over quantity. Since many modern organizations face one or both of these conditions—especially complex, inter-dependent jobs—but may still be unwilling to bypass the potential performance improvements promised by individual incentives, some researchers suggest that they have adopted merit plans and group incentive plans in an effort to reap those benefits without the negative consequences (Lawler, 1973; Mitchell and Broderick, 1991).

Merit Pay Plans

It is not difficult to view merit pay plan design as a means of overcoming some of the unintended consequences of individual incentive plans. This is especially true when merit plans are considered in the context of more com-plex managerial and professional jobs. As we document in the next chapter, merit pay plans are almost universally used for managerial and professional employees in large private-sector organizations. The most common merit plan design is a "merit grid" that directs supervisors to allocate annual pay increases according to an employee's salary grade, position in the grade, and individ-ual performance appraisal rating. The type of performance appraisal most commonly used for managerial and professional jobs involves a management-by-objective (MBO) format in which a supervisor and an employee jointly define annual job objectives—typically both qualitative and quantitative ones. The rating categories or standards generated from MBO appraisals are usually qualitative and broadly defined. Most organizations use three to five categories that differentiate among top performers, acceptable performers (one to two cat-egories), and poor or unsatisfactory performers (one to two categories), with the acceptable category (or categories) covering the majority of employees (Wyatt Company, 1987; Bretz and Milkovich, 1989; HayGroup, Inc., 1989). Merit plan payouts are relatively small (in the private sector the average payout for the last five years has hovered around 5 percent of base salary, compared with middle management/professional bonus payouts of 18 percent plus—HayGroup, Inc., 1989); however, they are added into an employee's base salary while bonuses typically are not. This addition of payouts to base offers the potential for cumulative long-term salary growth not typical of other salary plans.

The use of an objectives-based performance appraisal format might be reasonably viewed as recognition that it is difficult to capture all the important aspects of managerial and professional jobs in a single, comprehensive measure such as "sales volume"; multiple measures, quantitative and qualitative, might be developed in such appraisal formats, thus decreasing the probability that im-portant aspects of a job will be ignored. The choice of a performance appraisal format may also assume that the perspectives of both supervisor and employee are needed to set appropriate objectives and avoid gaming. The broader per-formance appraisal rating categories typical of merit pay plans may also tend to decrease clashes between work group norms and an individual performer, since the majority of employees are rated as acceptable. The relatively smaller payouts and their addition to base salaries could also make merit plans seem less economically threatening than individual incentive plans.

Merit plan design characteristics, intended to diminish the potentially negative consequences of individual incentive plans, can, however, also dilute their motivation and performance effects. Performance appraisal objectives are typically less specific than the quantitative ones found under individual incentive plans. Employees may thus see them as less doable and more subject to multiple interpretations, and their attainment may be less clearly linked to employee performance. Pay increases are smaller and may be viewed as less meaningful; the addition of pay increases into base salaries may also dilute the pay-for-performance link (Lawler, 1981; Krzystofiak et al., 1982). Many management theorists have suggested that employers focus on the process aspects of performance appraisal and merit plans in order to enhance their motivational potential (see Hackman et al., 1977; Latham and Wexley, 1981; and Murphy and Cleveland, 1991, for reviews). For example, employee-supervisor interaction and bargaining during performance appraisal objective-setting could increase an employee's commitment and understanding of goals and feelings of trust toward management. Training both supervisors and employees in how to use performance appraisal objective-setting, feedback, and negotiation effectively is recommended. Communication of merit pay plans as a means of differentiating individual base salaries according to long-term career performance is also suggested as a means of helping employees to see these plans as providing meaningful pay increase potential. Our review of merit pay practices in the next chapter shows that some organizations are following these recommendations.

There is very little research on merit pay plans in general nor on the relationship between merit pay plans and performance—either individual or group—in particular.

In a recent review of research on merit plans, Heneman (1990) reported that studies examining the relationship between merit pay and measures of individual motivation, job satisfaction, pay satisfaction, and performance ratings have produced mixed results. The field studies comparing managers and professionals under merit plans with those under seniority-related pay increase plans, or no formal increase plan, suggest that the presence of a merit plan positively influences measures of employee job satisfaction and employee perceptions of the link between pay and performance. In several of these studies, the stronger measures of job satisfaction and of employee perceptions of pay-to-performance links found under merit pay plans were also correlated with higher individual performance ratings (Kopelman, 1976; Greene, 1978; Allan and Rosenberg, 1986; Hills et al., 1988). However, other field studies, notably those of Pearce and Perry (1983) and Pearce et al. (1985), reported that over the three years following merit plan implementation among Social Security office managers, perceptions of pay and performance links declined, and department level measures of performance did not change.

Heneman's review and the reports of the other researchers cited all point out the many methodological limitations on the few existing studies: their correlational nature, the lack of good baseline measures, reliance on opinions for performance measurement, and the lack of control over organizational factors that might be expected to work against positive merit pay plan effects. Although many of these limitations probably reflect organizational reality, it is impossible to draw conclusions about the relationships between merit pay plans and performance from this research. The research also offers no means for comparing the short- or long-term performance effects of merit plans with those of other incentive plans.

Group Incentive Plans

The adoption of group incentive plans may provide a way to accommodate the complexity and interdependence of jobs, the need for work group cooperation, and the existence of work group performance norms and still offer the motivational potential of clear goals, clear pay-to-performance links, and relatively large pay increases. Most of the group incentives used today— gainsharing and profit-sharing plans—resemble individual incentive plans; they are tied to relatively quantitative measures of performance, offer relatively large payouts, and do not add payouts into base salaries. Unlike individual incentive plans, however, group incentives are tied to more aggregate measures of performance—at the level of the work group, facility/plant/office, or organization, so that the link between individual employee performance and payoff is sharply attenuated.

While group incentive plans might reasonably be predicted to offer some motivational potential for performance improvements, such a prediction requires a sizable inferential leap from the expectancy and goal-setting literature. Two of the three conditions of expectancy theory—that goals be doable and that the link between employee performance and pay be clear—are not well satisfied. The major motivational drawback to group incentives appears to be the difficulty an individual employee may have in seeing how his or her effort gets translated into the group performance measures on which payouts are based. Academics and other professionals experienced in the design and implementation of group incentive plans emphasize the importance of organization conditions that foster employees' beliefs about their ability to influence aggregate performance measures (O'Dell, 1981; U.S. General Accounting Office, 1981; Graham-Moore and Ross, 1983; Bullock and Lawler, 1984; Hewitt Associates, 1985).

Examples of such conditions include the following: management willingness to encourage employee participation in group plan design and in day-to-day work decisions; an emphasis on communications and sharing of information relevant to plan performance; joint employee-management willingness to change plan formulas and measures as needed; cooperation among unions, employees, and managers in designing and implementing the group plan and tailoring plans to the smallest feasible group; and an economic environment that makes plan payouts feasible. All of these suggestions seem reasonable but are largely the product of expert judgment, not empirical studies.

Renewed interest in gain sharing, profit sharing, and other types of group incentives during the 1980s (although not necessarily accompanied by increased adoption of such plans, as we document in the next chapter) has led to several reviews of research on group incentives (Milkovich, 1986; Hammer, 1988; Mitchell et al., 1990). Two methodologically rigorous gainsharing studies examined the productivity effects of traditional gainsharing plans covering nonexempt employees in relatively complex, interdependent jobs in manufacturing plants. Schuster's (1984a) was a controlled, longitudinal study (five years) examining the effects of introducing gainsharing plans on measures of plant productivity; he reported that for half of the 28 sites, there were immediate, significant productivity gains over baseline measures and continued effects over the study period. He noted that less successful plans tended to be in sites where many different plans were adopted to cover work group teams instead of a plant-wide plan, when infrequent bonus payments were made, when union-management relations were poor, and when management attempted to adjust standards and bonus formulas without employee participation. Wagner et al. (1988) also examined five years of plant productivity data before and after the introduction of gain sharing and also reported significant increases in plant productivity.

Much of the research on gain sharing is based on single case studies lacking rigorous methodological controls. There are few reports of gainsharing "failures." In general, the case studies report multiple, beneficial effects from gain sharing: enhanced work group cooperation, more innovation, and more effort; improved management-labor relations; higher acceptance of new technologies; worker demands for better, more efficient management; and higher overall productivity. Mitchell et al. (1990:69-71) note that an analysis of this case study literature leaves the impression that job design enabling team work, smaller organizational size and more flexible technology, employee participation, and favorable managerial attitudes about gainsharing plans may all be critical to their success in improving productivity, but that the research does not allow conclusions beyond "gainsharing may work in different situations for different reasons." This suggests that many beneficial effects attributed to gain sharing—including productivity effects—may be as much due to the contextual conditions as to the introduction of gain sharing. Indeed, there is an emerging case study literature supporting this view (see Beer et al., 1990). Some go so far as to suggest that organizational context should be the only focus of productivity improvement efforts; that pay-for-performance plans will ultimately depress productivity (Deming, 1986; Scholtes, 1987). The research evidence cannot confirm or deny any of these alternatives.

Gainsharing plans have been most common in manufacturing settings, covering mostly nonmanagement employees, and the research on gain sharing is thus restricted to these private-sector settings and employees. Mitchell et al. (1990) report that research on profit-sharing plans covering nonmanagerial employees is even more scarce and less rigorous than research on gain sharing. They note that the limited case study research available suggests that profit-sharing plans are less likely than gainsharing plans to improve performance of nonmanagerial employees. Expectancy and goal-setting theories would predict this result because it is difficult to see how these employees would translate their job efforts into organizational profit improvements. Advocates of profit-sharing plans (Metzger, 1978; Profit Sharing Council of America, 1984), however, point out other potential benefits of plan adoption, most notably the improved employee commitment to the organization and understanding of its business that can emerge when information relevant to profit generation is shared with employees as part of the plan. As we noted for gainsharing plans, it is possible that these benefits would result from organization conditions like information sharing absent a profit-sharing plan. Profit-sharing plans and managerial bonus plans have traditionally been used as part of executive and middle management compensation packages; typically they tie payments to organizational financial outcomes (such as return on assets, return on equity, and so forth). Most of the studies of executive compensation (reviewed by Ehrenberg and Milkovich, 1987), however, examine the relationship between overall compensation levels and firm performance, not between profit sharing and firm performance.

However, a recent study by Kahn and Sherer (1990) explored the impact of managerial bonus plans on the performance of managers in the year following a bonus award. The company studied had a bonus plan for which all middle- to higher-level managers were eligible, but which in practice targeted critical higher-level managers for the most substantial performance payments. Targeted managers were eligible for bonuses representing 20 percent of base salaries; other managers were eligible for 10 percent bonuses. The bonus plan was tied to a management-by-objective appraisal system that used some common individual-level behavioral and outcome measures for all managers. Controlling for pay level, previous performance, and seniority, Kahn and Sherer found that the targeted critical managers had significantly higher performance ratings in the year following bonus payment than less critical, nontargeted managers. They suggested that higher potential payouts were highly correlated with higher performance effects.

Another recent study by Gerhart and Milkovich (1990) analyzed five years of firm performance and compensation data for 16,000 mid-level managers and professionals in 200 large corporations. They controlled for individual, job, and organizational conditions and found that firms in which managers and professionals had higher profit-sharing bonus potential (measured as the percentage of base salary represented by the bonus) also had better performance (measured as return on assets) in the year following the bonus payment. Specifically, every 10 percent bonus increase was associated with a 1.5 percent increase in return on assets. This association, while not statistically significant, is certainly not trivial in absolute terms. Although the study did not control for prior profit history, these results suggest that profit-sharing plans may have a positive impact on organizational performance among the higher-level managerial and professional employees whose jobs are most directly related to financial outcomes. However, another study by Abowd (1990) qualifies these results, suggesting that profit-sharing bonuses for higher-level employees will be more likely to improve firm performance when economic conditions make such improvements realistic.

Summary

Most of the research examining the relationship between pay-for-performance plans and performance has focused on individual incentive plans such as piece rates. By design, these plans most closely approximate the ideal motivational conditions prescribed by expectancy and goal-setting theories, and the research indicates that they can motivate employees and improve individual-level performance. However, the contextual conditions under which these plans improve performance without negative, unintended consequences are restricted; these conditions include simple, structured jobs in which employees are autonomous, work settings in which employees trust management to set fair and accurate performance goals, and an economic environment in which employees feel that their jobs and basic wage levels are relatively secure. Because these conditions—especially the job conditions—are not found collectively in many organizations and do not apply to many jobs, some researchers suggest that organizations might adopt merit pay plans or group incentive plans in an effort to avoid the potentially negative consequences of individual incentive plans while still reaping some of their performance-enhancing benefits.

Merit pay plans have some design features, such as the addition of pay increases to base salary, and the use of individual performance measures, including both quantitative and qualitative objectives, that can help avoid some of the negative consequences of individual incentives plans; these characteristics may also dilute the plans' potential to motivate employees. Organizations, however, can take steps to strengthen the motivational impact of merit plans. While there is not a sufficient body of research on merit pay plans to confirm it, we think it likely that to the extent merit pay plans approximate the motivational strengths of individual incentive plans, they will, at minimum, sustain individual performance and could improve it. Our conclusion is based on inference from the research on individual incentives.

Given the restricted conditions under which individual incentive plans work best, some organizations have adopted group incentive plans. Gainsharing and profit-sharing plan designs retain many of the motivational features of individual incentive plans—quantitative performance goals, relatively large, frequent payments—but it is not as easy for individuals to see how their performance contributes to group-level measures, and the motivational pay-to-performance link is thus weakened. At the same time, group-level performance measures may be more appropriate than individual measures when work group cooperation is needed and when new technology or other work changes make it difficult to structure individual jobs, although there is little theory or research to substantiate this claim.

The research evidence (all based on private-sector experience) suggests that gainsharing and profit-sharing plans are associated with improved group- or organizational-level productivity and financial performance. This research does not, however, allow us to disentangle the effects of group plans on performance from the effects of many other contextual conditions usually associated with the design and implementation of group pay plans. Consequently, we cannot say that group plans cause performance changes or specify how they do so. Indeed, some researchers believe that it is the right combination of contextual conditions that is critical to improved performance, not the performance plans themselves.

This research provides us with at least a partial list of contextual conditions that may influence pay-for-performance plan effects. These include task, organizational, and environmental conditions. Task conditions reflect the nature of the organization's work, including the complexity and interdependence of jobs, the diversity of occupations and skills required, and the pace of technological change. Organizational conditions include work force size and diversity, levels of employee trust, the degree of participative management, existing performance norms, and levels of work force skill and ability (including those of management). Organizational conditions are all influenced by the organization's history, strategic goals, and personnel policies and practices. Environmental conditions include economic pressures and opportunities for growth, which influence the organization's ability to fund performance plans and the extent to which employees may feel economically threatened by the use of pay-for-performance plans. The presence of unions is another environmental factor that may influence pay-for-performance plan effects.

Employee Attraction and Retention

Organizations typically report that they want their pay systems to help them attract and retain higher-quality, better-performing employees. A conceptual case can be made for how pay-for-performance plans might influence the attraction and retention of these better employees. An underlying framework in many social science disciplines describes the employee-employer relationship as an exchange in which the employer offers inducements (certain working conditions, opportunities, pay, job security, and so forth) in exchange for employee contributions that include joining and remaining in the organization (see, for example, March and Simon, 1958; Mahoney, 1979). This framework assumes that employees globally assess the inducements (including pay) an employer offers relative to their own preferences, their abilities and skills, and their other employment opportunities, and then make decisions about joining the organization accordingly. Similarly, employees already within the organization make global assessments of the continuing inducements offered relative to their own contributions. (The employer side of this exchange is primarily concerned with the relative benefits gained given the cost of inducements; this is discussed in our review of research on pay for performance and cost regulation.)

Unfortunately, the empirical research examining the relationship of pay to an employer's ability to attract and retain high-performing employees is limited, and there is virtually no research examining the impact of pay for performance on these objectives. In a 1990 review of research on the strategies that organizations use to attract employees, Rynes and Barber note support for the importance of pay in employee assessments of the inducements an employer offers, and for the ability of relatively higher pay inducements (specifically salaries, recruitment and retention bonuses, and educational incentives) to increase the quality and quantity of an organization's recruitment pool. These findings provide some support for conceptual proposals about pay and the attraction of better employees, but they do not help us pinpoint the influence of pay for performance. In a review of research on turnover and retention, we found only one experimental study relating retention to the adoption of a merit pay system involving nonclerical, white-collar workers in U.S. Navy labs (U.S. Office of Personnel Management, 1988b). This study reported modest reductions in overall voluntary turnover and considerable reductions in turnover among superior performers (as rated by the performance appraisal system) in the labs using merit pay plans. One study is not sufficient to support any general propositions about the relationship of pay for performance and retention. However, if high wages generally reduce turnover, we can infer that merit pay probably has a positive influence on the retention of those employees who receive high performance ratings and, therefore, the largest pay increases from one year to the next.

In summary, the role that pay-for-performance plans can play in an organization's ability to attract and retain the best performers can be conceived in terms of an inducements-contributions exchange between employee and employer. This conceptual framework suggests that an employee assesses the pay-for-performance plan relative to other payments, working conditions, and other employment or promotional opportunities in deciding to join or remain with the organization. Certainly, if all else is equal, pay-for-performance plans should help attract and retain better performers. This framework assumes the importance of context; it also emphasizes that individuals will assess pay-for-performance plans and other payments relative to everything else the organization offers, thus placing pay in a potentially less prominent position than does the research on performance motivation. For example, some individuals, though opposed to pay-for-performance plans, might still be willing to stay with an organization offering a challenging job, pleasant working conditions, and opportunities for promotion. Unfortunately, although a conceptual case can be made for the ability of pay-for-performance plans to help an organization attract and retain the best performers, the research does not allow us to confirm it.

Fair Treatment and Equity

The adoption of pay-for-performance plans that treat employees fairly and equitably seems an inherently good and ethical pursuit in and of itself. While organizations undoubtedly recognize this, they also realize that different people have different definitions of what is fair and equitable. Organizations thus frame their objectives pragmatically. They want their pay systems to be viewed as fair and equitable by multiple stakeholders: employees; managers, owners, and top managers; other interested parties at one remove, such as unions, associations, regulatory agencies; and the public (Beer et al., 1985). Employee perceptions of pay system fairness are thought to be related to their motivation to perform, and this is one reason that organizations are interested in fairness. Organizations are also interested in pay system fairness because there are laws and regulations that require it, because employees and their representatives (unions and associations) demand it, and because society (representing potential constituents, clients, or customers) is thought to smile on organizations with a reputation for treating their employees fairly.

The research on fair treatment and equity in organizations has been mostly concerned with employee perceptions (as opposed to the perceptions of unions, associations, or other interested organization stakeholders). Theories of organizational justice distinguish between distributive and procedural concerns (Cohen and Greenberg, 1982; Greenberg, 1987; for a detailed review of theory and research on organizational justice, see Greenberg, 1990). In application to pay, theories of distributive justice suggest that employees judge the fairness of their pay outcomes by gauging how much they receive, relative to their contributions, and then making comparisons against the reward/contribution ratios of people or groups they consider similar in terms of contributions. If the employee judges that he or she is comparatively unfairly paid, negative reactions are predicted (such as higher absenteeism, lower performance, higher grievance rates, and so forth) (see Adams, 1965; Mowday, 1987). Pay distribution concerns would involve employee perceptions of the fairness of pay outcomes such as the level of pay offered, the pay offered for different types of jobs, and the amount of pay increase received.

Distributive justice theories also predict that some employees, particularly those managing or administering pay systems, will be concerned with distributing pay increases according to rules that the majority will view as fair, thereby reducing conflict (Greenberg and Levanthal, 1976). These distribution concerns encompass employee perceptions of the fairness of basic pay policies, especially those about how pay increases are allocated. Examples of pay increase policies include increases tied to performance, increases based on seniority, across the board (or equality) increases, and higher increases for those with greater needs.

Procedural justice theories suggest that employees have expectations about how organization procedures will influence their ability to meet their own goals, and that these expectations will be shaped by both individual preferences and prevailing moral and ethical standards (Walker et al., 1979; Brett, 1986). Work in procedural justice also suggests that the consistency with which procedures designed to ensure justice are followed in practice is an important determinant of their perceived fairness (Levanthal et al., 1980). In application to pay, procedural concerns would involve employee perceptions about the fairness of procedures used to design and administer pay. The extent to which employees have the opportunity to participate in pay design decisions, the quality and timeliness of information provided them, the degree to which the rules governing pay allocations are consistently followed, the availability of channels for appeal and due process, and the organization's safeguards against bias and inconsistency are all thought to influence employees' perceptions about fair treatment (Greenberg, 1986a).

Research examining distributive and procedural theories in a pay context is scarce; there are no studies that can directly answer questions about the perceived fairness of different types of pay-for-performance plans. The existing research on distributive justice does suggest that employee perceptions about the fairness of pay distributions do affect their pay satisfaction. Research on procedural justice suggests that employee perceptions about the fairness of pay design and administration procedures can also affect their pay satisfaction, as well as the degree to which they trust management and their commitment to the organization. None of this research, however, allows us to determine causality.

Early research (mostly case studies and laboratory experiments) examining employee perceptions of the fairness of pay distribution focused on differences in pay for different jobs or specific tasks (Whyte, 1955; Livernash, 1957; Jaques, 1961; Adams, 1965; Lawler, 1971). It supported theoretical predictions that employees do judge the ratio of their pay outcomes to their work contributions against selected comparison groups, and that negative reactions—primarily pay dissatisfaction—can occur if comparisons are unfavorable. It also suggested at least three major pay comparison groups—employees in similar jobs outside the organization, employees in similar jobs within the organization, and employees in the same job within the organization—to which pay designers should be sensitive. Recent reviews of work on pay satisfaction (Heneman, 1985; Miceli and Lane, 1990) also suggest that pay satisfaction is multidimensional; that employees make judgments about their satisfaction with multiple distributive outcomes: base salaries, pay increases, and so forth. This research does not, however, allow us to determine whether dissatisfaction with one type of pay outcome (such as base salary) affects satisfaction with other pay outcomes (such as merit increases).

There have been a few correlational field studies on employee perceptions of procedural fairness—most of them examining the procedures surrounding performance appraisal ratings used to allocate pay (Landy et al., 1978, 1980; Dipboye and de Pontbriand, 1981; Greenberg, 1986b; Folger and Konovsky, 1989). These studies suggest that opportunity for employees to have input into performance evaluations is a key determinant of their perceptions about its fairness. For example, when employees are able to interact with supervisors in setting performance objectives, when they have some recourse for changing objectives due to unforeseen circumstances, and when there are channels for appealing ratings and pay increase decisions, they will be more likely to see performance appraisals and any pay allocations based on them as fair. Other studies suggest the importance of explanations about how performance appraisal works, basing appraisals on accurate information (for example, current job descriptions), and good interpersonal relationships between supervisor and employee in determining employee perceptions of fairness.

As we noted earlier, this research is all focused on employee perceptions of procedural fairness, but the findings are consistent with the body of judicial cases shaping the legal definition of fair (and nondiscriminatory) performance appraisal practices (Feild and Holley, 1982). These findings are also consistent with some of the research on pay satisfaction suggesting the importance of pay administration procedures (communication of pay policies, employee participation in job evaluation, and so forth) to higher pay satisfaction (Dyer and Theriault, 1976; Weiner, 1980; Heneman, 1985).

There is no body of research on employee perceptions of the fairness of different pay increase policies—those based on performance, seniority, or equality/across the board or according to need. Several studies (Dyer et al., 1976; Fossum and Fitch, 1985; Hills et al., 1987) suggest that private-sector managers believe that pay increases should be tied to performance; the perceptions of other employee groups are not well documented. Evidence from public-sector professional and managerial employees suggests that their beliefs differ from those of private-sector managers. Although there appears from attitude surveys of federal workers to be support of merit pay in principle, there is other evidence of a disinclination to differentiate among employees. For example, several managers' associations have proposed that performance appraisals have but two scale points, satisfactory and unsatisfactory (Professional Managers

Association, 1989). And a recent report of the Advisory Committee on Federal Pay (1990) suggests that there is a fairly strong impulse to see equity in terms of standardization or comparability of pay levels for employees in the same grade and with the same length of service.

The research on fairness and equity does not allow us to draw distinctions among the different pay-for-performance plans illustrated in Figure 5-1. Presumably distributive and procedural fairness will be important considerations in the adoption of any type of pay-for-performance plan. Mitchell et al. (1990) do, however, point out that individual and group incentive plans that offer relatively large pay increases, which are not added into base (matrix cells two and three), will over time place more of an employee's total pay at risk, regardless of whether an employee is in a very high- or very low-paying job. While such risks have been common in many higher-paying jobs (for example profit-sharing plans in top management), their fairness in lower-paying jobs has been questioned. Organizations may want to consider this in adopting individual and group incentives for lower-paid employee groups.

In summary, we believe that this research suggests several points relevant to the relationship between pay-for-performance plans and fair treatment or equity, although none of it allows us to draw any conclusions about specific types of pay-for-performance plans. The research does confirm that the perceived fairness of the distribution of pay increases will influence employees' pay satisfaction. It suggests at least three groups against which employees may assess the fairness of their pay—people in similar jobs outside the organization, people in similar jobs inside the organization, and people in the same job or work group inside the organization. This implies that employers might consider how their pay systems measure up to these three groups in designing the system, in deciding whether to use the same system throughout the organization, and in communications about pay in their efforts to improve employee perceptions about the fairness of pay distributions.

The research also suggests that employee perceptions of procedural fairness can influence their satisfaction with pay, their level of trust in management, and their overall commitment to the organization. Evidence of procedural fairness also appears to be important to other organization stakeholders such as regulatory agencies and unions and associations. This implies that organizations might usefully invest in communications, training, appeals channels, and employee participation in order to ensure procedural fairness.

Finally, the research suggests that there are different beliefs about how pay increases should be allocated—performance, seniority, across the board, and so forth—throughout U.S. society, although pay-for-performance beliefs appear to dominate among managerial employees in the private sector. The very existence of different beliefs, however, suggests that organizations trying to change their pay increase policies may have to deal with employees' perceptions of these policies as unfair. We base this notion on theories of procedural fairness that propose that employees' assessments of what is and is not fair depend on their expectations about organization procedures. These expectations will be shaped by their individual preferences, their organizational experiences, and their moral and ethical beliefs.

Regulating Costs and Making Trade-Offs

The necessity of regulating costs is a fact of life in all organizations. Financial status and pressures from competition or funding sources force organizations to make choices about the amount of money that can be allocated to technology, capital and material investments, and human resources. Trade-offs must obviously be made. Whether they are couched in terms of an inducements-contributions exchange between employee and employer, or simply as keeping an eye on the budget, trade-offs must also be made among multiple human resource systems (selection, training, and so forth) and their objectives. Ideally, organizations try to meet their overall human resource objectives as best they can given cost constraints. Pay system objectives and the policies and plans adopted to meet them are no exception to this give and take.

An organization's decisions about whether to adopt a pay-for-performance policy and, if adopted, the type of plan to use are, in principle, subject to assessment of trade-offs among performance, equity, and costs. In practice, these assessments have been notoriously difficult to make (Cascio, 1987). Nevertheless, economists have developed models of the basic performance/cost trade-offs and some of the contextual conditions that influence them. Brown's (1990) study of firms' choice of pay method provides a summary of many of these models. He proposes that a firm's choice among plans basing pay increases on seniority or across-the-board criteria, merit plans, or piece rate (individual incentive) plans would depend on its assessment of each plan's ability to accurately measure employee performance and the costs of implementing the plan in the firm context. By design, piece rate plans, tied to specific, quantitative measures of employee productivity, are viewed as the most accurate of the three alternatives. Merit plans, tied to supervisory judgments about employee productivity, are the next best alternative in terms of accuracy. Standard rate plans, in which pay increases are tied to seniority or across-the-board criteria, are considered the least accurate alternatives.

The costs of actually implementing and monitoring each plan so as to reap the benefits of accurate performance measurement vary with firm context. Brown describes several contextual variables that many economists have predicted will influence these costs: the organization's size, its occupational diversity, the demands its technology makes on job structure, skill variation and quality versus quantity measures of performance, the organization's labor intensity, and the degree of unionization in the organization, industry, or sector. In general, the less the occupational diversity and the less complex and varied the job structure and skill demands, the more appropriate the quantitative measures of performance. The higher the labor intensity, the less costly it will be to implement and monitor piece rate plans and still maintain the benefits of their accurate measurement. As occupational diversity increases, job structure become more complex, skill demands more varied, and quality measures of performance more important; as labor intensity decreases, merit plans may represent the best trade-off between accuracy of performance measurement and cost. Brown proposes that unionization may be the best predictor of a firm's adoption of seniority or across-the-board plans. He also suggests that, in some firm contexts, job complexity and interdependence will make measurement of individual performance so difficult that only group-level measures will be accurate. He does not, however, speculate about the organization conditions that would make group plans the cost-effective choice, and we know of no economic models that do.

Brown finds support for most of his predictions about the relationships between firm context and choice of pay plans. His study focused on manufacturing firms and production workers. We can only speculate that these predictions might be applicable to professional and managerial jobs and a firm's choice of individual bonus (based on mostly quantitative measures), merit, or seniority or across-the-board pay increase plans. A simulation study by Schwab and Olsen (1990) suggests that, in firms with highly developed internal labor markets and in managerial and professional jobs, supervisory estimates of individual performance used with conventional merit plans may provide a higher level of accuracy for the cost than previously thought. One simulation, however, is not enough to enable us to generalize about performance and cost trade-offs for management and professional jobs.

Economic models provide some conceptual basis for describing the potential trade-offs between performance and cost that an organization faces in choosing a pay increase policy and selecting pay-for-performance plans. We have no similar conceptual foundation for potential trade-offs between fair treatment or equity and costs. It seems reasonable to think that contextual arguments about these trade-offs could also be made. That is, the costs of ensuring that different types of pay-for-performance plans are viewed as fair and equitable will be influenced by firm context (Milkovich and Newman, 1990). However, the arguments for cost and equity trade-offs quickly become complicated when multiple organization stakeholders are considered. For example, when organization conditions all favor the use of individual incentives, investments in such procedural protections as appeals may be lower than under merit plans because it is easier for employees to accept quantitative performance measures as fair. Yet unions and associations often consider individual incentives plans unfair unless they are involved in the development of individual performance measures and in monitoring when measures should change. Some organizations may consider that the costs of union participation cancel out the benefits from individual incentive plan use.

Our discussion of pay-for-performance plan costs and trade-offs has thus far dealt with the indirect labor costs that might be associated with plan design and implementation. There are, in addition, the direct labor costs that merit, individual, and group incentive plans like gain sharing and profit sharing pay out in increases. It has often been claimed that individual and group incentive plans that do not add payments into base salaries will, over time, make an employer's direct labor costs more competitive. These claims, however, depend on many other factors, such as the employer's competitive wage policies and tax treatment of these variable payments. They also do not consider the potentially high indirect costs associated with successful individual and group incentive plan design and implementation. To date, no research has convincingly supported these claims (see Mitchell et al., 1990).

In summary, the research on cost regulation and the cost-benefit trade-offs associated with pay-for-performance plans is sparse and limited to production jobs and manufacturing settings. The research available does suggest that certain contextual conditions believed to reflect indirect labor costs are associated with organization decisions about adopting a pay-for-performance policy and selecting among merit, individual, or group incentive plans. The more contextual conditions depart from those considered most cost-effective in the implementation of individual incentive plans (structured, independent jobs, low occupational diversity, high labor intensity, and so forth), the more likely it is that merit or group plans will be considered. We have no evidence that any particular pay-for-performance plan is superior to another or to no pay-for-performance plan in regulating direct labor costs.

There is no research on cost and fairness or equity trade-offs, so the most precise summary we can offer is that we believe they exist. In adopting a merit plan or any other pay-for-performance plan, organizations should consider the likely equity perceptions of their various stakeholders, the process and procedural changes that might be required to improve them, and the resulting costs (economical, political, and social) of making those changes.

PAY FOR PERFORMANCE: RESEARCH FINDINGS AND THEIR IMPLICATIONS FOR THE FEDERAL GOVERNMENT

Organizations have multiple objectives for their pay systems; they want them to attract, retain, and enhance the performance of successful employees, be perceived as fair and equitable, and help regulate labor costs. Our review of research on pay-for-performance plans was organized around these objectives, and the conclusions we have drawn from it have implications for federal policy makers' decisions about pay for performance for federal employees and, specifically, the use of merit pay plans. The committee's task did not extend to any detailed analyses of the federal work forces and working conditions, so we cannot discuss research implications exhaustively or specifically. We can, however, discuss general implications.

Although virtually no research on the performance effects of merit pay exists, we conclude by analogy from research that examines the impact of individual and group incentive plans on performance that merit pay plans could sustain, and even improve, individual performance to the extent that they approximate the ideal motivational conditions prescribed by expectancy and goal-setting theories. There are some features of merit plan design that depart from these conditions, namely the use of less specific, less quantitative measures of performance (typically performance appraisal measures) that employees may find unclear and thus undoable, and the relatively small pay increases that are added to base salary. Employees may view such increases as too small to warrant additional effort, and their addition to base salary may make them seem less linked to performance.

However, organizations can and do take steps to strengthen the motivational impact of merit plans. For example, they can emphasize joint employee-supervisor participation in setting performance goals, thus increasing employee understanding about what is expected. They can emphasize the long-term pay growth potential offered under a merit program, thus making each pay increase seem more meaningful. This suggests that performance appraisal formats that allow some give and take between employees and supervisors, that make investments in training managers and employees in how to jointly set clear performance objectives, and that implement pay communication programs stressing the links between merit payouts, individual performance, and long-term pay growth could enhance the performance improvement potential of federal merit programs. The research on performance also led us to conclude that merit pay plans might best be adopted under certain contextual conditions. (Group incentive plans such as profit sharing or gain sharing might also be considered, but our focus here is on merit plans.) There is evidence that, when jobs are complex, require work group cooperation, and are undergoing rapid technological change, employees are less likely to find specific, quantitative measures of performance—such as those typical of individual incentive plans— acceptable. There is also evidence that when the organization is facing economic pressures and reduced growth, tying relatively large payments to performance— as is more common of individual and group incentives—is especially threatening to employees. Moreover, the research suggests that when individual incentive plans are adopted under these conditions, they are often associated with negative consequences, such as employees' ignoring important aspects of their jobs, falsifying performance data, and actively restricting work group performance by "punishing" high performers.

The federal government obviously represents a diverse set of job and organization conditions, and individual agencies face different economic pressures and growth projections, but when jobs are complex and require work group cooperation (as is true of many professional and managerial jobs), and when there are significant economic and growth constraints, merit plans may deliver some of the individual performance improvements associated with individual incentive plans, yet have fewer of the negative consequences. The emphasis on the importance of context in organizational decisions to adopt different types of pay-for-performance plans also implies that an organization as diverse as the federal government might adopt several types of pay-for-performance plans (merit, individual, or group incentives) or, in some agencies, no pay-for-performance plans, depending on its agency-by-agency analysis of context.

Although the research on cost regulation and the cost-performance trade-offs associated with pay-for-performance plans is sparse, it is consistent with the research on performance effects in that both support the importance of contextual conditions in an organization's decision to adopt different types of pay-for-performance plans. It suggests that firms will adopt merit plans (or perhaps group incentive plans) when their occupational diversity, job complexity, and labor intensity are higher than would be ideal for individual incentive plans such as piece rates. Though piece rates offer the most potential for accurate performance measurement (and are thus the best indicator of actual individual performance), the cost of successfully implementing them under these organization conditions might be prohibitive. Merit plans offer the next best level of accurate individual performance measurement at a reasonable cost.

This research also suggests that firms that are heavily unionized tend to adopt seniority-based or across-the-board pay increase plans, presumably because unions are opposed to merit plans and this increases the cost of their adoption. The federal government may face higher costs in implementing merit plans than less unionized organizations.

There is no research that examines the relationship between different pay-for-performance plans and an organization's ability to attract and retain high-performing employees. We know that pay influences employees' decisions to join and to stay in an organization, but we cannot disentangle the influence of overall pay—let alone pay-for-performance plans—from all the other inducements (working conditions, promotions, job security, etc.) the organization has to offer. This suggests that the federal government consider the entire work experience offered to employees in its efforts to attract and retain the best performers; it should probably not expect a merit pay program alone to have a substantial effect.

Like the research on employee attraction and retention, research on fairness and equity does not allow us to distinguish among different types of pay-for-performance plans. Our conclusions from this research do, however, have some implications for an organization's adoption of pay-for-performance plans. First, the research suggests that there are different beliefs about how pay increases should be allocated—pay for performance, seniority, across the board, etc. The fact that these different beliefs exist suggests potential problems for organizations like the federal government that are trying to change their allocation policies. Since increases are seldom doubled or denied, it appears that, in practice, the federal government used an automatic step increase policy for years. Although survey data indicating wide support for merit pay exist, a sizable portion of the work force may view the automatic step system as most fair and will thus be dissatisfied with any pay distributions based on performance criteria (Advisory Committee on Federal Pay, 1990). Managers who try to implement a pay-for-performance policy in this situation will be strongly tempted to manipulate pay-for-performance plans to maintain the status quo.

At the same time, the research suggests that organizations investing in measures to assure employees about the fairness of the procedures surrounding pay-for-performance plan design and implementation can positively influence pay satisfaction, perceptions of pay fairness, and employee trust and commitment. In application to merit plans, certain procedures would be included: providing employees with information about the way appraisal works, training managers in conducting appraisals, employee participation in setting performance objectives, and channels for appealing ratings and pay increases. Procedural fairness is also a concern of other organization stakeholders, such as regulatory agencies and unions or associations. When employees believe pay-for-performance procedures are fair, managers administering these programs may face less hostility, despite employee dissatisfaction with ratings or increases. We know that the federal government has many procedural protections in place for its employees, but given the historical precedent for seniority-based pay increases, the representation of unions and associations in the federal work force, and the regulatory and public scrutiny that agencies face, an examination of how those procedures are operating and a focus on employee perceptions of fairness may be an important aspect of merit pay reform.

We began this chapter by observing that the pay systems of organizations have multiple objectives reflecting the various interests of multiple stakeholders. An organization's ability to meet those objectives will not depend on pay-for-performance plans alone. It depends on many organizational factors including other pay decisions, its human resource systems, its job structures, its management style, its work force, and its institutional goals. It will also be influenced by external conditions such as economic pressures, unionization, and pressures from regulations and public opinion. Switching to a pay-for-performance policy, adoption of a particular pay-for-performance plan, or change in current plans is unlikely to help an organization meet and balance its pay system objective unless the changes make sense within the total pay system, the personnel system, and the broader organizational context. No one pay-for-performance plan will be right for every organization.

The implications of the federal context for merit plan adoption are taken up in Chapter 7. We turn next to a review of performance appraisal and pay-for-performance practices in the private sector.

6

Private-Sector Practice and Perspectives

This chapter offers a broad-brush picture of contemporary organization performance appraisal, merit pay, and individual and group incentive pay practices as they apply to the managerial and professional jobs that are the focus of the committee's review. As the previous chapters demonstrate, the research on performance appraisal and pay for performance is limited in its ability to offer federal policy makers specific guidelines. A review of contemporary private-sector practice that covers the types of appraisal and pay-for-performance plans organizations use, the way they design and administer these plans, the contexts in which plans are operating, and the criteria many use to judge the effectiveness of these plans may offer some additional insights. Our aim is to identify points of convergence between sometimes tentative research findings and predominant private-sector practices.

The committee reviewed several sources of information on private practice: major proprietary surveys, a special survey of Conference Board firms conducted at the committee's request, and invited interviews with the personnel managers of five Fortune 100 firms whose appraisal and merit plans are generally regarded as successful. More details on the surveys reviewed by the committee appear in Appendix A. The Fortune 100 firms we consulted represented large, financially successful manufacturing firms in high-technology industries with employee populations of more than 50,000. Three of the five operated with U.S. unions. Most of them had been using their current performance appraisal systems for 20 years without major changes. For all our surveys and interviews, the respondents were predominately personnel managers who may be presumed to have some interest in presenting a favorable picture of their organization's practices—a point noted in our earlier chapter on the nature of the evidence, and one to keep in mind throughout this chapter.

The chapter is organized into two major sections. The first reviews performance appraisal practices: the predominant types of appraisal used, the typical objectives of performance appraisal, common performance appraisal design and administrative characteristics, and measures of plan effectiveness. The second provides a similar review of merit pay and individual and group incentives. We focused on the individual and group incentive plans that do not add pay increases into base salaries, and we have labeled these *variable pay plans*. In each section we describe general trends concerning performance appraisal and merit and variable pay plans to provide a profile of "average" practice; we then use information from our interviews with the personnel managers of the five Fortune 100 firms to provide richer detail about performance appraisal, merit, and variable pay plan practices that are generally considered successful. Such details are not available in survey reports of performance appraisal practice. Each section ends with a brief discussion of the convergence or divergence between practice and the research findings presented in earlier chapters.

PERFORMANCE APPRAISAL: CURRENT PRACTICE AND EMERGING TRENDS

Our review of research in the previous chapter made it clear that performance evaluation is thought critical to the success of pay-for-performance plans in achieving performance improvements, in being accepted and thought fair and equitable by employees and other organization stakeholders, and in helping the organization to regulate costs wisely. Performance appraisals that focus on individual performance and typically use a combination of quantitative and qualitative performance objectives are the type of performance evaluations most often associated with merit pay plans.

General Trends in Performance Appraisal

Prevalence, Distribution, and Objectives

Between 93 and 99 percent of private-sector organizations use performance appraisal plans for their exempt and nonexempt salaried employees (Bretz and Milkovich, 1989; HayGroup, Inc., 1989; Hewitt Associates, 1989; Wyatt Company, 1989b). Larger organizations (> 1,000 employees) are slightly more likely than smaller ones to use performance appraisal (Bretz and Milkovich, 1989; Hewitt Associates, 1989). Hourly employees—especially unionized hourly—are less likely to be covered by performance appraisal plans; even so, over half the organizations surveyed in the last few years had performance appraisal plans for hourly employees (Bureau of National Affairs, 1981; Hewitt Associates,

1985, 1989; Bretz and Milkovich, 1989). The prevalence and distribution of performance appraisal plans appears to have increased since the mid-1970s. In particular, small companies are now more likely to use these plans, and executive and hourly employees are more likely, in all companies, to be covered by them (Bureau of National Affairs, 1974; Conference Board, 1977; Bretz and Milkovich, 1989).

Organizations have historically used performance appraisal to accomplish multiple organization objectives (Conference Board, 1977; Bretz and Milkovich, 1989; Wyatt Company, 1989b). Improvements to work performance, tying pay to performance (via merit plans), and communicating work expectations to employees are the three objectives that were consistently rated as the highest priorities among the surveys we reviewed. There was more interest in using performance appraisal results to validate selection and promotion decisions in the late 1970s—especially for hourly and nonexempt salaried employees—but this interest is not a high priority today (Bureau of National Affairs, 1974; Conference Board, 1977; Bretz and Milkovich, 1989).

Design Characteristics

The Conference Board (1977) reported that, despite the fact that most personnel managers believe job analysis, description, and evaluation provide necessary foundations to effective performance appraisal plans, less than half the companies in its survey even reviewed job descriptions prior to plan development or revision. Only about one-fourth of the larger organizations in the Conference Board sample had conducted any sort of pilot testing of performance appraisal plans prior to their implementation.

Management by objective (MBO) or "objective" work standard approaches were the performance appraisal formats most commonly reported for executives, managers, and professionals (Bretz and Milkovich, 1989; Wyatt Company, 1989b). The MBO format is a very loosely defined one and thus difficult to compare across organizations. MBO is really both a planning and an appraisal process in which the organization's strategic plans are supposed to shape broad goals that are passed down to employees through the management hierarchy. Both employees and their supervisors then participate in setting individual performance objectives against these goals. For work standard appraisals, management defines important job factors or dimensions that may be applied uniformly throughout a major job group, such as managers, or may be customized for particular jobs. Factors may be either qualitative (such as "provides group leadership") or more quantitative (such as "finishes projects within days assigned"), and they are scaled to denote different levels of performance ("well above average" to "well below average"). Both these performance appraisal approaches require raters to assess an employee against performance objectives or factors. The employee's ratings on these factors are then combined into one overall rating. The typical appraisal rating includes three to five performance intervals or "buckets," ranging from "below expected standards" to "meets expected standards" to "far exceeds expected standards" (Conference Board, 1977; Wyatt Company, 1987, 1989b; Bretz and Milkovich, 1989).

Most organizations reported skewing in their performance appraisal ratings—that is, ratings that do not follow the normal distribution; most employees are rated as fully satisfactory or above (Wyatt Company, 1987; Bretz and Milkovich, 1989). About 20 to 25 percent of the organizations in the Bretz and Milkovich survey required that summary appraisal ratings be either ranked (that is, individual employees in similar jobs are ranked top to bottom) or forced to approximate a normal distribution; others may suggest informally that managers rank or force distributions (Conference Board, 1984).

Administration Characteristics

The typical organization, as reflected in our survey review, used different performance appraisal plans for different employee groups (executives, managers/professionals, clerical employees, etc.) and has used the same plan, without major revisions, for about nine years (Bretz and Milkovich, 1989). Most organizations also reported that policy guidelines for performance appraisal design and administration were centralized (Hewitt Associates, 1989; committee's survey of Conference Board firms, 1990).

The Bretz and Milkovich survey (1989) reported that most organizations required an employee's immediate supervisor to conduct performance appraisals annually. Appraisals for managers and professionals were likely to be reviewed by a second level of management. There was no evidence that organizations are making increasing use of peer, subordinate, or self-review for performance appraisals, despite the reported popularity of these practices in the business press (Kiechal, 1989:201). Formal evaluations of managers' use of performance appraisal and penalties for poor use were rarely reported. The average time that managers spent on annual appraisals per employee was four to six hours.

Several surveys (Bretz and Milkovich, 1989; Wyatt Company, 1989b; committee's survey of Conference Board firms, 1990) reported that employee participation in performance appraisal design and administration was mostly limited to personnel staff; line managers were involved in administration only via actual assessments of their employees; employees were involved only if there was joint manager-employee setting of performance objectives for the appraisal and, in some cases, the appeals process. Only about one-fourth of the organizations in the Bretz and Milkovich survey (1989) had a formal employee appeals process.

The Wyatt Company (1989b) reported that most organizations did not provide managers and employees with much assistance in understanding and using performance appraisal. When assistance was provided, it was to the managers who are expected to conduct appraisals, not to the employees being appraised. Only a small proportion of companies have written objectives for their performance appraisal systems or provide written instructions for supervisors about how to use performance appraisal plans. Performance appraisal training was typically conducted for managers only when a new performance appraisal plan was first implemented. Training focused on using forms, measuring performance, conducting interviews, providing feedback, and setting performance objectives. There was more training emphasis on avoiding bias (perceptual, memory, and racial/ethnic types of bias) in the 1970s than there is today.

Measures of Success

Fewer than half the organizations participating in the surveys the committee reviewed reported any formal measurement of performance appraisal success. Among those who did measure, managerial and employee opinion surveys were typical measurement approaches. These surveys ask personnel managers, other managers who administer the plans, and employees covered by the plans about how effective they perceive the plan to be both overall and in accomplishing specific plan objectives (improving performance, tying pay to performance, and communicating work expectations). Personnel managers (the designers of performance appraisal plans) were the most likely employees to be questioned in opinion surveys, as well as the most likely to view plans as "very effective" or "partially effective," but even they recognized problems. In general, less than 20 percent of personnel managers polled in recent surveys gave their performance appraisal plans an overall rating of "very effective"; another 60 to 70 percent, however, rated their plans "partially effective." Other managers and employees were similarly unenthusiastic. On average, less than one-third rate their organization's performance appraisal plans as "effective" in tying pay to performance or in communicating organizational expectations about work (HayGroup, Inc., 1989; Wyatt Company, 1989b).

Richer Detail on Performance Appraisal Practices

These survey statistics on performance appraisal success paint a fairly bleak picture. It appears that most employees do not believe their organizations do a very good job of managing performance appraisal. However, the personnel managers we interviewed from the five Fortune 100 firms reported that they used similar measures of performance appraisal effectiveness, and that between 40 and 70 percent of all employees surveyed believed that performance appraisals were meeting objectives. In this section we discuss some of the detail these personnel managers provided about their firms' performance appraisal practices. To organize the discussion, we use the distinctions between effective and ineffective performance appraisal practices drawn from a 1989 Wyatt survey of performance management. This survey defined *effective* and *ineffective*

TABLE 6-1 Elements of Performance Appraisal Plans

Appraisal Plan Elements	Percentage of All Companies Surveyed n = 3,052	Percentage of Companies With Effective Plans n = 427	Percentage of Companies With Ineffective Plans n = 518
Written goals	66	84	39
Supervisor instructions	69	77	47
Supervisory guides	42	54	26
Annual training	18	32	6
Senior management training	64	79	45
Training covers:			
objective setting	79	88	62
providing feedback	71	78	53
Joint supervisor-employee objective setting	34	54	14
Measurement of supervisors' plan use	10	21	2
Integration with the pay system	65	74	48

Note: Table reports survey results for a sample of 3,052 companies, which are also broken out for companies with effective and ineffective plans. Percentages in each cell are based on total number of companies in the column. Of the personnel managers responding, 14 percent (427) considered their firm's plan effective; 17 percent (518) considered their firm's plan ineffective; and 66 percent considered it partly effective.

Source: The Wyatt Communicator: Results of the 1989 Wyatt Performance Management Survey, Fourth Quarter, 1989 (Chicago: The Wyatt Company) pp. 7-8.

according to personnel managers' opinions about whether their performance appraisal plans met objectives. Effective and ineffective performance appraisals were distinguished along the elements shown in Table 6-1. These elements include process factors such as written goals, manager training, joint objective setting, and a structural factor, integration with the pay system. Each of the elements is more likely to be associated with companies that consider their performance appraisal systems effective, than with those that judge them ineffective.

The Performance Appraisal Process

The Wyatt performance management survey reported that performance appraisal plans involving annual training for managers—especially on how to set objectives and provide feedback—and encouraging joint participation of supervisors and employees in developing appraisal objectives and standards were more likely to be considered effective. So too were plans including written policy guidelines and instructions to managers about administration—especially with regard to merit increases and those requiring that managers be evaluated on their use of performance appraisal.

The performance appraisal details provided to the committee by the five personnel managers we interviewed follow effective practice as reported by Wyatt. Four of the five Fortune 100 firms had MBO performance appraisal plans covering exempt employees; the fifth had several types of performance appraisal plans for exempt employees, and one of these was an MBO plan. (Only one of the plans described covered unionized employees; it was not an MBO format.) In most cases, employees and their managers jointly developed the plan objectives against which performance would be measured, typically using a set of corporation-wide factors (e.g., customer satisfaction, affirmative action responsibilities, people development) and a set of more specific job-related responsibilities as guides. In one of the five firms, employees and their managers actually developed job descriptions together and could revise these descriptions in preparation for setting objectives. In two firms, there were formal interim reviews in which managers and employees could discuss the need for changes in performance appraisal objectives due to changes in priorities, working conditions, and so forth.

One firm demonstrated an array of communication tools (written and audio-visual) for instructing both managers and the individual employee about their roles in the performance appraisal process and the organization's goals for performance appraisal.

All five firms held managers accountable for their management of performance appraisal—primarily by reviews of performance appraisal results by the next higher level of management and by making effective performance appraisal management one of a manager's own performance appraisal objectives. Two firms had automated several aspects of the performance appraisal process and routinely notified managers about upcoming performance appraisals for their employees and any delinquencies in completing them.

The training efforts of most of these firms did not appear to go beyond those described earlier as average. Most offered two-day training sessions to introduce managers to the performance appraisal process. At a minimum, training covered objective-setting and how to provide feedback.

These process details from the interviews and the Wyatt results suggest that many personnel managers believe the process surrounding performance appraisal design and administration to be at least as critical to employee acceptance as the appraisal format used, the number of intervals used in summary ratings, or whether the distribution of ratings is ranked or forced. It also suggests that these managers believe that employee acceptance or perceptions about performance appraisals as fair are important measures of plan success. Indeed, other sources (Bretz and Milkovich, 1989, the committee's survey of major Conference Board firms, 1990) confirm that the emphasis on process represents the latest thinking among personnel managers about how performance appraisal should be managed. These views are generally described as a shift away from what has been viewed as traditional performance appraisal toward "performance management." Bretz and Milkovich (1989) also suggested that this emphasis on process is consistent with current trends in performance appraisal research.

How Performance Appraisal Ratings Are Used for Pay Allocations

The Wyatt Company's comparison of effective and ineffective plans (see Table 6-1) also illustrated that organizations with effective performance appraisal plans were more likely to integrate them with their pay systems. Presumably, a rationale for how performance appraisal ratings influence merit increases and a clear statement of the place of merit increases in the organization's overall pay plan increases the likelihood that both employees and managers will understand the connection. The research reviewed in the previous chapter suggests that the better employees understand this connection, the more likely that performance will be improved. Since our profile of the typical organization's performance appraisal plan indicates that most organizations do use performance ratings for merit pay allocations, the integration of performance appraisal and the pay system that is characteristic of more effective plans makes sense.

However, a traditional rule of thumb among managers of performance appraisal has also suggested the wisdom of decoupling the appraisal process from merit pay. The rationale for this has been that both employees and their managers will be too focused on the money involved with the appraisal rating to attend to its developmental objectives. In particular, the concern has been that managers will deliberately inflate performance appraisal ratings to distribute merit pay, thus decreasing the chances that employees with real training needs will be identified or increasing the chances that overrated employees will be promoted beyond their capabilities. In this regard, it is interesting to note that four of the five firms we interviewed used performance appraisal ratings as one of the inputs to a ranking process. The rankings were then used to support merit increase, promotion, and reduction-in-force or dismissal decisions. This practice contrasts with our summary of general organization trends, which showed that fewer than 25 percent of the organizations surveyed used ranking schemes in addition to their performance appraisal summaries.

The ranking schemes presented by the four firms were similar. Managers within the same functional responsibilities (for example, marketing) or divisional areas (for example, small appliances) gather at least annually, bringing the performance appraisal summaries of their employees with them. They are joined by their own managers. They emerge with a relative ranking for each employee that reflects joint decisions, negotiations, and shared goals regarding the group's norms for employee performance. The role of the higher-level managers is to help shape the group's definition of employee performance norms in a fashion consistent with other groups throughout the organization. Employees are told whether they are in the top, middle, or bottom ranks. In one of the four firms, ranking was used throughout the corporation; in the other three, ranking was used only in specific divisions.

The personnel managers in these firms believed that ranking helped to separate the performance appraisal process from the decisions about merit pay and promotion, thus strengthening managers' and employees' association of the appraisal process with counseling and development. They also believed that the joint management meetings involved in the ranking process helped managers calibrate and define their expectations about individual employee performance. This was viewed as especially important in middle-management ranks, where there is high mobility and thus a less shared sense of employee performance norms for a specific function or division. They believed that joint meetings also provide an added incentive for managers to do a careful job of performance appraisal because they would have to defend their rating decisions before their peers and superiors. Two other benefits of these meetings were noted: (1) they give managers familiarity with a wider set of employees and (2) they permit managers to attribute low rankings to the group.

Fit With Organization Culture and Personnel Practices

Surveys do not convey a sense of how an organization's performance appraisal plans are wedded to its culture, its work force, and its other personnel practices. The five firms that presented their performance appraisal plans to the committee all believed their plans were successful because they fit firm culture and personnel philosophy. In most cases, personnel philosophies were essentially meritocratic—that is, these firms hire, place, develop, reward, promote, and dismiss employees according to their contributions to a range of organizationally defined and ranked positions. Employees are continually made aware of this philosophy, from their first employment interview to their retirement. It would seem strange under a meritocratic philosophy if performance appraisal was not closely tied to other personnel programs. Indeed, all five firms had used performance appraisal plans for at least 20 years. The personnel managers also said they believed that meritocratic beliefs were fundamental to U.S. culture, and that employees would perceive personnel practices with no reference to merit to be unfair.

Consistent with this meritocratic personnel philosophy, the five personnel managers we interviewed emphasized that their firms were perceived as good, even elite, places to work. Both formal organization communications and informal social norms reinforced these perceptions. Indeed, all the personnel managers we interviewed considered the identification of employees far above or below acceptable performance norms as a primary performance management objective of their plans.

This private-sector view of a meritocratic personnel philosophy and the role that performance appraisal plays in it appear to differ from the federal government's meritocracy, especially in practice. For example, the importance of identifying top and bottom performers in order to sustain high levels of work force contributions is accompanied in the private sector by relative discretion of managers to promote top performers and dismiss employees with consistently poor performance. Federal managers have more limited discretion to make such decisions. This lack of discretion may reduce the potential organizational benefits of performance appraisal and make its role in the federal meritocracy less clear.

All five of the personnel managers we interviewed indicated that their firms regularly canvassed employee opinions regarding performance appraisal plans; they were most concerned with indicators related to specific objectives—such as "the plan helps communicate work expectations" or "the plan links pay to performance"—than to overall satisfaction ratings. They believed these more specific indicators provide a better yardstick against which personnel managers can judge whether employees perceive that performance appraisal plans are operating as intended. They believed that employees' sense of consistency between what the organization says performance appraisal is supposed to do, and what it does, is basic to their perceptions about its fairness and that employees' sense of fairness about personnel programs in general is basic to a meritocratic personnel philosophy.

Four of the five firms had a centrally developed performance appraisal plan for exempt employees. The fifth, itself a major division (45,000 employees) of a larger corporation, had traditionally decentralized all performance appraisal decision making within the division, but had recently proposed a common MBO-type plan for all the division's exempt employees. In all cases, centralization meant that headquarters personnel staff provided managers with sample communications defining the firm's performance appraisal philosophy and its relationship to other personnel practices, a set of broadly defined performance areas (such as people management and development or customer satisfaction), a set of administrative guidelines, and training materials. Managers then had considerable discretion to adapt these to their own departments.

Convergence/Divergence Between Research and Practice

There are two major points on which research and practice converge and diverge. The major point of convergence involves the emphasis on process in performance appraisal design and implementation. The details of performance appraisal practice provided by the five personnel managers we interviewed, as well as the distinctions drawn between effective and ineffective performance appraisal plans in the Wyatt report (1989b), both suggest the importance of performance appraisal process and its fit with the organization's culture and personnel philosophy. This emphasis is consistent with some emerging research trends in industrial-organizational psychology and human resource management.

However, it is also important to understand that this emphasis on process and fit comes mostly from the managers of performance appraisal plans and from their beliefs about how process investments will enhance employees' sense of the fairness of performance appraisal. We do not know whether line managers and other employees are equally enthusiastic about the process aspects of performance appraisal, and there are no generally available surveys that frame questions about performance appraisal in ways that would allow us to judge employees' beliefs about its fairness.

The major point of divergence between research and practice is in the area of measurement. Certainly the opinion survey measurement reported by most organizations does not exhaust potential measurement of the objectives typically reported for performance appraisal—work improvements, communication of work expectations, and tying pay to performance. For example, in the area of work or performance improvement, surveys indicate that most organizations do not attempt to validate their performance appraisals, or even to revise job analyses and descriptions prior to performance appraisal plan changes. Yet some validation efforts and good job information appear important to improving performance via appraisals and to enhancing employee perceptions about an appraisal's fairness. The research on performance appraisal focused for many years almost exclusively on psychometric properties but, as we noted in our review of performance appraisal research, the research focus has now given way to a much greater interest in operational aspects of appraisal.

The lack of measurement of performance appraisal effectiveness contributes to problems for policy makers. For example, performance appraisal does have serious detractors, such as Deming (1986) and his interpreters (Scholtes, 1987), who view the appraisal of individual employees as a "deadly disease" (Scholtes, 1987:1). In particular, they argue that individual performance appraisals cannot lead to significant improvements in organization productivity and quality. In fact, Deming believes that any use of individual performance appraisal is deadly; that organizations should focus on system-level, not individual-level, performance. While this view may represent an extreme, the evidence from research and practice on performance appraisal is not sufficient to either confirm or deny it.

MERIT AND VARIABLE PAY PLANS: CURRENT PRACTICE AND EMERGING TRENDS

The committee's review of practice covered both merit and variable plans and included many of the same proprietary surveys covered in the review of performance appraisal practice, as well as interviews with the personnel managers of the five Fortune 100 firms.

General Trends in Merit and Variable Pay Practice

Prevalence, Distribution, and Objectives

Recent surveys report that merit pay plans cover exempt employees in 95 percent of private-sector organizations (Wyatt Company, 1987b; HayGroup, Inc., 1989; Hewitt Associates, 1989). Executives and hourly employees, especially unionized hourly employees, are less likely to be covered by merit pay plans, and larger organizations are slightly more likely than smaller ones to have merit pay programs (Bureau of National Affairs, 1984; Hewitt Associates, 1989). There is no evidence of a decline in the use of merit pay programs, despite some predictions to the contrary (O'Dell, 1987; Hewitt Associates, 1989).

Merit pay objectives are related to an organization's compensation objectives. We observed in the previous chapter that most organizations report at least three objectives for their pay systems and their pay-for-performance plans: attracting and retaining high-performing employees and sustaining or improving the performance of these employees, ensuring that pay-for-performance plans are fair and equitable, and regulating costs.

Most surveys, however, do not directly address the question of why merit pay plans are used. Paying for performance is a top-ranked compensation objective for over 80 percent of the organizations responding to a 1984 Conference Board survey. When asked why, many top managers stated that U.S. managers and employees believe pay increases should be related to performance (Wm. M. Mercer, Inc., 1983; Conference Board, 1984). Because merit pay plans are so prevalent, these survey statistics suggest that organizations view merit pay as a means of at least sustaining employee performance in a way that will be viewed as fair or equitable by the majority of employees. More explicitly, merit pay plans appear, by design, to help regulate payments consistently according to performance ratings—that is, everyone with the same rating and position in the salary range receives the same payment. This could help regulate labor costs and enhance employees' perceptions of the fairness of merit pay. Merit pay plan design practices are discussed in the next section.

The prevalence and distribution of variable pay plans are difficult to gauge via surveys. There is such a variety of plans that it is difficult to tell exactly which plans are being counted in any given survey. A recent survey (O'Dell, 1987) reported phenomenal growth in organizational interest in variable pay plans, but such growth must be assessed against a 40- to 50-year history of scant use of or interest in variable pay in U.S. industry (Mitchell et al., 1990). There is no doubt that variable pay plans are much less prevalent and less widely distributed across employee groups than merit plans. For example, O'Dell's 1987 survey of incentives (conducted by the American Compensation Association and the American Productivity Center) indicated that 13 percent of the firms they surveyed (n = 1,598 private-sector firms) were using gainsharing plans. The Hewitt Associates 1989 compensation survey reported that 16 percent of their survey respondents (n = 705 private-sector firms) were using gain sharing; the Conference Board's 1990 survey of variable pay (n = 435 private-sector firms) reported 13 percent. Hewitt noted that two-thirds of the gainsharing plans in their survey had been in place less than three years. Similarly, Hewitt reported that 16 percent of the firms they surveyed reported using cash profit-sharing plans; the Conference Board reported 19 percent. Hewitt also reported that half of the cash profit-sharing plans in their survey had been in place for less than three years.

Executives have traditionally had profit-sharing and bonus plans, sales people are often on commission plans, and a limited number of hourly employees work on piece rate plans (such as in the garment industry); however, the vast majority of employees have not been covered by variable plans. The 1989 Hewitt survey suggests that variable pay plans may now be covering some nontraditional employee groups. For example, 35 percent of the organizations in the survey (n = 435) reported using gainsharing plans for exempt employees, although these plans have been more commonly used for nonexempt employees. Profit sharing, traditionally used for executives, covered nonunion hourly employees in 47 percent of the organizations surveyed. TPF&C/Towers Perrin (1990) reported that variable pay plans are less likely to be found in union environments.

The objectives claimed for variable pay plans are legion. The 1990 TPF&C report on group incentives indicates that 73 percent of the organizations they surveyed (n = 144) gave "supports personnel strategy as it relates to competitive or revitalization business strategies" as their most important reason for adopting variable pay plans. They noted that this objective encompassed other goals: encouraging employee participation, increasing organization productivity and quality, increasing employees' sense of ownership in the organization, and moving employees away from a sense of entitlement to automatic annual pay increases. O'Dell's 1987 report (700 organizations in their sample used gainsharing or profit-sharing plans) listed increasing organization productivity and financial performance as one of the most important reasons for organizations' adoption of variable plans. Controlling costs was another important reason given. The Conference Board (1990) reported that, of the 57 organizations with gainsharing plans in their survey, over half thought organization productivity and quality improvements were the most important reasons for adopting the plans; between 25 and 30 percent indicated that they used gain sharing to increase employee involvement and promote teamwork; 19 percent reported controlling labor costs as important. Taken as a whole, these reports suggest that organizations adopt variable pay plans to improve organization performance, increase employee acceptance and involvement in organization goals, and regulate costs.

Plan Design Characteristics

Merit pay plans are typically implemented via a merit grid (see Figure 6-1). Hewitt Associates (1989) reports that 58 percent of the organizations in their survey used merit grids that determined individual merit payments according to appraisal performance ratings, positions in the pay range, and the size of the merit budget. Typically, the distribution of pay increase percentages in a merit grid is based on assumptions about the percentage of employees at each performance level and position in the pay range. (Approximately 70 percent of organizations employing 10,000 or more use merit grids. Another 20 percent use merit grids that allocate payments according to individual ratings and the size of the merit budget.) Merit payments are usually expressed as a percentage of each employee's base salary and distributed annually. For budget and cost regulation, merit grids are often designed so that the higher an employee is in a pay range, the lower the recommended merit payment for a given performance appraisal rating. When organizations are in growth periods, higher-performing employees in the top of their ranges can be promoted into the next pay range; in low-growth periods, such moves are less likely. Under today's lean staffing policies, some organizations are considering dropping this cap on merit payments and offering lump sum bonuses. These latter are essentially merit payments that are not depressed by an employee's position in the range. In contrast to conventional merit pay plans, some organizations do not add lump sum bonuses to the employee's base pay. Hewitt (1989) reports that 15 percent of the organizations in their survey were using lump sum bonuses for exempt employees.

Merit budget setting is centralized in most organizations (79 percent) (Hewitt, 1989). Top managers report that their organizations' "ability to pay" or its profitability and the pay offered by its labor market competitors are the most important factors determining budgets (Wyatt Company, 1989a). Merit budgets are typically allocated to each business unit or department as a percentage of its payroll (Conference Board, 1984).

Just as there are many types of variable pay plans, there are many variations on plan design. Although it is beyond the scope of our review to describe the

Performance Rating	Percentage of Employees*	Position in Salary Range				
		Low ⟶ A	B	C	D	High E
Outstanding	6%	9%	8%	7%	6.5%	5%
Exceeds expectations	20%	7%	6%	5.5%	5%	4%
Fully satisfactory	70%	5%	4.5%	4%	3.5%	3%
Needs some improvement	3%	1%	1%	1%	1%	No increase
Unsatisfactory	1%	No increase	No increase	No increase	No increase	No increase

* Employees distributed across performance ratings

FIGURE 6-1   Sample merit grid.

spectrum of variable pay plan designs, there are some common design issues that must be addressed in all such plans: determining the performance measure to be used, identifying employee eligibility, specifying the payout distribution rules, and setting payout form and frequency (Milkovich and Newman, 1990). As under merit plans, the distribution rules help to regulate costs or the distribution of the plan funds and ensure that individual employees are treated consistently.

An example will suffice to illustrate these issues. Under a gainsharing plan, determining the performance measure involves deciding what level of system performance (work group, department, plant) is best and what type of measurement (ratios of labor costs to hours or of production value to volume) should be used. Employee eligibility might include only hourly employees, hourly plus nonexempt salaried, or all employees in a work group, plant, or department. Decisions about payout distributions in gain sharing might involve both potential splits of any gains between the company and the employees and whether to distribute the gains to individual employees as a percentage of base salary or across the board. Finally, decisions must be made about how often to assess and distribute gains (monthly, quarterly, twice a year, and in what form) as part of the regular check, as a separate check, as cash, or as some form of deferred payment. (For an overview of variable pay plan design and a source of further references, see Milkovich and Newman, 1990.)

Plan Administration Characteristics

We reported earlier that top managers tend to talk about merit pay as an important part of their overall compensation systems (Conference Board,

1984). This suggests that organizations define the role of merit pay in their pay communications to employees. Yet we found no recent surveys detailing what information organizations provide their employees about pay. A 1976 Conference Board survey indicated that up to 70 percent of the organizations in their survey had a policy of telling employees their pay range, but fewer than 20 percent discussed the organization's overall pay structure, let employees know what other organizations were used as a comparison group for determining salary market competitiveness, or told employees the size (percentage) of the average merit increase. This is certainly in direct contrast to the federal government, where this pay information is available to employees.

There is no average set of administrative guidelines for variable pay plans. Unlike merit plans, however, variable pay plan administration—or perhaps the better word here is implementation—often goes hand in hand with much broader organization changes such as job redesign, team development, changes in management style, increased investments in employee participation, major communication efforts, more sharing of information with employees, more explicit provisions for job security, training for plan administration, and so forth (Conference Board, 1990; TPF&C, 1990; Wallace, 1990). (For more information on variable pay plan implementation and further references, see Milkovich and Newman, 1990.)

Measures of Plan Effectiveness

There is no direct survey evidence of the effectiveness of merit pay programs in improving individual performance, enhancing employee perceptions of pay fairness, or regulating labor costs. The Bureau of National Affairs (1984) reports that fewer than 6 percent of the organizations in their pay survey attempt any formal assessment of their merit plans. The little evidence that does exist comes from opinion or attitude surveys of managers and employees. This evidence suggests that most do not see clear links between their performance and their merit increases. For example, the Wyatt Company's report on employee attitudes (1989b) found that only about 28 percent of the employees they surveyed saw a link between their pay and their job performance.

The surveys on variable pay plans also tend to report variable plan effectiveness in terms of managers' opinions about a plan's success in meeting the organization's objectives. TPF&C's 1990 report, for example, indicates that the managers involved in plan design and administration believed that their plans yielded quantifiable improvements in group or organization measures of quality and productivity and in employee involvement, communications, and commitment. All recent surveys of variable pay plans (O'Dell, 1987; TPF&C, 1990; Wallace, 1990) suggest that plan design variables and the organizational context in which the plan operates are critical to a plan's effectiveness. Careful specification of performance measures, the distribution of gains, the information exchanged with employees, the steps taken to enhance employee involvement, and an emphasis on how the plans fit the organization's broader mission were all considered important to plan effectiveness.

At first glance these measures of variable pay plan effectiveness appear more positive than those for merit pay. They must be placed, however, in perspective. There are few survey measures of the specific effects of merit plans. We also know very little about how employees react to variable pay plans—whether they view them as fair, whether they view them as linking pay to performance, and so forth. There is, after all, a downside to variable pay that is not usually emphasized in these survey reports, namely that variable plans do not pay out when there are no performance improvements. Wallace (1990) also reports that, based on his study of 46 firms, the costs of implementing variable pay plans are significant.

Richer Detail on Merit Pay Plan Practices

Our review of survey results on merit pay suggests that most private-sector organizations use merit pay plans for their exempt employees, that there is little variation in plan design and administration, and that most top managers and personnel managers report that merit pay is an important part of their pay systems—in part because they believe that U.S. social values support the rightness or fairness of tying pay to individual performance.

The personnel managers (representing five Fortune 100 firms) interviewed by the committee all reinforced the importance of viewing merit pay as part of a broader pay system that, in turn, supports meritocratic personnel practices. Merit plan design and administration in their organizations do not depart from the typical company described in our survey review but, as was true in their discussion of performance appraisal, all the personnel managers emphasized the efforts they make to place merit pay in a broader meritocratic context. They noted that pay communications, in particular, are designed to demonstrate to employees that their base pay is competitive with a relatively elite group of corporations, that the organization plans to continue to provide base pay that at least meets competition, that each employee is doing an important job, and that merit plans allow the organization to provide returns to individual contributions. In general, the tone was "This is a good place to work, we pay competitively, we expect a great deal from employees, and thus each one of you who meets those expectations is one of an elite group." These managers also indicated that they share little specific pay information with employees, which is consistent with the survey information we reviewed.

As noted in our discussion of performance appraisal and its role in a meritocracy, there appear to be differences between the private-sector and federal meritocracies that may influence the role of merit pay. For example, in the federal government, managers have little control over the pay information available to employees. This may make it more difficult to persuade employees that they are paid competitively overall and that merit plans provide returns for individual contributions and long-term salary growth. Instead, employees may simply view merit pay as a means of making their base salaries more (or less) competitive.

The five personnel managers we interviewed believed that merit pay plans helped their organizations regulate the distribution of the annual merit payments so that employees were treated consistently and payments were within budget.

The committee did not interview the five personnel managers regarding variable pay plans in their organizations.

Convergence Between Research and Practice

There appear to be two major points of convergence between research on merit pay and variable plans and current private-sector practices. The first is the lack of measures of effectiveness for merit plans in meeting any pay-for-performance plan objectives. In comparison, the measures of effectiveness of variable pay plans seem prolific. Despite the prevalence of merit pay plans, we cannot determine their effects. And the relative scarcity, the recency, and the air of advocacy surrounding variable pay plans also means that the existing survey measures of their effectiveness must be taken with more than a few grains of salt.

The second is that both research and practice consider context important to organization decisions about adopting and implementing merit or variable pay plans. The five personnel executives we interviewed stressed that merit pay plans reflected their firms' meritocractic personnel philosophies and that merit principles were an important part of their cultures. The survey literature on variable pay plans reveals that firms with some experience in implementing these plans stress the importance of management support for the plan, work cultures that reflect good employee-management relations and participative management styles, and training for those involved in administering the plan. The research literature also suggests the importance of context variables such as job or task structure, the organization's technology, occupational diversity, labor intensity, and personnel practices, as well as environmental variables such as unionization and rate of economic growth.

PRIVATE-SECTOR PRACTICE: CONCLUSIONS AND THEIR IMPLICATIONS FOR THE FEDERAL GOVERNMENT

Our review of practice indicates that performance appraisal and merit plans are extensively used for professional and managerial employees in private-sector firms. However, surveys report little formal measurement of the effects of performance appraisal and merit plans on individual performance, on employee perceptions of the fairness of these plans, or of the direct and indirect labor costs associated with plan development and administration. The measures that are reported involve opinion surveys of either employee perceptions about the success of appraisal and merit plans in linking pay to performance, or of personnel managers' assessments of how well these plans work. In general, neither employees nor personnel managers are overly enthusiastic. These opinion survey trends appear consistent with the federal government's experience, yet they have not been accompanied by any decline in the private sector's use of performance appraisal and merit pay.

Our interviews with the personnel executives of five Fortune 100 firms that considered their performance appraisal and merit plans successful provided the committee with richer details. These details may offer one explanation for the persistence of performance appraisal and merit pay plans in the face of less than universal enthusiasm about them. These five personnel managers all stressed that their performance appraisal and merit plans are embedded in meritocratic personnel philosophies and work cultures that support merit pay. They believed that the majority of their employees would find a pay system with no connections to their performance unfair, and that no plan for pay distribution would meet with unqualified employee approval and satisfaction. These beliefs are consistent with surveys of managerial and professional employees that report support for merit pay.

These interviews also pointed out some differences between meritocratic personnel practices in the five Fortune 100 firms and in the federal system, differences that have implications for federal performance appraisal and merit plans. For example, the personnel managers noted that a major benefit of performance appraisal is the identification of top and bottom performers. However, private-sector managers have more flexibility (and incentive) in promoting top performers and dismissing consistently poor performers than is typical in the federal government. Similarly, the personnel managers stressed the importance of communicating merit pay as one element of a broader, competitive pay system that recognizes a variety of employee contributions and needs. These managers, however, also have more control over the pay information that employees receive than is typical in the federal government. Finally, the personnel managers we interviewed stressed the importance of process in managing performance appraisal and merit plans. However, in at least one process area—that of procedural protections—the private sector appears to have less formal, more flexible procedures in place to handle employee appeals than is true of the federal government.

These examples suggest that, at least in these five firms, a sizeable degree of management flexibility accompanies a meritocratic personnel philosophy and performance appraisal and merit plan administration.

Management flexibility is just one of many context factors that may influence the federal government's merit pay reforms. We have listed a number of other potentially influential context factors throughout this report. In the next chapter, we discuss these factors and their implications for the federal government in more detail.

7

The Importance of Context

Our reviews of performance appraisal and merit plan research and practice indicate that plan success or failure are substantially influenced by the context within which they are embedded. Research on performance appraisal now encompasses a broader set of organizational factors, along with the individual and task factors that it has traditionally studied (Murphy and Cleveland, 1991). Research on pay now stresses the importance of viewing pay and pay-for-performance plans in the context of an organization's personnel system, its structure and managerial styles, and its strategic goals (Balkin and Gomez-Mejia, 1987a, 1990; Carroll, 1987). Managers of performance appraisal, merit pay, and variable pay plans stress that these plans must fit or be consistent with the organization's personnel practices, culture, and strategic mission or goals if they are to work as the organization intends. Both researchers and managers acknowledge the influence of environmental conditions on organization decisions about adopting and implementing these plans.

The rationale underlying this concern with context is a simple one. In Chapter 5, we noted that theory and research on individual motivation show that individuals are motivated by pay to the extent that they value pay, understand performance goals, and believe that pay is contingent on that performance. Variations in an organization's context attributable to its strategy, structure, job design, culture, management systems, personnel systems, and work force culture and characteristics can strengthen or attenuate the links between pay and individual motivation. Design and implementation of performance appraisal and merit plans that fit or are consistent with context factors tend to strengthen these links.

Unfortunately, on the basis of the existing research evidence, it is difficult to be specific about what fit really is. However, it may be useful to briefly summarize several points about the concept of fit that are relevant to the federal government's interest in performance appraisal and pay for performance and that appear to receive support in the existing quantitative, clinical, and/or practice literatures.

This chapter is organized around the three categories of related contextual factors identified in reviews of research and practice on performance appraisal and pay for performance: (1) the nature of the organization's work—primarily its technology and job designs; (2) the broader features of organizational context such as size, management systems, personnel systems, and work force culture and characteristics; and (3) features of the organization's environment, such as its economic growth, the presence of unions and associations, and the pressures exerted by multiple public regulators and interest groups. We do not offer any comprehensive review of the very diverse research literatures that might be brought to bear on the influence of context on performance appraisal and merit pay. Instead, our discussion focuses on the factors that may be particularly relevant to the federal government (Perry and Porter, 1982) and provides some general research findings suggesting how these factors may influence performance appraisal and merit pay. We end with a description of the federal bureaucratic context and its implications for performance appraisal and merit pay.

TECHNOLOGICAL FIT:
THE NATURE OF THE ORGANIZATION'S WORK

An organization's technologies and the pace of change characteristic of those technologies will influence the way an organization defines its jobs and work methods (Scott, 1981). The performance evaluation measures most suitable to an organization will depend in part on the effects of technology on job complexity, interdependence, and stability; on job goal specificity; and on the ease of measuring or supervising job performance (Dornbusch and Scott, 1975; Murphy and Cleveland, 1991). For example, stable jobs characterized by low complexity, in which performance goals can be easily specified for each employee and in which employee performance is easily observed, are compatible with more quantitative, carefully scaled individual evaluations based on specific work output or behavior.

However, using highly specific, individual performance appraisals and incentives with jobs that are complex and involve multiple and ambiguous goals can result in employees ignoring important aspects of their jobs or distorting job information to make their performance look good. Blau (1955) provided a classic description of how explicit performance measures in a public employment agency induced interviewers to behave in ways that were consistent with their performance goals but destructively competitive and nonproductive for the organization. Pfeffer and Baron (1988) suggested that one factor promoting the increased reliance on "contingent" labor (such as part-time, temporary, leased, or subcontracted labor) was managerial performance appraisals that assessed outputs per capita, in which the denominator of that ratio was based only on full-time equivalents. In both these cases the use of quantitative performance measures created incentives for employees to behave in ways that were rational but organizationally detrimental.

Many scholars have pointed out that managers and professionals in public-sector organizations face conflicting, diffuse goals that make it difficult to develop meaningful performance criteria (e.g., Buchanan, 1975). It has also been suggested that it may be easier to establish concrete and appropriately challenging goals in jobs in which the bottom line is measurable (staff sales, units produced) than in more typically bureaucratic jobs, such as managing strategic planning or policy development. Yet the examples of the possible unintended consequences of explicit performance measures cited above are equally pertinent in the private and public sectors. Indeed, one could argue that the potential problems are greater for private-sector employers because they have moved away from developing standards and elements based on job analysis for their managerial and professional employees, and instead rely on management-by-objective kinds of appraisal. The premium that such appraisal systems place on specific, narrowly defined goals and the likelihood that negotiated goals will tend to be lenient would seem also to increase the likelihood that important aspects of the job will be ignored or the appraisal otherwise distorted.

BROADER ORGANIZATIONAL FACTORS

While the relationships among an organization's technology, job designs, performance evaluation plans, and pay-for-performance plans have been the contextual factors most directly examined, many others are thought to influence an organization's success in adopting and implementing these plans. For the purposes of this chapter, we classify them broadly as: (1) factors related to organization strategy, goal clarity, and cohesiveness; (2) factors related to organization size, structure, and management systems—including personnel systems; and (3) factors related to work force climate and employee-labor-management relations.

Organization Strategy, Goal Clarity, and Cohesiveness

The business policy and strategy literature suggests that organizations vary in their perceptions of their environments and in their definitions of the strategic goals meant to help them compete in those environments. Many different strategic orientations have been identified in this literature (see, for example,

Schendel and Hofer, 1979; Lamb, 1984; Porter, 1985; and Harrigan, 1988). Two primary strategic postures have been applied in studies of the association between strategy and performance evaluation and pay systems in private-sector firms: a dynamic, growth-oriented model and a steady-state model. Most of these studies are cast at the headquarters level and examine executive compensation systems. For our purposes they are interesting because they suggest that different strategic goal orientations are associated with different emphases on performance evaluation and pay-for-performance plans. We emphasize the word *suggest* here, since these studies are, at best, descriptive and cannot be viewed as generalizable.

A 1985 study by Kerr, for example, used a multiple case study methodology to classify firms according to their corporate strategies and to distinguish patterns of performance evaluation and pay plans within strategic classes. The 20 firms that Kerr classified were pursuing either an "evolutionary/dynamic growth" or an "steady-state/maintenance" strategic approach to their market environments. Evolutionary strategies were defined as emphasizing increasing market growth through active pursuit of new markets via acquisitions, joint ventures or mergers, and innovative products or services. Steady-state strategies were defined as emphasizing holding onto current market positions through internal development of technology, improvements in products or services, increasing work force productivity, internal coordination, and economies of scale.

Kerr found that executives in firms successfully pursuing evolutionary strategies were more likely to be evaluated strictly on quantitative, organization-level measures of strategic performance tied to bonus plans that offered high returns (40 percent or more of base salary). Executives in firms successfully pursuing steady-state strategies were more likely to be evaluated against a mix of subjective and quantitative performance measures cast at both the individual and the organization levels. Their bonuses paid out at a lower rate (20 percent of base salary). (Kerr's results were consistent with earlier work on corporate strategy and executive pay such as Berg [1965], and Pitts [1976].)

In a 1984 study of electronics manufacturing firms, Balkin and Gomez-Mejia found that firms pursuing strategic innovation and growth goals through new research and development were more likely to offer their engineers and scientists a higher proportion of their pay in the form of incentives (bonuses, profit sharing, and stock) than firms with less investment in innovation and new development.

In both these studies, organizations pursuing riskier (i.e., evolutionary, innovative) strategies were evaluating their managers or professionals on quantitative, specific, organization-level performance goals. They offered them pay incentives that would be paid out only if the organization was successful, but would then pay out very well. We can speculate that by tying performance evaluations strictly to strategic goal attainment and by offering high payouts, organizations are sending a signal to current and prospective employees about the importance of more entrepreneurial, innovative behavior to the organization. Organizations pursuing maintenance-oriented strategies evaluated their managers on a mix of more qualitative individual behaviors and quantitative organization-level goals; bonus payouts were typically a lower proportion of base salaries than in firms pursuing riskier strategies. We can likewise speculate here that by using this combination of performance evaluation and bonuses, these organizations are sending a signal to employees about the importance of professional management skills in meeting specific organization performance goals, and of getting along as individuals within the performance norms shaped by the work force culture. These remain, at this point, speculations, although many researchers have voiced them (Salter, 1973; Galbraith, 1977; Lawler, 1981; Balkin and Gomez-Mejia, 1987a; Carroll, 1987).

There are also theoretical perspectives suggesting that organizations vary in their ability to define strategic goals so that they are likely to be understood and seen as legitimate by their employees, their other stakeholders, and the public. For example, organizations in highly institutionalized sectors or those relying significantly on public trust may be more likely to adopt very formal, precise performance evaluations in response to external pressures or regulations (Meyer and Rowan, 1977). In such cases, organizations may use performance appraisals and pay-for-performance plans (like merit plans) to make their management decisions appear more legitimate to both employees and other organization stakeholders. (See, for example, Tolbert and Zucker's 1983 study of the adoption of civil service reforms.)

The reason for this, some scholars would argue, is that when organization goals are most difficult to define and job performance is thus difficult to evaluate against some agreed-upon criteria, organizations feel compelled to adopt more formal, precise evaluations in order to assure their constituents that they are operating rationally and efficiently. For instance, a government agency with a fairly straightforward mission and relatively easily defined performance criteria, such as the Internal Revenue Service, might exhibit less formal and precise performance evaluation than one with a less clearly defined mission and performance criteria, such as the Environmental Protection Agency. It is precisely the difficulty in identifying effective job performance in the latter case that induces decision makers to emphasize formal evaluation. Moreover, it is symbolically important for employees and other organization stakeholders to perceive that meaningful evaluation criteria are used and that differential outcomes are not capricious (Salancik, 1977; March and March, 1978). As March (1981:232) writes, "decision making is, in part, a performance designed to reassure decision makers and others that things are being done appropriately." In reality, desired performance may be difficult or impossible to specify or identify a priori, especially in higher-skilled and information-intensive lines of work. Ironically, this may make it all the more likely for an organization to try and do so in order to leave the impression among members that things are not done arbitrarily.

Organizational Structure, Management Systems, and Size

Structure and Management Systems

The perspectives on organizational choice of strategic goals and organizational ability to define strategic goals assume that such choices are influenced by internal structure, management systems, and personnel systems. By virtue of their history, growth patterns, strategic goals, and the environmental challenges they face, organizations make decisions about their physical and geographic structures, their job designs and hierarchies, their management systems, and so forth. While the conceptual writing and the research undertaken to examine the relationships between organization strategy, structure, management, and environment are extensive, we focus here only on selected work used in normative proposals about the relationship between organization structure, management systems, and performance appraisal and pay systems. This includes work by Burns and Stalker (1961), Miles and Snow (1978, 1983), Balkin and Gomez-Mejia (1987a, 1990), and Carroll (1987).

Burns and Stalker's classic study (1961) proposed two ideal types: (1) the organic organization—young, innovative, aggressively pursuing growth in highly uncertain environments—and (2) the mechanistic organization—less risk-oriented, more stable, more focused on internal efficiencies. They described the organic organization as one in which jobs or tasks are undifferentiated; performing them requires employees with general problem-solving or professional skills. Job definition is flexible and changes with the organization's goals and technology. Decision-making responsibility is decentralized, and employee input is not only valued but expected. Management hierarchies are flat; evaluations are tied to external professional standards and broadly defined organization goals. Policy and work rule standardization and formalization are low; communication is open, offering information rather than supervisory instruction.

Burns and Stalker's mechanistic organization, by contrast, is described as one in which jobs or tasks are highly defined, requiring employees with specialized, functional skills and specific organizational experience. Job definition is stable but difficult to change, as change would require new skills. Decision making tends to be centralized, with each supervisor having a distinct span of control and set of responsibilities, and employee input is low. In the mechanistic genre, hierarchies are steep, and control systems tend to be behavioral and tied to employee loyalty and diligence in carrying out assignments. Policy and work rule standardization and formalization are high; communication tends to be restricted, vertical (and one-way: top to bottom), and focused on instruction rather than an information exchange. Burns and Stalker proposed that the mechanistic type provided the context an organization needed to capitalize on the managerial and technical efficiencies possible in more stable, certain environments.

Miles and Snow (1978, 1983) proposed a similar pattern in the context variables of an organization's structure and management system in their prospector and defender types, adding more detail on the personnel management systems appropriate to each. (Miles and Snow's work echoes that of Doeringer and Piore, 1971, on variations in a firm's internal labor market development.) In their large-scale, systematic case studies and writings, Miles and Snow distinguished two distinct strategic goal orientations—one that emphasizes innovation and market growth (prospector firms) and one that emphasizes holding current market position by pursuing cost efficiencies, quality, and productivity improvements (defender firms). The personnel management systems of the more entrepreneurial organizations emphasize general skills, hiring at all levels of the organization, higher investments in recruiting than in training and development, and performance measures tied to innovation and competitive market outcomes; retention is not considered a primary personnel management goal. Defender firms are described as emphasizing job-specific skills; promotion from within; retention; higher investments in selection, training, and development; and performance measures tied to cost efficiencies, social norms, and historical standards. In short, in the Miles and Snow typology, prospectors spend personnel dollars to buy a work force; defenders, to make or build one.

Drawing on this and other work, Carroll (1987) and Balkin and Gomez-Mejia (1987a, 1990) have proposed that organizations pursuing growth-oriented, innovative strategies, which have organic structures and management systems and personnel practices that emphasize buying an entrepreneurial work force will be best served by performance evaluations that emphasize competitive, organization-level performance and by pay systems that emphasize group incentives and bonuses. Organizations pursuing cost efficiencies and maintenance strategies, with mechanistic structures and management systems and personnel practices that emphasize internal skill development and the importance of work force norms, would be better served by more traditional performance appraisal and merit plans or other policies that recognize an employee's long-term contributions to the organization.

There is considerable anecdotal literature that supports these prescribed patterns of association or fit between performance evaluation and pay-for-performance on one hand and organizational strategy, structure, management, and personnel systems on the other (Cook, 1981; Salschieder, 1981; Ellig, 1982; Smith, 1982). However, there is little research specifying the exact dimensions of fit among organizational systems, nor are there generally accepted theories concerning how such fit contributes to organizational performance.

Case study research on high-performance organizations and on organizational innovation also suggests that effective performance appraisal and pay allocation practices must be closely aligned with an organization's culture, structure (e.g., number of layers of management, job structure), management style (e.g., centralization versus decentralization), and work force (Beer et al., 1990). A number of commentators have argued that the success of so-called high-commitment organizations illustrates the power of well-integrated personnel systems to increase motivation and organizational effectiveness (Walton, 1979, 1980). In some cases, new manufacturing facilities have been built from the ground up, with all of the elements of the organization planned and designed to be congruent from the outset to increase motivation, teamwork, and effectiveness. Although there have been instances of failure and regression over time, the record of these high-commitment work systems suggests that motivation, attachment, quality, and productivity are positively affected when the human resources policies and practices of the organization are highly congruent.

Motivation in high-commitment organizations seems to be governed not by one dimension such as pay, or a relationship with the boss, or the nature of the work, but by a multiplicity of organizational practices such as organization design, pay practices, management style, information and feedback, employee involvement, and the types of employees recruited and socialized into the organization. The internal consistency of these practices is thought to reinforce employee perceptions of the organization's fairness and concern for equity (Greenberg, 1986b).

Size

The work discussed so far does not capture the size or scale, the scope of operations, the complexity of joint working arrangements, and the diversity of work forces typical of many large, modern organizations. In particular, in large organizations with diverse operating units and work forces, there is always the question of where in the organization's structure decentralization of performance appraisal and pay systems is most likely to facilitate the achievement of strategic objectives. We know, for example, that even within a discrete business unit, personnel systems, including performance evaluation and pay-for-performance plans, may vary by employee group (Hewitt Associates, 1989).

The business policy studies of the 1960s and 1970s illustrated two basic approaches to corporate structuring and control of large, diverse businesses: one in which corporate management took a hands-off or holding company approach to managing business divisions; the other in which the corporate management tried to set basic policy guidelines and used both performance evaluation and pay systems to tie division managers to corporate as well as divisional goals (Chandler, 1962; Berg, 1965; Pitts, 1976). Recent case studies of globalizing or transnational firms have noted that, while some firms try to manage and coordinate diverse businesses and work forces by developing more elaborate bureaucratic and centralized structures and controls, most have moved to global statements of corporate values that are intended to guide, but not dictate, business unit actions at a decentralized level (Doz and Pralahad, 1981; Galbraith and Kazanjian, 1986; Bartlett and Ghoshal, 1988; Evans, 1989). The work of Vancil and Buddrus (1979) also supports decentralized control of performance appraisal and pay-for-performance plans based on the nature of the work being performed (e.g., team-based, task interdependence, task concreteness, stability of technology, etc.).

Work Force Climate and Employee-Management-Labor Relations

The research we reviewed earlier on pay-for-performance plans indicated that such factors as employees' confidence and trust in management, their opportunities to participate in setting performance goals, and the availability of channels for appeals of performance appraisal ratings and merit allocations can influence both their motivation to perform and their assessments of the fairness of performance appraisals and pay-for-performance plans. There is considerable case study and anecdotal literature documenting problems that can occur when individual and group incentive plans, for example, are implemented in an organization unit in which employee-management-labor relations have been traditionally hostile (Whyte, 1955; Lawler, 1973; Schuster, 1984b; Mitchell et al., 1990). Problems include the development of work force norms restricting performance, and gaming or providing false performance information in order to get plan payoffs without changing actual performance. This literature provides some warning to organizations attempting to implement new pay-for-performance plans in hostile work climates that they must understand the risks involved. Lawler (1981) suggests that, in such situations, organizations should improve the work climate before implementing pay changes.

ENVIRONMENTAL FACTORS

While there are a host of environmental factors that may influence organizational arrangements, we focus here on three sets of institutional forces of particular interest to performance evaluation and pay-for-performance systems: economic pressures and growth; the presence of unions and professional associations; and the pressure of laws and regulations governing personnel systems.

Economic Pressures and Growth

Our review of research on pay-for-performance plans suggested that the economic environment the organization faces and its projected employment and financial growth can influence employees' acceptance of pay-for-performance plans. Lawler's (1973) review of case studies on individual incentive plans suggested that employees were less likely to accept the plans (and thus be motivated by them) when they believed the plans might eventually result in reducing the organization's demand for people in their jobs. Likewise, the case studies of gainsharing plans suggest that employees are more likely to accept these plans when there is some form of job guarantee attached or the organization's future economic success and growth look promising (Schuster, 1984b). Conventional merit plans also offer more incentive potential for employees when the organization is growing. As we noted in our review of practice, the opportunity to promote high-performing employees who are also high in their salary range makes it more likely that merit plans will, over time, provide higher-performing employees with higher pay levels. Some organizations, faced with limited employment growth, are now considering avoiding restrictions on merit allocations for employees already high in their salary ranges by offering some portion of merit increases as lump sums (i.e., not added into base salaries). In short, some assurances that pay-for-performance plan payouts are feasible and that job security is not jeopardized by the plan appear to be important to employee acceptance and motivation under pay-for-performance plans. Both may be influenced by the organization's economic and growth prospects.

Unions and Professional Associations

Unions in the United States have resisted performance appraisal systems and pay-for-performance arrangements because they view them as cloaking managerial exploitation (hence worker distrust of performance appraisal ratings) and reducing worker solidarity by substituting wage competition (merit or incentive plans) for a community of interest among laborers (Stone, 1974). Unions aim to raise the wage levels of the whole collective, rather than the wages of individual members. The practical effect of union resistance and aims is well documented. Most surveys of incentive systems in use (including merit plans) indicate that unionized employees are far less likely than nonunionized employees to be covered by such pay arrangements (Bureau of National Affairs, 1981, 1984). Freeman and Medoff (1984), in a comprehensive study of unions, noted that unionization tended to reduce wage differentials among union members, while raising their overall wage level relative to that of first line management (also see Kalleberg and Lincoln, 1988). To the extent that pay-for-performance plans might increase any disparities between the rewards of managers and those of the employees they supervise, the relatively high degree of unionization in the federal government might make employees more resistant to pay-for-performance plans (Advisory Committee on Federal Pay, 1990).

The 1980s saw some slight reduction in union resistance to alternative pay arrangements in the private sector. The particular pay arrangements conceded, however, typically were profit-sharing and lump sum plans, which do not differentiate among individual employees (Mitchell, 1985).

Industrial unions typically emphasize the power of numbers in reaching wage bargains; craft unions and professional associations typically emphasize skills. Professional associations might be expected to resist centralized or standardized performance measurement systems and related pay-for-performance plans on the grounds that only members of the profession can appropriately judge performance. To the extent that such systems might reduce the power or wages of their groups, they would be resisted. The exception here might be personnel professionals who have a particular stake in the institution of these systems (Baron et al., 1986).

Overall, then, the extent of unionization and professionalization in an organization's labor markets will tend to reduce support for the adoption of performance evaluation and pay-for-performance plans. In the federal government, there are four associations that represent managers and professionals and at least four employee unions. Survey responses of government managers suggest that, although there is agreement in concept with merit pay, there is dissatisfaction with its administration to date.

Laws and Regulations Governing Personnel

External laws and regulations impose additional goals for organizations (for example, equal employment opportunity) and often prescribe internal structures and controls for achieving them. These imposed goals and internal systems may be incompatible with the organization's other goals and internal systems. In the federal government, details of many personnel programs are dictated by law and audited by the General Accounting Office and the Office of Personnel Management. The extent to which external laws and regulations have pressured organizations to adopt internal structures and programs that are at cross-purposes with mainline organizational goals is debatable. The laws and regulations prohibiting employment discrimination, for example, have brought dramatic changes in the way companies conduct and document their personnel management procedures. Although these laws were designed to implement important constitutional and policy goals, they have also had an impact—many would argue a positive impact—on such things as the quality of employment tests and the resources that companies devote to human resource management. Other legal protections may not be compatible with effective performance appraisal systems. For example, the legal protections available to federal employees have put significant pressure on the design and administration of the performance appraisal system.

In the case in which employees have explicit procedures for grievance and due process, there is generally more emphasis placed on the development of clear and concrete performance standards and dimensions that have at least the appearance of validity to both the supervisor and the employee. There is always the danger that, in an environment with heavy legalistic protections for employees, the performance appraisal system will be asked to provide an unrealistic level of measurement rigor. The results of our analysis of the technology of performance appraisal (see Chapter 4) suggest that moderate levels of validity can be achieved under highly controlled conditions, but that we have probably reached the point of diminishing returns in the search for measurement precision. Moreover, although research analyzing court decisions on performance appraisal systems indicates that appraisal focusing on specific behaviors or results are more likely to find judicial approval, recent measurement and cognitive research fails to support a preference for these approaches over the appraisal of broad traits.

There are some specific concerns with regard to the protections afforded federal employees. While due process requirements giving employees the right to appeal their evaluations are common in the public sector and are related to the concept of fairness in the public and private sectors, some of the bases for appealing performance appraisals under the Civil Service Reform Act may hamper effective managerial discretion. For example, the Civil Service Reform Act requires that performance standards be objective to the maximum extent feasible. Lack of objectivity of the performance standard can be the basis for appealing an unsatisfactory performance evaluation. We have discussed in Chapter 4 the inappropriateness of the terms objective and subjective, particularly with reference to managerial appraisal. We have also established that managerial performance does not lend itself to job-specific measurement. Providing employees a right to appeal their performance appraisals if the standards are not objective enough is likely to be a time-consuming exercise with no valid or beneficial outcome.

FINDINGS

1. Using very precise individual performance measures and incentives systems for managerial and professional jobs can have potentially negative consequences for the organization; many organizations use more global appraisals combined with merit plans for such jobs.

2. Organizations differ in their ability to articulate strategic goals that provide direction throughout the management hierarchy in setting meaningful performance appraisal goals. Some organizations—especially public-sector organizations—find it difficult to articulate overall mission or strategic goals.

3. Public-sector organizations may use more formal, precise performance appraisals in an effort to make management decisions appear legitimate both to employees and to other constituents. While this may be useful in satisfying some constituents (for example, Congress) it may make employees skeptical of their performance appraisals and any pay system based on them, and it may reduce management incentives to administer the systems as the organization intends.

4. The literature related to fit suggests that there is a general match between certain patterns of organization strategy, structure, management on one hand and performance evaluation and pay systems on the other. For example, traditional performance appraisal and merit pay plans appear to be most suited to steady-state organizations, which emphasize skill development and work force norms. Group incentive systems appear better suited to innovative entrepreneurial organizations.

5. Many large firms with diverse goals and work forces have moved towards decentralized management strategies, with the home office providing policy and audit functions and the local units designing and implementing performance evaluation and pay systems.

This general discussion of contextual factors shaping performance appraisal and pay practices suggests not only that performance appraisal and pay practices must be aligned with the rest of an organization and its environment but also, presumably, that the reverse is true. In other words, to the extent that the federal government is seriously devoted to pay for performance, success in implementing it is unlikely unless the broader context supports it.

8

Findings and Conclusions

The Office of Personnel Management (OPM) requested this study in preparation for reauthorization hearings, scheduled for 1991, on the troubled Performance Management and Recognition System (PMRS). Our charge was to review the research on performance appraisal and on its use in linking compensation to performance. To supplement the research findings, we were asked to look at private-sector practice as well, to see if there are successful compensation systems based on performance appraisal that might provide guidance for policy makers in reforming PMRS. We construed this charge as requiring an investigation of whether and under what conditions performance appraisal in the context of merit pay systems could assist the federal government in managing performance, fostering employee equity, improving individual and organizational effectiveness, providing consistent and predictable personnel costs, and—not least—enhancing the legitimacy of public service.

The Civil Service Reform Act (CSRA) of 1978 provides the backdrop for this study. That act required the development of job-related and objective performance appraisal systems, the results of which were to be used as a basis for training, promotion, reduction in grade, removal, and other personnel decisions. The act also created performance-based compensation systems for middle and senior managers. Designed to revitalize the civil service, in part by bringing private-sector management strategies to the federal bureaucracy, the reforms have by most measures fallen short of expectations, despite fairly substantial midcourse corrections. Yet the belief in merit principles remains strong, as does the expectation that performance appraisal and linking compensation to performance can provide incentives for excellence.

135

Policy makers already have extensive documentation of the problems and employee dissatisfactions with the Merit Pay System (MPS) and the successor PMRS: consistent underfunding of the merit pool, the lag of merit salaries behind the salaries of employees still under the General Schedule, the widely held and annually reinforced belief that federal salaries have fallen far behind their private-sector equivalents, and the perceived politicization of the civil service and the merit pay system that seemed to be an outgrowth of the Civil Service Reform Act. This study is intended to supplement that knowledge and experience with information drawn from the private sector, beginning with a systematic investigation of the research on performance appraisal and pay-for-performance systems and including an assessment of private-sector practices in the years since the passage of the Civil Service Reform Act.

We began the report with a cautionary note about the difficulties inherent in trying to measure social phenomena in general, and about the particular evidentiary obstacles presented by the subject at hand (Chapter 3). Our research has taken us into the literature of a variety of disciplines as we tried to piece together from fragmentary evidence the best possible scientific understanding of the adequacy of performance appraisal as a basis for making personnel decisions and of the effectiveness of using pay to improve performance. Investigation of the effects of linking compensation to performance led us from the question of individual effectiveness to organizational effectiveness and required an examination of both merit and variable pay plans. Recent research trends also broadened the scope of the study beyond measurement instruments and appraisal processes to an examination of context and the attempt to identify conditions under which performance appraisal and merit plans operate best.

In the course of our investigations it became clear that the theoretical and empirical literatures have posited at least four different types of benefits in discussing performance-based pay systems: (1) positive effects on the work behaviors of individual employees (including decisions to join an organization, attend, perform, and remain); (2) increased organization-level effectiveness; (3) facilitating socialization and communication; and (4) enhancing the perceived legitimacy of an organization to important internal and external constituencies.

We have been ecumenical in pulling together evidence and information that speak to these criteria for gauging the effectiveness of an organization's performance appraisal and pay systems. The preceding pages have taken account of theory, empirical research, and clinical studies not only from many disciplines, but also from any research topics that seemed relevant. The formal evidence has been supplemented with information about current practices in private-sector firms.

The study's findings and conclusions are presented in this chapter as follows. The first section deals with the science and practice of performance appraisal, focusing first on measurement research, then on applied research, and ending with overall findings and conclusions. The second section covers performance-based pay systems, focusing first on evidence from research, then on findings from practice, and again ending with overall findings and conclusions. The third section deals with the influence of context on performance appraisal and merit pay systems. The fourth section deals with the implications of the study's findings and conclusions for federal policy making.

I. THE SCIENCE AND PRACTICE OF PERFORMANCE APPRAISAL

The evaluation of workers' performance is directed toward two fundamental goals. The first of these is to create a measure that accurately assesses the level of an individual's performance on something called *the job*. The second is to create a performance measurement system that will advance one or more operational functions in an organization: personnel decisions, compensation policy, communication of organizational objectives, and facilitation of employee performance.

Although all performance appraisal systems encompass both goals, the two are represented in the literature by two distinct, albeit overlapping, lines of development in theory and research. In part the difference in approach to performance appraisal reflects disciplinary orientation, in part historical development. One approach grows out of psychometrics and the measurement tradition, with its emphasis on standardization, objective measurement, psychometric properties (validity, reliability, bias, etc.). The other comes from the more applied fields—human resource management, industrial and organizational psychology, organization science, sociology—and focuses on the organizational context and the usefulness of performance appraisal for such things as promoting communication between managers and employees; clarifying organizational goals and performance expectations; providing information for managers to guide retention, dismissal, and promotion decisions; informing performance-based pay decisions; and motivating employees.

Both research fields are interested in the use of rating scales to evaluate job performance, although they have tended to focus on different questions and have different expectations of performance appraisal. At the risk of overemphasizing the distinctions, we have presented our discussion in this report in two parts, one focused on the measurement research, the second on the applied research. It is, however, a matter of general orientation, not unrelated polarities.

Of the two goals, accuracy and organizational utility, most of the research in the measurement tradition has concentrated on aspects of accuracy, the implicit assumption being that if the measures are accurate, the functional goals will be met. Research in the more applied fields tends to focus not on the measurement instrument and the accuracy of inferences drawn from the measurement, but on the whole operational system of which it is a part. The applied or management perspective tends to evaluate the performance measurement component by how well the whole operates, e.g., whether the system distributes pay as it was designed to, whether the system is accepted by all players. Accuracy of performance measurement tends to be ignored, not because it is considered unimportant, but because it is assumed, at least implicitly, that if the system-level criteria are met, then the measurement component must be sufficiently accurate.

Apart from our own convenience in presenting findings from the measurement and applied traditions separately, it is important that federal policy makers, managers' groups, and employees understand these differences and tailor their language and expectations appropriately. Current federal policy is couched in the language of the measurement tradition. In the manner of the 1978 *Uniform Guidelines on Employee Selection Procedures*, which elaborates the requirements of Title VII of the Civil Rights Act of 1964, Office of Personnel Management regulations implementing the Civil Service Reform Act of 1978 called on federal agencies to develop job-related and objective performance appraisal systems. The regulations required that performance standards and critical job elements be specified consistent with the duties and responsibilities outlined in an employee's position description. OPM suggested that performance standards be based on a job analysis to identify the critical elements of a job, and that each agency develop a method for evaluating its system to ensure its validity. Although courts have not demanded of performance appraisal systems the degree of rigor required of tests and other selection instruments, the terms *validity*, *objectivity*, and *job-relatedness* are all drawn from the context of psychological testing and performance measurement.

The Measurement Tradition

Psychometrics grows out of the theory of individual differences, namely, that humans possess characteristics and traits (e.g., height, verbal ability, upper-body strength); that each possesses these characteristics in some amount; and that the amounts can be measured. Drawing on findings in the biological sciences about the distribution of characteristics in a given plant or animal population, the founders of psychological measurement developed statistical techniques for expressing human mental characteristics and for relating the standing of one individual to that of a population of individuals. From the beginning, these theories and measurement techniques were thought to hold great promise for matching people to jobs and for measuring job performance. They were also particularly compatible with the concept of meritocracy and the particularly American idea that jobs ought to be allocated on the basis of talent or ability and not as a function of family connection, social class, religious persuasion, or other criteria that are irrelevant to job performance.

In the realm of psychometrics, the scientific imperative is accuracy of measurement. Standardized multiple-choice tests, the most familiar type of instrument in this mode, are a product of that drive for precise measurement.

Just as test administration can be controlled to provide a high degree of consistency and uniformity in the conditions of testing, so does the format of the tests constrain response possibilities to allow direct comparison of the performance of all test takers. Over the years a variety of sophisticated statistical analytics have been developed to evaluate the consistency of measurement (reliability analyses) and the accuracy and relevance of inferences drawn from the measurement results (validity analyses).

Prior to 1980, most research on performance appraisal was generated from within the psychometric tradition. Performance appraisals were viewed in much the same way as tests: they were evaluated against criteria for validity and reliability and freedom from bias, and a primary goal of the research was to reduce rating errors.

Our findings on how closely performance appraisal has been found to conform to these aspirations of measurement science follow.

Research on Job Analysis

Findings: Job Analysis

Applied psychologists have used job analysis as a primary means for understanding and describing job performance. There have been a number of approaches to job analysis over the years, including the job element method, the critical incident method, the Air Force task inventory approach, and methods that rely on structured questionnaires to describe managerial-level jobs in large organizations. All of these methods share certain assumptions about good job analysis practices, and all are based on a variety of empirical sources of information.

1. There is an enormous body of job analysis research, the preponderance of which has been conducted for relatively simple, concrete jobs—military enlisted jobs, auto mechanics, sales, and other jobs characterized by observable behaviors or tangible products. The literature on complex, interactive, cognitively loaded jobs, and specifically on managerial jobs, is comparatively sparse and less conclusive.

2. With few exceptions, the analysis of managerial performance is cast at a high level of abstraction; far less attention has been given to the sort of detailed, task-centered definition typical of simpler, more concrete jobs. This global focus is reflected in managerial appraisal instruments, which typically present very broad performance dimensions for evaluation.

3. A job may be more or less routinized, structured, and constrained by the requirements of machinery or defined by training, but the evaluation of job performance will always depend in the final analysis on external judgments about what is most important (number of units produced or quality of the

units produced; everyday performance or response to the infrequent emergency; single-minded pursuit of profits or avoidance of environmental damage).

4. As a consequence, describing job performance is not a straightforward or obvious process. Even for simple jobs, it involves judgment and inference combined with careful study of the job by such means as interviews, observation, and collection of data on tasks performed and skills required. For managerial jobs, the task of adequate description becomes even more difficult, because much of what a manager does is fragmented, amorphous, and involves unobservable cognitive activities.

5. Job descriptions and the appraisal systems based on them reflect organizational values and judgments as well as some independent constellation of job tasks and performance requirements. To speak of objectivity with regard to job analysis and performance appraisal does not imply the absence of human judgment, but rather the absence of irrelevant or inappropriate judgments.

Conclusions: Job Analysis

1. The commonly made dichotomy between objective and subjective measurement is more misleading than useful in the field of performance appraisal.

2. Organizations cannot use job analyses or other methods of specifying critical elements and performance standards as replacements for managerial judgment; at best such procedures can inform the manager and help focus the appraisal process.

3. The abstract character of the behaviors (e.g., leadership, oral communications, overall performance) that typifies much of the research on managerial job performance conveys a message from the research community about the nature of managerial performance and about the infeasibility of capturing its essence through lists of tasks, duties, and standards that can be objectively counted or quantified. Reliance on global measures guarantees that evaluation of a manager's performance is of necessity based on a substantial degree of judgment. An overly literal interpretation of the requirements of the Civil Service Reform Act—taking *job-related* to mean job-specific, or treating *objective* as the opposite of judgment, would be particularly destructive for managerial appraisal.

Research on Psychometric Properties

Reliability

Reliability analysis provides an index of the consistency of measurement, from occasion to occasion, from form to form (if there are several versions of a test or measure that are all intended to measure the same thing), or from rater to rater. The first- and last-mentioned types of reliability analysis are particularly pertinent to performance appraisal. If the measurements are to have any meaning, one would expect the rater to reach the same judgment from one week to the next (assuming the employee's performance did not change significantly), just as one would hope that several raters would reach substantially the same decision about a single individual's performance. Data on reliability derive in part from operational settings and in part from laboratory experiments or from research projects undertaken in field settings, using special rating instruments developed for the purpose and administered with the proviso that no operational decisions will be based on the results.

Findings: Reliability

1. There is substantial evidence in the research literature to support the premise that supervisors are capable of forming reasonably reliable estimates of their employees' overall performance levels. For the mostly nonmanagerial jobs studied over the years, raters show substantial agreement in rating workers' performance. There is also some data showing interrater agreement on managerial performance.

It is important to remember, however, that consistency among raters cannot be taken simply at face value as proof of the accuracy of performance appraisal procedures; it can also cloak systematic bias or systematic error in valuing performance. Systematic bias is difficult to detect, the more so if it is the product of unexamined views and conventional assumptions. There is evidence of such bias, fragmentary but suggestive, in a small number of studies showing that white supervisors tend to rate white employees as a group somewhat higher than black employees and, conversely, that black supervisors rate black employees higher on average. The studies have not been able to distinguish between real performance differences and rater bias but suggest the presence of both, although the variance accounted for by bias appears to be quite small.

Validity

From the psychometric perspective, the central question posed by any measurement system is whether it produces an accurate assessment of relevant performance. *Validity* is the technical term used to refer to the degree of accuracy and relevance that characterizes a measurement procedure. It is not meant to imply a static characteristic of a test or rating scale; rather, the term has to do with the structure of meaning that can be built up to support the assessment results. Validity, therefore, is an accretion of evidence from many sources; it describes a research process that gradually lends confidence to the interpretations or judgments made on the basis of the measure.

In the realm of job performance, validation begins in an important sense with an analysis of the job or category of jobs for which performance measures are to be developed. If an employment test or appraisal system can be linked to important aspects of the job—say typing accuracy and speed or a sonar technician's skill at recognizing patterns—then one building block is in place. The evidence of interrater reliabilities described above can provide another sort of clue to the accuracy of measurement systems like performance ratings, hands-on job sample tests, and other procedures that depend on an observer to judge the performance. Statisticians and psychometricians have developed an array of sophisticated statistical methods to explore the relationships between the test or measure under study and other relevant variables (correlational and regression analysis, multivariate analysis and ANOVA techniques).

Findings: Validity

1. Performance appraisal does not lend itself to the full complement of validation strategies that have been found useful for standardized tests. Criterion-related validity, for example, is rarely as useful for evaluating performance appraisals as it is with selection tests. The strength of the approach lies in showing that a healthy relationship exists between, say, test results and some independent, operational performance measure (e.g., college admissions test and grade-point average). When the measure being validated is itself a behavioral measure, it is difficult to find relevant operational measures for comparison that have the essential independence. As a consequence, what is frequently considered a compelling type of evidence in validation research is usually not possible for performance appraisals. Furthermore, in those limited conditions in which independent criteria do exist, the jobs themselves tend to be much more simple and straightforward than those for which appraisals are typically used.

2. It is, however, possible to compare performance appraisals to other measures of job performance using the conventional statistical methods of psychometric analysis. Recent military job performance measurement research, for example, demonstrated moderate correlations between supervisor ratings and each of the other types of criterion measures developed (hands-on test scores, training grades, written job knowledge tests), which lends credibility to the claim that carefully developed performance appraisals can bear a meaningful degree of relationship to actual job performance.

3. Supervisor ratings have been used in thousands of studies designed to examine the power of cognitive and other ability tests to predict job performance—in other words, they have been used to validate employment tests. These studies consistently show a low to moderate observed correlation between employment tests and supervisor ratings; job incumbents who score well on the test tend also to receive good ratings and those with low test scores tend to be rated as mediocre performers. While admittedly circular, this relationship provides further indirect evidence that supervisors can rate their employees with some degree of (but by no means perfect) accuracy; whether they will do so in an operational setting is another matter.

Scale Characteristics

A wide variety of rating scale formats, defining performance dimensions at varying levels of specificity, exist. Commonly used rating dimensions include personal traits (e.g., initiative, leadership, perseverance), job behaviors (e.g., follows safety procedures in engine room, financial management, interpersonal relations), and performance results (e.g., quality of work, quantity of work). The number of scale points has ranged as high as 11, but most appraisal scales have between 3 and 5.

In terms of scale format, a general distinction can be made between scales that include specific behavioral examples of good, average, and inadequate performance and those that do not. The latter, called graphic scales, simply list the dimension of interest and present a number of scale points along a continuum. The scale points, or anchors, can be numerical or adjectival (e.g., consistently superior, average, consistently unsatisfactory).

Behaviorally anchored rating scales (BARS) were developed to reduce some of the rating error typical of graphic scales. Proponents thought that BARS would help to clarify the meaning of the performance dimensions used and would help calibrate various raters' definition of what constitutes superior, average, and unsatisfactory performance on the dimension. It was also felt that the behavioral descriptions would discourage the tendency to rate on broad, general traits by focusing attention on specific work behaviors. Mixed standard scales, also behaviorally based, went one step further in trying to control rater error, particularly bias and leniency. These scales present the behavioral descriptions in random order and not in conjunction with a particular performance dimension. The rater's responses are computed by someone else into a performance score for each dimension measured.

Findings: Rating Format

1. Reviews of the relevant research suggest that behaviorally based scales have not met early expectations. Although the research findings are not entirely consistent, the consensus seems to be that scale formats have relatively little impact on psychometric quality, when impact is indexed by interrater agreement, rater errors, and convergent and discriminant validity of ratings. In other words, the use of behavioral versus nonbehavioral language and the physical arrangement of the scale do not appear to be critical in terms of the validity of the overall judgments about performance.[1]

---

[1] A weakness in the comparative research on rating approaches and formats, however, was noted by Landy and Farr (1983). It is, namely, that in many studies the scales compared were actually developed in the same way. The performance dimensions and behavioral examples were developed according to BARS methodology. This means that only the presentation modes were actually compared. Many authors have also pointed to the lack of rigor in the selection and scaling of anchors, which suggests that the final word has not been spoken on the merits of behavioral approaches to rating scales.

2. This proposition is given support by the research on the cognitive processes involved in performance appraisal done in the 1980s. This body of research suggests that the distinction between behaviors and traits is not as salient as once thought. Raters appear to rely less on specific behaviors than on their general evaluation of each employee when they make ratings, regardless of the focus of the rating scale. These general evaluations substantially affect raters' memory for and evaluation of actual work behaviors.

Finding: Job-Specific Versus Global Ratings

1. In litigation dealing with performance appraisal, the courts have shown a clear preference for job-specific dimensions. There is little research that directly addresses the validity of ratings obtained on job-specific, general, or global dimensions. Indirect evidence suggests that raters may work at the global level in any case. First, there is the evidence from the research on cognitive processes mentioned in finding number 2 above. In addition, there is a substantial body of research on halo error in ratings that shows that raters do not, for the most part, distinguish between conceptually distinct aspects of performance in rating their workers. This suggests that similar outcomes can be expected from rating scales that use global or job-specific performance dimensions.

Finding: Number of Scale Points or Anchors

1. The weight of the evidence suggests that the reliability of ratings drops if there are fewer than 3 or more than 9 rating categories. Recent work indicates that there is little to be gained from having more than 5 response categories. Within that range (3 to 5), there is no evidence that there is one best number of scale points in terms of scale quality.

Conclusion: Psychometric Properties

1. The combination of research on job analysis, research on the reliability of appraisal results, and the direct and indirect evidence of a modest relationship between performance ratings and other sorts of measures (employment tests, other measures of job performance) leads us to conclude that the performance appraisal process, while by no means high-precision measurement, can achieve moderate levels of accuracy within the assumptions of the measurement tradition.

It is also the case that the choice of approach (traits or behaviors) and format (BARS or graphic format) may make a difference in the usefulness, if not the accuracy, of the ratings. Scales containing specific behavioral examples may be more useful for providing feedback to employees; trait scales may be more useful for ranking those rated.

The Applied Tradition

The focus of psychometric theory and research tends to be on the rating instrument, its measurement properties, and standardization of raters to reduce error. Researchers in the organizational sciences and human resource management tradition, which is more attuned to applied settings and operational systems, concentrate more on the appraisal system and how it functions to serve organizational ends. From this point of view, performance ratings are not the equivalent of testing technology, and the concentration of research energies on questions of job analysis, scale development, scale format, and measurement precision is misguided.

There are others closer to the measurement tradition who also have begun to feel that the psychometric lines of inquiry have become arid and are unlikely to bring about large additional improvements in the way performance appraisals are used in organizations (Banks and Murphy, 1985; Ilgen et al., 1989). A number of industrial psychologists in the last decade have begun to move away from the traditional view of performance appraisal as a measurement problem; rather than treating it as a measurement tool, they have begun to look on performance appraisal as a social and communication process (Murphy and Cleveland, 1991). Although such scholars do not reject the idea of accuracy, they tend to take a more commonsense approach, talking of the "relevance" of the appraisal to job performance, and to concentrate much more on the contextual factors that support or distort appraisal systems.

From this perspective, the interesting research questions about performance appraisal systems are whether they enrich managerial judgment and improve employee understanding of organizational goals and standards of performance; encourage more communication between managers and employees; communicate a sense of equity and fair play in the distribution of rewards and penalties by making visible the grounds of these decisions; and enhance employee trust and acceptance. While none of these questions can be divorced from the accuracy-validity issues, the answers tend to be sought in evidence of system-level outcomes. Research on the effectiveness of performance appraisal looks at such questions as employee attitudes toward the system, the degree to which it serves individual needs (feedback, employee development) or organizational needs (communication of mission, meritocratic principles), and the degree to which it enhances (or destroys) cohesion in the work unit or organization. And, as many of these points of emphasis indicate, there is a great deal of emergent interest in the organizational context in which appraisals occur.

Although this reorientation is quite recent among applied psychologists, our review of the literature included several bodies of research in organizational psychology and management science that contribute to an understanding of how appraisal systems function as part of an organization's performance management system. These include: (1) performance appraisal and motivation, (2) approaches to assisting supervisors in making high-quality ratings, and (3) the types and sources of rating distortion that can be anticipated in an organizational context, particularly when the results of the performance appraisal are linked to decisions about employees' pay increases.

Performance Appraisal and Motivation

Information about performance is believed to influence work motivation in three ways. First, in expectancy theory, performance information is thought to provide the basis for the employee to form beliefs about the causal connection between performance and pay. Second, performance information is believed to affect motivation by creating a sense of accomplishment; this sense of accomplishment provides an incentive to maintain high performance. Third, it is proposed that performance information provides cues to the employee about which behaviors should be continued and which should be dropped or modified.

Findings: Performance Appraisal and Motivation

1. The empirical research needed to support these motivational models is ambiguous as well as spotty. There is some survey data, including data on the federal Performance Management and Recognition System, that indicates that the feedback from performance appraisal helps some employees understand the job and performance expectations better. Whether that translates into better performance is unclear. At the same time, there is survey evidence indicating that appraisal information is less likely to be an accurate source of information than informal interactions with the supervisor, talking with coworkers, specific indicators provided by the job itself, and personal feelings.

2. The performance feedback literature, which also draws heavily on survey data, indicates that the credibility of the supervisor is crucial to acceptance of appraisal information. That credibility appears to depend heavily on the supervisor's perceived degree of knowledge about the employee's job and degree of interest in the employee's welfare.

3. A frequent research finding is that employees rate their own performance higher than do their supervisors. This is supported by evidence that people are likely to accept positive information about themselves and to reject negative information. Both of these inclinations would tend to dilute the motivational influence of any critical performance appraisals.

Approaches to Increasing Rating Quality

Several approaches have been used to increase the quality of performance ratings. These have included developing training programs for supervisors responsible for providing performance appraisals and developing appraisal scales that explicitly guide the rater through both performance observation and performance assessment.

Finding: Increasing Rating Quality

1. The research results on rater training are mixed. A number of recent research reviews have concluded that rater training has not been highly effective in increasing the accuracy of ratings. However, there is some contrary evidence suggesting that training can lead to more accurate ratings—particularly training that focuses on the rating process and on the use of specific rating tools. Thus training seems indicated if the performance appraisal system involves scales that require complicated procedures or calculations.

Sources of Rating Distortion

Performance ratings are subject to distortion from many quarters, no matter how carefully designed the appraisal instrument. The measurement research has concentrated on statistical analysis to detect rater bias and rater errors such as halo and leniency. The organizational context adds greatly to our understanding of likely sources of distortion. It is widely assumed, for example, that the uses of the rating data in an organization will influence the appraisal process and outcomes. There are also strains in the motivational literature suggesting that supervisors distort ratings, among other reasons, to achieve outcomes they value, to bolster feelings of fairness in the work group, or to avoid demotivating employees with brutal ratings.

Findings: Sources of Rating Distortion

1. There is evidence from both laboratory and field studies to support the assumption that the intended use of performance ratings influences results. The most consistent finding is that ratings used to make operational decisions (e.g., pay, promotion) are more lenient than ratings used for research purposes or for feedback.

2. While the predictions from the motivational literature seem reasonable, empirical research on motivational factors in rating distortion is understandably rare. Little is known about the factors actually considered by raters when they decide how to fill out their rating forms. There is some revealing clinical evidence, however. A number of researchers have reported, based on interview data, that supervisors consciously manipulate appraisals to achieve desired outcomes, such as maximizing the chances that deserving employees get promoted.

3. Whatever the exact nature of the environmental sources of rating distortion, organizations have adopted a number of devices to deal with it. Some

private-sector firms deal with rating inflation by requiring a forced distribution in which the majority of ratings are allocated to the middle two or three categories—this provides for only a few outstanding ratings and encourages a few less-than-satisfactory ratings. Some companies decouple the performance rating from pay decisions by interposing a negotiation among relevant supervisors to rank all employees with similar jobs, thereby hoping to combat inflation and lessen the negative consequences of disappointing pay outcomes on the relationship of supervisor and employee.

Findings From Practice

Our review of performance appraisal practices in the private sector suggests that most organizations focus on the process, rather than the design aspects, of performance appraisal. For example, few organizations conduct regular updates to job analyses and job descriptions or fund validation studies. Indeed validity and reliability do not seem to enter the vocabulary of private-sector human resource managers as a rule, a finding of no great surprise since only a few of the larger companies (Sears, AT&T) have an in-house personnel testing and measurement research capability. In contrast, there is nearly universal use of objective-based formats for managers and professionals; this format allows for joint manager-employee participation in defining performance objectives and, in some organizations, interim changes to objectives according to organization or individual needs.

In addition, some organizations use joint management meetings for ranking employees after initial performance ratings are completed; these meetings provide a forum for negotiating the basic norms of "acceptable" individual performance for similar jobs or job areas. Such meetings recognize the process aspects of performance appraisal—that norms change, that raters change, that context is important, that individual judgments need to be calibrated against group norms. Our interviews with personnel managers suggested that their process emphasis also includes communications to managers and other employees about the role of performance appraisal in the context of the organization's other meritocratic practices and culture, and the insistence that performance appraisal is an important, ongoing part of a manager's job. These companies tend to assess the effectiveness of performance appraisal via its influence on employee perceptions of equity and job satisfaction, rather than with measures of performance improvements or cost reductions.

All of this emphasis on process and the use of performance appraisal systems to reinforce the idea of a meritocratic personnel context is consistent with the current research interest in performance appraisal as a social and communication process rather than a measurement tool. However, it does not address the question of the accuracy of the rating decisions or the effects of using an appraisal system on individual or corporate performance.

PERFORMANCE APPRAISAL: OVERALL FINDINGS

We have to some extent caricatured two different approaches to performance appraisal—the one preoccupied with psychometrics and precision measurement, the other focused on the utility and acceptance of performance appraisal. Clearly, both sets of considerations are important. The appropriate balance in devoting resources to measurement issues versus process issues will obviously depend on the specifics of the situation.

However, we wish to call attention to two sets of findings that suggest that there may be diminishing returns to focusing on the measurement properties of appraisal scales in the federal context.

Findings: Quality of the Instrument

1. There is no compelling evidence that one appraisal format is significantly better than another. The improvements in accuracy and precision that were at one time anticipated from the use of behaviorally anchored rating scales have not been convincingly demonstrated as yet—not in a way that would justify the very expensive and labor-intensive development of such scales for federal jobs generally. Although there is far less evidence on the subject, global ratings do not appear to produce very different results from job-specific ratings.

2. Assuming that reasonable care has been taken in the development of scales and the training of raters, the reliability and validity of performance appraisal systems does not appear to be improved by fine-tuning the format of the appraisal instrument or the number of rating anchors used.

3. The reliability and validity of performance appraisal systems established in the context of research or laboratory settings cannot necessarily be expected to translate directly into operational settings. We know, for example, that when performance ratings are used in the context of merit pay allocations, managers tend to inflate ratings. We know too that specifying behaviors of interest in the appraisal format (e.g., BARS or management-by-objective systems) can lead managers to ignore other aspects of job performance, particularly those that are difficult to reduce to concrete terms, that may be equally important to successful performance.

4. There is virtually no research establishing the predictive validity of performance appraisal measures, tools, and approaches for measures of organizational effectiveness aggregated to the level of the office, division, or firm. (This statement says more about the state of the analytical tools available to social scientists than perhaps about performance appraisal.)

Findings: Costs of Psychometric Sophistication

1. Psychometrically sound performance measures based on job analysis and supported by a substantial empirical research base are both difficult and costly to generate and to maintain.

2. One could infer from current practice that the payoffs of trying to maximize and demonstrate the scientific validity of measures of job performance are not perceived to justify the costs—or that there is simply little felt need to do so. Few organizations attempt to establish the scientific validity of performance appraisal using typical psychometric procedures. The focus in applied settings appears to be on performance appraisal as a means of supporting an ethos of meritocratic personnel decisions, and on the development and administration of performance appraisal in ways that foster employee perceptions of equity and fairness—using goal setting formats, using joint management negotiations to define job performance norms, and measuring employee perceptions of performance appraisal fairness. There is virtually no measurement of the effects of performance appraisal on ongoing organization-level performance or cost reduction measures.

PERFORMANCE APPRAISAL: OVERALL CONCLUSION

Given the expense and difficulty of developing appraisal systems that conform to the exacting requirements of the measurement tradition; given the very modest returns to that investment that have been documented empirically; given the widespread lack of concern with this level of precision among firms using performance appraisal; given the absence of convincing evidence linking performance appraisal to organization-level outcomes—we find it impossible to conclude that federal policy makers should commit vast new human and financial resources to job analyses and the development of performance appraisal instruments and systems that can meet the strict constructionist challenge of measurement science.

Many applied psychologists and management experts feel that the search for such a high degree of precision in measurement is not economically viable in most applied settings—some believe that there is little to be gained from this level of precision over currently accepted sound practices.

Policy makers need to consider carefully where on the spectrum, between psychometric measurement and impressionistic measurement, performance appraisal for the civil service should be aimed. The purposes of the appraisal system should enter into the decision. There seems little doubt that for purposes of communication and feedback, the demands for scientific precision will not overwhelm cost considerations. For controversial decisions such as dismissal or pay, the question becomes more difficult.

However, it is important to remember that line supervisors are usually in a position to know their employees well and to have far more information available to them than the consumers of standardized test results—say, a college admissions committee.

1. These considerations lead us to conclude that for most personnel management decisions, including annual pay decisions, the goal of a performance appraisal system should be to support and encourage informed managerial judgment and not to aspire to a degree of standardization, precision, and empirical support that would be required of, for example, selection tests.

In this context, informed judgment means that there are demonstrable and credible links between the performance of the individuals being rated and the supervisor's evaluation of that performance.

II. PERFORMANCE-BASED PAY SYSTEMS

The label *pay for performance* covers a broad spectrum of compensation systems that can be clustered under two general categories: merit pay plans and variable pay plans. The latter category can be further divided in two, namely, individual incentive plans and the currently popular group incentive plans. Although the charge to the committee was couched in terms of merit pay plans, we extended the scope of our review to include pay-for-performance and compensation research more generally. This was in part for the sake of expedience—we found virtually no research on the effects of merit pay systems on the performance of individuals or organizations, and so were forced to turn elsewhere to explore the question. But we also rapidly realized that the effects of performance-based pay plans on individual and organizational performance cannot be easily disentangled from the broader context of an organization's structures, management strategies, and personnel systems.

We have distinguished performance-based pay plans along two dimensions. The first represents design variation in the level of performance measurement—individual or group—to which payouts are tied. The second represents design variation in the plan's contribution to base pay—some are added into base pay, some are not.

In merit pay plans, the locus of attention is individual performance. As an important element in a meritocratic personnel system, merit pay plans link annual pay increases, at least in part, to how well the incumbent has performed on the job. As a consequence, performance appraisal is at the heart of most merit plans. Payouts allocated under merit plans are commonly added into the individual's base salary. The payouts are typically not large (on average 5 percent, with a range of 2 to 12 percent), but their addition to base pay offers the potential for significant long-term salary growth.

In the most common individual incentive plans—piece rate plans and sales on commission—payouts are not added to base salary. Although the payouts can be large, they also carry the risk to the individual of no payout if performance thresholds are not met.

Group incentive plans differ from the two preceding types in basing compensation decisions on unit or system performance rather than individual performance. Thus profit-sharing plans or equity plans link employees' payouts to the overall fortunes of the firm as measured by some indicator of its financial health. Although payouts can be large in good times, they are not usually added to base pay—hence the designation *variable pay* plan.

All pay-for-performance plans are designed to deliver pay increases to employees based, at least in part, on some measure of performance. In theory, such plans offer several potential benefits:

• They can support the organization's personnel philosophy by helping to communicate the organization's goals to its employees. For example, if financial goals are paramount, then a pay-for-performance plan tied to the achievement of financial goals (e.g., a profit-sharing plan) helps reinforce their importance for employees.

• Goal theory also suggests that performance-based pay plans can support a certain level of performance that is consistent with the organization's mission. For example, a plan that pays out when financial goals are almost met (80 percent) sends a different message to employees than one that pays out only when goals are completely met (100 percent). Likewise, if employees receive no pay increase when their performance appraisal is below some work force norm, then they are more likely to attend to that norm.

• They can help ensure consistency in the distribution of pay increases. For example, under a plan that ties pay increases to a specific financial goal, payouts are distributed only when that goal is met. Under a merit plan, pay increases are distributed consistently to employees who are in the same pay grade, who are in the same position in grade, and who have the same performance appraisal ratings. This helps the organization predict and regulate the price tag for merit increases.

• Motivation theory suggests that pay for performance can positively influence individuals to achieve goals that are rewarded. To the extent that these goals contribute to organizational effectiveness, we can infer that pay for performance can influence individual and organizational effectiveness.

Before turning to the research findings, it is important to note that performance-based pay is only one dimension of employee compensation; other dimensions include competitiveness of salaries with the marketplace, benefits packages, cost-of-living considerations, and others. The effects of merit or variable pay plans will depend in good measure on this larger compensation context.

EVIDENCE FROM RESEARCH

Organizations design pay systems to accomplish three objectives: attracting, retaining, and motivating employees to perform; advancing the fair and equitable treatment of employees; and regulating labor costs. We have reviewed the research literature to see how pay-for-performance plans, and particularly merit pay plans, influence an organization's ability to meet these objectives.

Employee Motivation

The research most directly related to questions about the impact of performance-based pay plans on individual and organizational performance comes from theory and empirical study of work motivation. Motivation theories that have been well tested empirically predict that employee motivation is enhanced, and the likelihood of desired performance increased, under pay-for-performance plans when: (1) employees understand performance goals and view them as "doable" given their own abilities and skills and the restrictions posed by organization context; (2) there is a clear link between performance and pay increases, consistently communicated and followed; and (3) the pay increase is viewed as meaningful.

Findings: Employee Motivation

1. Most of the research examining the relationship between pay-for-performance plans and performance is focused on individual incentive plans such as piece rates. By design, these plans most closely approximate the ideal motivational conditions prescribed by expectancy and goal-setting theory.

2. Empirical research indicates that individual incentive plans can motivate employees and improve individual performance.

3. Individual incentive plans are most likely to improve performance in (a) simple, structured jobs in which employees are relatively autonomous; (b) work settings in which employees trust management to set fair performance goals; and (c) a stable economic environment.

4. Merit pay plans do not conform as closely as individual incentive plans to the theoretical conditions thought to be conducive to improved performance. Although merit plans also focus on individual performance, the link between performance and pay increase is less concrete; pay increase guidelines typically consider position and time in grade as well as performance rating; and pay increases tend to be small and therefore do not clearly differentiate outstanding from average or even poor performance. These characteristics may dilute their potential to motivate employees.

5. There is very little empirical research on merit pay plans. What exists is mixed and defies firm conclusions about the relationship between such plans and either individual or group performance. There are a number of field

studies suggesting that managers and professionals under a merit pay system (as opposed to a straight seniority system or no formal system) express more job satisfaction and perceive a stronger tie between pay and performance. Other studies suggest that these effects may be tenuous.

6. Some group incentive plans retain many of the motivational features of individual incentive plans (quantitative performance goals, relatively large and frequent payouts), but it is not easy for individuals to see how their performance contributes to group- or organizational-level measures, so the motivational link is weakened. More to the point, payouts may occur only in good times and are dependent on larger environmental and economic forces beyond the control of the individual employee.

7. There is a modest body of research evidence drawn from private-sector experience that suggests that gainsharing and profit-sharing plans are associated with improved group- or organizational-level productivity and financial performance. This research does not, however, allow us to disentangle the effects of the pay plans on performance from many other contextual conditions. We cannot say that group plans *cause* performance changes or specify how they do.

Finding: Attraction and Retention

1. The empirical research examining the relationship of pay to an employer's ability to attract and retain high-performing employees is limited, and there is almost no research on the impact of pay-for-performance plans on these objectives. We have found but one experimental study (involving white-collar workers in Navy labs) that relates retention to the adoption of a merit pay system. The study reported considerable reduction in turnover among superior performers. One study, however, is not sufficient to support a general finding.

Fairness and Equity

Organizations want their pay systems to be viewed as fair by multiple stakeholders: employees, managers, owners, and top managers; those at one remove, such as unions, associations, and regulatory agencies; and the public. Theories of organizational justice distinguish between distributive and procedural justice. The former predicts that the employee judges the fairness of pay level or pay raises in comparison with other people or groups considered similar in terms of contribution. Theories of procedural justice link employees' job satisfaction to their perceptions about the fairness of procedures used to design or administer pay, for example, the fairness of performance appraisals or the availability of mechanisms for appealing pay decisions.

Findings: Fairness and Equity

1. Research examining distributive and procedural fairness theories in real-world pay contexts is scarce; there are no studies that can directly answer questions about the perceived fairness of different types of pay-for-performance plans.

2. The existing research does suggest that employee perceptions of fairness with regard to pay distributions and the design and administration of pay systems does affect their job satisfaction, their trust of management, and their commitment to the organization. The research suggests at least three groups against which employees may assess the fairness of their pay: people in a similar job outside the organization; people in similar jobs inside the organization; and others in the same job or work group.

3. The research shows that there are different beliefs about how pay increases should be allocated (performance, seniority, equal percentage of base, etc.). Several studies suggest that private-sector managers believe that pay increases should be tied to performance. Surveys of federal managers have shown support of the concept of performance-based pay increases in principle, but there is also a tradition, stemming from the concern to protect the bureaucracy from political manipulation, that equates equity with equal pay for all people in the same grade and step.

Regulating Labor Costs

All organizations have to regulate labor costs. An organization's choice of pay system by definition involves trade-offs among performance, equity, and costs. The various performance-based pay systems studied in this report approach these trade-offs differently. The design of merit pay plans appears to emphasize predictability and stability over time. Pay increases are administered via a merit grid that uses performance rating and position in the pay grade to determine a prespecified percentage increase. The increases are typically modest, but since they are added to base pay, the gradual accumulation over years becomes significant.

Variable pay plans are intended to be more immediately market sensitive. Many of the group incentive plans, for example, are tied to clearly defined measures of organizational productivity or financial performance. Generally, improvements in these performance measures generate the bulk of the pay increase pool. Since the increases are not added to base pay, employee pay is tied closely to the fortunes of the firm. In good times, the payouts are relatively large; in bad times, the employee has more at risk than under a merit system.

Findings: Regulating Labor Costs

1. Although economic models provide a conceptual basis for understanding the potential trade-offs between cost and performance and some of the contextual factors that might be presumed to favor one pay policy over another, the research on cost regulation and the cost-benefit trade-offs associated with pay-for-performance plans is sparse and limited to production jobs and manufacturing settings.

2. We have no evidence that any particular pay-for-performance plan is superior to another in regulating labor costs.

FINDINGS FROM PRACTICE

1. Our review of private sector practices revealed that pay for performance is an important part of compensation philosophy and the overwhelming choice of U.S. private-sector firms. Merit plans are almost universally used for managerial and professional employees (95 percent); variable pay plans are much less frequently used (between 16 and 40 percent, depending on the type of plan), but increased competition worldwide appears to be kindling interest in them.

2. Our interviews with personnel managers of five Fortune 100 companies indicated that merit plans are viewed primarily as a means of guiding managers' decisions about pay increases in a way that is consistent with a meritocratic personnel philosophy—that is, it ensures that pay increases are, at least in part, tied to individual contributions, and that the increases are consistently distributed to employees in a way that is fair and predictable.

3. This strong attachment to a meritocratic ethos explains the predominance of merit pay plans in the private sector. Merit plans are the only pay-for-performance plans currently used that base pay increase decisions on the combination of individual contributions (skills, experience, and performance) that are the foundation of a meritocratic philosophy.

4. The personnel managers interviewed noted that a major benefit of performance appraisal and merit pay was the identification of top and bottom performers. They emphasized the flexibility of private-sector managers to bring top performers into a job at any position in the pay range, and the comparative ease of dismissing those who cannot meet company performance standards.

5. Surveys indicate that organizations do not evaluate the effect of merit plans on performance, but rather focus on employee perceptions of plan fairness and workability and of the link between pay and performance.

6. The personnel managers interviewed also emphasized the importance of communicating merit pay increases as part of an overall pay system and a meritocratic personnel philosophy. For example, most of these managers emphasized the competitiveness of base pay and benefits and the general excellence

of the company and work force in their pay communications to employees. Notable, also, is that most of these managers said that their organizations did not share specific pay information—such as average annual increase percentages, market competitors and wage survey methods, the organization spectrum of pay ranges—with employees. This is in contrast to the federal meritocracy in which employees appear to have information about their pay from many different (and conflicting) sources.

7. In contrast to the nearly universal presence of merit pay plans, our survey reviews revealed that less than 40 percent of private-sector firms have bonus plans for middle managers; less than 20 percent have gainsharing or profit-sharing plans in place. Baseline data for the frequency and distribution of specific plans is difficult to obtain, but there appears to be some increase in interest in these plans and in their application to groups of employees not traditionally covered.

8. There are a limited number of surveys on the use of group incentive plans. They report that most organizations adopt these plans to improve productivity and financial outcomes and, more generally, to "revitalize the organization consistent with business strategy." These same surveys report that organizations that have adopted these plans believe that they have achieved the desired effects, but also acknowledge the importance of contextual factors such as employee involvement, information sharing, and ongoing marketing and communication to the employees covered. One survey acknowledged that design and implementation costs were high. None of these surveys reported employee perceptions about the equity or efficacy of variable pay plans.

PERFORMANCE-BASED PAY SYSTEMS: OVERALL FINDINGS AND CONCLUSIONS

Taken together, the evidence from research and practice suggests the following findings and conclusions about the effects on individual and organizational performance of pay-for-performance plans.

Findings: Individual Performance

1. The evidence on the effects of pay for performance, pieced together from research, theory, clinical studies, and surveys of practice, suggests that, in certain circumstances, variable pay plans produce positive effects on individual job performance.

2. There is insufficient research to determine conclusively whether merit pay can enhance individual performance or to allow us to make comparative statements about merit and variable pay plans.

Conclusion: Individual Performance

1. We nevertheless infer that merit pay can have positive effects on individual job performance, on the basis of analogy from the research and theory on variable pay plans. These effects might be attenuated by the facts that, in many merit plans, increases are not always clearly linked to employee performance, agreement on the evaluation of performance does not always exist, and increases are not always viewed as meaningful. However, we believe the direction of effects is nonetheless toward enhanced performance.

Finding: Organizational Performance

1. There is some evidence from the private sector suggesting that gainsharing plans are associated with improved organizational performance. However, it is not possible from existing research to conclude that these plans cause performance changes, to specify how they do so, or to understand how the behavior of individuals under these plans aggregates to the organization level.

III: THE IMPORTANCE OF CONTEXT

Our reviews of performance appraisal and merit pay research and practice indicate that their success or failure will be substantially influenced by the broader features of the context in which they are embedded. Research on performance appraisal has recently turned to organizational factors that might support or hinder the appraisal system from functioning as intended. Research on pay plans stresses the context of the organization's personnel system, technological systems, and strategic goals.

Overall Findings

1. There is a broad consensus among practitioners—as well as some research evidence—that personnel systems in general and performance appraisal and pay systems in particular must exhibit "fit" or congruence to be effective.

2. Three categories of contextual factors of particular relevance to performance appraisal and pay for performance emerged from our reviews of research and practice: (a) the nature of the organization's work, or what might be called *technological fit*; (b) the broad features of the organization's structure and culture; and (c) external factors such as economic climate, the presence of unions, and legal or political forces exerted by external constituents.

Technological Fit

The strongest evidence on congruence has to do with the fit between appraisal and pay systems and the nature of work. The literature on the links between pay and individual motivation, for example, demonstrates the importance of job independence, concrete and easily measured products, and production standards that are perceived as fair (doable) to effective individual incentive pay plans. Only a limited number of jobs, mainly in some executive, sales, and manufacturing work, have proved to be amenable to this sort of performance measurement and incentive pay. Conversely, it has been shown that using highly specific individual performance appraisals and incentives with jobs that are complex, interdependent, and have multiple and amorphous goals can result in employees' ignoring important aspects of their jobs or distorting performance in order to meet the appraisal goals. This sort of gaming is a particular danger with objectives-based appraisal systems. Group incentives avoid some of the problem. They recognize the interdependent nature of work and focus on organization-level performance. However, they suffer from unclear links between individual actions and organization-level results.

Organizational Structure and Culture

Although there is little systematic evidence to suggest precisely what the congruence of pay system and organizational culture looks like, there is a growing body of case studies that look at organizational structure and culture, particularly studies of high-commitment organizations and of organizational innovation. The business policy literature, for example, describes two archetypal strategic postures—the dynamic firm and the steady-state firm—and the performance appraisal and pay systems that appear to go along with each. Firms pursuing innovation and growth tend to offer their employees a higher proportion of their pay in the form of incentives than do firms in steady state. The more entrepreneurial firms tend to evaluate their managers and professionals on quantitative, organization-level performance goals and to offer high payouts if strategic goals are met. Studies of organizational structure confirm this pattern. They describe the entrepreneurial firm as emphasizing general skill, higher investment in recruiting than training, and performance measures tied to market outcomes. Retention is not a primary management goal.

Firms pursuing a maintenance strategy tend to evaluate managers on more qualitative, individual behaviors. Their personnel practices emphasize internal skill development, the importance of work force norms, and the employee's long-term contribution. Such firms would seem to be well served by traditional performance appraisal and merit pay plans.

There are also theoretical literatures that suggest that organizations in highly institutionalized sectors or that rely greatly on public trust may be more likely to adopt very formal, precise performance appraisal systems. In such organizations, personnel and pay systems can have an important legitimizing function.

There is a considerable literature that supports these general patterns of association between performance appraisal and pay systems on the one hand and organizational strategy and structure on the other. However, all of this work is theoretical or descriptive and should be viewed as suggestive, but not necessarily generalizable.

External Forces

The final dimension of congruence has to do with external factors that constrain an organization's choice of evaluation and pay systems. One of the most relevant to federal policy makers is the widespread resistance of unions in the private sector to performance appraisal and pay-for-performance systems. Most surveys show that unionized employees are far less likely than nonunionized employees to be covered by incentive systems (including merit plans). To the extent that this changed in the 1980s, the incentive pay arrangements accepted by unions (e.g., profit sharing) were not ones that differentiate among individual employees.

Also of particular salience to the issue of pay for performance is the role of external laws and regulations. Fair labor standards, occupational health and safety, and equal employment opportunity are a few of the areas of law that prescribe internal structures, policies, and procedures that may be more or less compatible with an organization's chosen evaluation and pay systems. Federal equal employment opportunity policy has had an enormous impact on personnel management in every organization of any size in the nation.

In addition to these requirements, the federal government as an employer faces a set of constraints imposed by the laws and regulations surrounding its merit system. The desire to shield civil servants from the exigencies of politics has placed serious constraints on the managerial flexibility needed to make pay for performance work.

IV. IMPLICATIONS FOR FEDERAL POLICY

Since its formal adoption by the federal government, performance appraisal for merit pay has been a matter of continuing controversy and periodic amendment. One view of this experience is an explicit criticism of the federal government and its inability to "get right" what is now widely used in the private sector with (at least) less criticism. While there are many features of the merit pay system that could be improved, we do not attribute these failings to mismanagement or stupidity in implementation. Instead, we would emphasize the constraints, many of which derive from features unique to the federal sector.

The federal government faces special, if not entirely intractable, problems that work against any easy transferability of private-sector experience. The very term merit pay carries far more meaning in the context of a public civil service than in the private sector—above all, the absence of partisan political considerations in the determination of pay levels of career employees. Where private-sector practice relatively easily accepts manager-employee exchanges about performance objectives, both individual and organizational, such a practice in the public sector could be perceived as opening the civil service to partisan manipulation.

Hence, one of the most difficult questions facing federal policy makers is whether and how the experience of private-sector organizations with performance appraisal and pay-for-performance plans is applicable to civil service organizations. The portrait of high-commitment organizations that emerges from case studies highlights some fundamental differences between private firms in which performance-based pay seems to work well and the typical government agency. In high-commitment organizations, the following conditions appear to obtain:

• Pay for performance would be one part of a total management system, which provides full financial and organizational support for effective administration of the plan;

• The organization would be characterized by an emphasis on managerial discretion and flexibility and by the recognition that individual managerial authority is critical to effective performance appraisal;

• The climate would be characterized by shared values and high levels of trust throughout the organization;

• On the basis of those values, the ability to link individual performance and activities to organizational goals and objectives would be strong;

• There would be widespread agreement about individual and organizational standards of success; and

• There would be low turnover at the managerial levels.

Most of these conditions pose a problem for public-sector organizations because of the division of leadership between the political and career employees; the lack of managerial control over personnel and resource systems; the ambiguity of goals and performance criteria; and multiple authority centers for employee accountability. The very publicness of government creates organizations that are at once more open to external influences and less able to respond to them. These conditions have led to a working environment in which managers are frustrated in their ability to make personnel decisions and employees are distrustful of the performance appraisal and pay allocation systems—most do not see a link between their performance and their pay.

The issue of divided leadership provides a particularly salient example of the inherent difficulties of creating a successful merit pay system in the federal context. A continuing theme in modern government has been the need to make the bureaucracy more responsive to the chief executive. One tool available to presidents is appointing employees to positions outside the career civil service. But if the presence of political executives in leadership positions in federal agencies institutionalizes the continuing mandate for change, the authority and communication structures within those agencies often create obstacles to change (Ingraham, 1987). For example, the "dual executive" characteristic of many public agencies tends to create a system in which decisions are made according to short-term policy goals at the upper levels of the organization and according to longer-term program goals elsewhere.

In many ways federal agencies function as two loosely coupled organizations with authority, control, and communication between them much more tenuous than prescribed by the classic paradigm. Even if the policy goals were not so often diffuse, unclear, and contradictory (Heclo, 1978; Ingraham, 1987), the ability to communicate them to the career bureaucracy is attenuated by the lack of experience and short tenure of many political executives (Heclo, 1978). All too often, in the judgment of experts in federal management, organization-wide goals are either not articulated or are not communicated down through the organization to the career employees responsible for their implementation. Functioning with two sets of managers makes congruence and coherence hard to achieve. In most models of organizational fit, there is a single leadership that creates a coherent culture and shared values that are necessary conditions to enable a successful performance appraisal system.

The issue of organizational boundary (at which the controlling influences shift from internal to external actors), particularly as it relates to the ability to control or direct organizational resources, is also a central concern. Many have observed that public organizations are notable for the porosity of their boundary (Waldo, 1971; Kaufman, 1978; Gawthrop, 1984). The federal government has been structured deliberately to disburse authority among competing institutions (Allison, 1983); members of Congress, administration officials, interest groups, concerned citizens, and others can, and do, influence bureaucratic actors. This further obfuscates goals and objectives within the organization. Of equal significance is the fact that many of these external influences, but most notably the Congress, have a controlling influence on the resources available to the organization, thus further complicating the authority issue.

Other institutional influences that profoundly shape federal agencies and their activities include civil service laws and regulations that impose great complexity and rigidity on the system. Recruiting, testing, hiring, firing and rewarding are all constrained in the federal government (National Academy of Public Administration, 1983). As a result of these externally imposed constraints, managerial discretion has traditionally been limited and has, in fact, been discouraged by the provisions of the merit system (Ingraham and Rosenbloom, 1990). Although there is emerging evidence that some federal managers do use whatever flexibilities that are available, including those provided by existing performance appraisal systems, there is also strong evidence that procedural constraints deter all but the strongest of heart (unpublished document, U.S. General Accounting Office, 1990).

A frequently cited example of the boundary problem is demonstrated by the fact that Congress retained statutory control over development of the federal government's performance appraisal system, rather than delegating both the development and implementation components to the Office of Personnel Management. The rationale was to balance managerial discretion with employee rights in the context of a system that made it easier for agencies to fire incompetent employees; the result was to hobble the decision making of managers. On one hand, Civil Service Reform Act legislation provided the requirement for detailed performance appraisal standards that could be used by managers as proof of unsatisfactory performance. On the other hand, the managers' ability to act regarding unsatisfactory performance was limited in the statute by providing employees with strong substantive rights, such as the opportunity to improve before an unacceptable performance action can be taken and the ability to appeal performance appraisal ratings both within the agency and externally to the Merit Systems Protection Board. This has led to situations in which, at best, a number of years are required to release an inadequate employee, and the costs borne by managers serve as a strong disincentive against appraising mediocre performance accurately.

Another feature of the federal context that warrants consideration is whether the dominant motivations among employees are comparable to those of private-sector workers who work where pay for performance has been implemented. Although there has been a long tradition of simply applying private-sector motivation theory and techniques to the public sector, some recent studies are finding different sources for motivation and different motivational patterns among public employees. Perry and Wise (1990) explore the role of public service as a motivator; Rainey (1990) documents a fairly consistent pattern of differences in public and private managers in relation to money, job satisfaction and security, and organizational commitment. In a 1982 review article, Perry and Porter noted that public-sector employees had higher achievement needs and tend to value economic wealth less than do entrants into the private sector.

Furthermore, there is some evidence that public managers, particularly those at the highest levels of the organization, are keenly attuned to public perceptions of their effectiveness and the overall usefulness of the policies and programs they administer (Ingraham and Barrilleaux, 1983). Federal Employee Attitude Surveys in 1979 and 1980 demonstrated that upper-level managers perceived generalized "bureaucrat bashing" as a personalized attack. More recent studies by the Merit Systems Protection Board (1989) and the U.S. General Accounting Office (1987) indicate that managers continue to tie their overall job satisfaction to their perceptions of "appreciation" by the public. These findings suggest that policy makers would do well to give their attention to nonmonetary motivators in concert with their plan to strengthen the ties of pay to performance.

Finally, one of the most important contextual factors that governs how any new performance appraisal or pay-for-performance system is likely to function is the less than satisfactory experience of federal employees with the merit pay systems implemented during the last 12 years.

CONCLUSIONS

We have conducted a wide-ranging study of performance appraisal and pay for performance in the private sector to help the director of the Office of Personnel Management and other federal policy makers as they rethink the Personnel Management and Recognition System. What we have learned does not provide a blueprint for linking pay to performance in the federal sector or even any specific remedy for what ails PMRS. Instead, we conclude with some general suggestions about priorities.

1. Performance appraisal ratings can influence many personnel decisions, and thus care in the development and use of performance appraisal systems is warranted. There is, however, no obvious technical (psychometric) solution to the performance management issues facing the federal government. Further refinements in the technology of performance appraisal (e.g., extensive new job analysis, modifications of existing rating scales or rater training programs) are unlikely to provide substantially more valid and accurate appraisals than those currently in force, particularly for managerial and professional jobs. There is also no evidence that one particular appraisal format is clearly superior to all others. For example, we do not know that the objective-based format for managerial appraisal, so popular in the private sector, yields more (or less) valid appraisals than the supervisory ratings used in the government.

There appears to be at least as much effort expended on performance appraisal in the federal government as elsewhere. More generally, the pursuit of further psychometric sophistication in the performance appraisal system used in the federal government is unlikely to contribute to enhanced individual or organizational performance.

2. Where performance appraisal is viewed as most successful in the private sector, it is firmly embedded in the context of management and personnel systems that provide incentives for managers to use performance appraisal ratings as the organization intends. These incentives include managerial flexibility or discretion in rewarding top performers and in dismissing those who continually perform below standards. When performance appraisal ratings are used to distribute pay (as in a merit plan) the size of the merit pay offered allows managers to differentiate outstanding performers from good and poor performers, and thus provides them with incentives to differentiate. For example, top performers may receive 10 percent of their base salary in merit pay, good performers, 5 percent, and poor performers, no merit increase. Finally, managers are themselves assessed on the results of their performance appraisal activities.

We have been struck by the apparent contrast between incentives for private and federal managers to use performance appraisal and merit plans effectively. Whatever incentives there are for federal managers seem currently dwarfed by the disincentives.

3. In order to motivate employees and provide them incentives to perform, a merit plan or any pay-for-performance plan must theoretically (a) define and communicate performance goals that employees understand and view as doable; (b) consistently link pay and performance; and (c) provide payouts that employees see as meaningful. These conditions seem straightforward, and the notion of pay for performance thus becomes deceptively simple. Our reviews of research and practice indicate, however, that selecting the best pay-for-performance plan and implementing it in an organizational context so that these conditions are met is currently as much an art as a science. We cannot generalize about which pay-for-performance plans work best—especially for the federal government, with its considerable organizational and work force diversity.

We can suggest that, given this diversity and the importance of matching pay-for-performance plans to organization context, federal policy makers consider:

a. Decentralizing the design and implementation of many personnel programs, including appraisal and merit pay programs, within the framework of central policy guidelines and to the extent possible given the government's legitimate concerns about facilitating interagency mobility, standardization and comparability, and equity.

b. Supporting careful, controlled pilot studies of a variety of pay-for-performance systems in a variety of agencies. These studies would serve to identify important design, implementation, and evaluation issues for users, policy makers, and the research community, along with incentives to investigate these issues. They could take a variety of forms, but to be useful must provide careful measures of pre- and postintervention conditions.

4. Ensuring fair and equitable treatment for all employees is an important objective of any personnel system. Yet the heavily legalistic environment surrounding the federal civil service has led to dependence on formal procedures and an elaboration of protections, requirements, and procedures that ultimately provide powerful disincentives for managers to use personnel systems as the organization intends. Although these protections are meant to ensure employee equity, it is not clear that their proliferation provides federal employees with a greater sense of equity than seen in many private-sector organizations. Effective reform of personnel management and pay systems in the federal government may well need to be part of a more fundamental rethinking of past notions of political neutrality, merit, and their protection in the civil service.

5. Our entire review has stressed the importance of viewing performance appraisal and merit pay as embedded in broader pay, personnel, management, and organizational contexts. For example, while by no means the only relevant

contextual factor, the issue of comparability of federal base salaries with pay for equivalent private-sector jobs may pose severe problems for the acceptance of merit pay or any other pay-for-performance system if the promise of recently enacted legislation proves illusory. We realize that the broader changes suggested by an analysis of context can be costly, but we suggest that making programmatic changes to the Performance Management and Recognition System in isolation is unlikely to enhance employee acceptance of the system or improve individual and organizational effectiveness significantly and, in the long run, may prove no less costly.

References

Abowd, J.
  1990   Does performance based management compensation affect corporate performance? *Industrial and Labor Relations Review* 43(3):52-73.
Adams, J.
  1965   Inequity in social exchange. Pp. 272-283 in L. Berkowitz, ed., *Advances in Experimental Social Psychology*. New York: Academic Press.
Advisory Committee on Federal Pay
  1990   *Advisory Committee on Federal Pay: 19th Annual Report to the President of the United States*. Washington, D.C.: Advisory Committee on Federal Pay.
Allan, P., and Rosenberg, S.
  1986   An assessment of merit pay administration under New York City's managerial performance evaluation system: three years of experience. *Public Personnel Management* 15:297-309.
Allison, G.
  1983   Public and private management: are they fundamentally alike in all unimportant ways? In J. Perry and K. Kraemer, eds., *Public Management: Public and Private Perspectives*. Palo Alto, Calif.: Mayfield.
American Compensation Association
  1987   *Report on the 1987 Survey of Salary Management Practices*. Scottsdale, Ariz.: American Compensation Association.
American Educational Research Association, American Psychological Association, and National Council on Measurement in Education
  1985   *Standards for Educational and Psychological Testing*. Washington, D.C.: American Psychological Association.

167

Angoff, W.
  1988   Validity: an evolving concept. Pp. 19-32 in H. Wainer and H. Braun, eds., *Test Validity.* Hillsdale, N.J.: Erlbaum.
Argyris, C.
  1964   *Integrating the Individual and the Organization.* New York: Wiley.
Babchuk, N., and Goode, W.
  1951   Work incentives in a self-determined work group. *American Social Review* 16:679-687.
Balkin, D., and Gomez-Mejia, L.
  1984   Determinants of R and D compensation strategies in the high tech industry. *Personnel Psychology* 37(4):635-650.
  1987a   An integrated framework for the compensation system. Pp. 1-6 in D. Balkin and L. Gomez-Mejia, eds., *New Perspectives on Compensation.* Englewood Cliffs, N.J.: Prentice-Hall.
  1987b   Toward a contingent theory of compensation strategy. *Strategic Management Journal* 8:169-182.
  1990   Matching compensation and organizational strategies. *Strategic Management Journal* 11:153-169.
Banks, C., and Murphy, K.
  1985   Toward narrowing the research-practice gap in performance appraisal. *Personnel Psychology* 38:335-345.
Bann, C., and Johnson, J.
  1984   Federal employee attitudes toward reform: performance evaluation and merit pay. P. 79 in P. Ingraham and C. Ban, eds., *Legislating Bureaucratic Change: The Civil Service Reform Act of 1978.* Albany: N.Y.: SUNY Press.
Baron, J., Dobbin, F., and Jennings, P.
  1986   War and peace: the evolution of modern personnel administration in U.S. industry. *American Journal of Sociology* 92:350-383.
Bartlett, C., and Ghoshal, S.
  1988   Organizing for worldwide effectiveness: the transnational solution. *California Management Review* Fall:54-74.
Beer, M., Eisenstat, R., and Spector, B.
  1990   *The Critical Path: Mobilizing Human Resources for Corporate Renewal.* Cambridge, Mass.: Harvard Business School Press.
Beer, M., Spector, B., Lawrence, P., Mills, D., and Walton, R.
  1985   *Human Resource Management: A General Manager's Perspective.* New York: The Free Press.
Berg, N.
  1965   Strategic planning in conglomerate companies. *Harvard Business Review* May/June:79-92.
Berkshire, J., and Highland, R.
  1953   Forced-choice performance rating—a methodological study. *Personnel Psychology* 6:355-378.
Bernardin, H.
  1977   Behavior expectation scales versus summated scales: a fairer comparison. *Journal of Applied Psychology* 62:422-427.

Bernardin, H., and Beatty, R.
1984   *Performance Appraisal: Assessing Performance at Work.* Boston: Kent
        Press.
Bernardin, H., and Buckley, M.
1981   Strategies in rater training. *Academy of Management Review* 6:205-212.
Bernardin, H., Morgan, B., and Winne, P.
1980   The design of a personnel evaluation system for police officers. *JSAS
        Catalog of Selected Documents in Psychology* 10:1-280.
Bialek, H., Zapf, D., and McGuire, W.
1977   *Personnel Turbulence and Time Utilization in an Infantry Division.* Re-
        port #FR-WD-CA 77-11. Alexandria, Va.: Human Resources Research
        Organization.
Bjerke, D., Cleveland, J., Morrison, R., and Wilson, W.
1987   Officer Fitness Report Evaluation Study. Navy Personnel Research and
        Development Center Report, TR 88-4.
Blanz, F., and Ghiselli, E.
1972   The mixed standard scale: a new rating system. *Personnel Psychology*
        25:185-199.
Blau, P.
1955   *The Dynamics of Bureaucracy.* Chicago: University of Chicago Press.
Blinder, A., ed.
1990   *Paying for Productivity.* Washington, D.C.: Brookings Institution.
Borman, W.
1978   Exploring upper limits of reliability and validity in job performance ratings.
        Journal of Applied Psychology 63(2):135-144.
1983   Implications of personality theory and research for the rating of work
        performance in organizations. Pp. 127-172 in F. Landy, S. Zedeck, and
        J. Cleveland, eds., *Performance Measurement and Theory.* Hillsdale, N.J.:
        Erlbaum.
1987   Personal constructs, performance schemata, and "folk theories" of subordi-
        nate effectiveness: explorations in an Army officer sample. *Organizational
        Behavior and Human Decision Processes* 40:307-322.
Borreson, H.
1967   The effects of instructions and item content on three types of ratings.
        Educational and Psychological Measurement 27:855-862.
Brett, J.
1986   Commentary on procedural justice papers. Pp. 81-90 in R. Lewicki, B.
        Sheppard, and M. Bazerman, eds., *Research on Negotiation in Organizations.*
        Greenwich, Conn.: JAI Press.
Bretz, R., and Milkovich, G.
1989   Performance Appraisal in Large Organizations: Practice and Research Im-
        plications. Working paper #89-17. Center for Advanced Human Resource
        Studies, Cornell University, Ithaca, N.Y.
Brown, C.
1990   Firms' choice of pay method. *Industrial and Labor Relations Review*
        43(3):165-182.

Buchanan, B., II
 1975   Red tape and the service ethic: some unexpected differences between public
         and private managers. *Administration and Society* 6:423-438.
Bullock, R., and Lawler, E.E., III
 1984   Gainsharing: a few questions and fewer answers. *Human Resource Man-
         agement* 23:23-40.
Bureau of National Affairs
 1974   Management performance appraisal programs. *Personnel Policies Forum
         Survey No. 104*. Washington, D.C.: Bureau of National Affairs.
 1981   Wage and salary administration. *Personnel Policies Forum Survey No. 131*.
         Washington, D.C.: Bureau of National Affairs.
 1984   Productivity Improvement Programs. *Personnel Policies Forum Survey No.
         138*. Washington, D.C.: Bureau of National Affairs.
Burnett, F.
 1925   An experimental investigation into repetitive work. *Industrial Fatigue Re-
         search Board Report No. 30*. London: H.M. Stationery Office.
Burns, T., and Stalker, G.
 1961   *The Mangement of Innovation*. London: Tavistock.
Campbell, A.
 1988   Statement Before the U.S. Senate Subcommittee on Government Affairs.
         U.S. General Accounting Office, Hearings on Design of the Civil Service
         Reform Act of 1978.
Campbell, D., and Fiske, D.
 1959   Convergent and discriminant validation by the multitrait-multimethod matrix.
         Psychological Bulletin 56:81-105.
Campbell, J., and Pritchard, R.
 1976   Motivation theory in industrial and organizational psychology. Pp. 63-130 in
         M. Dunnette, ed., *Handbook of Industrial and Organizational Psychology*.
         Chicago: Rand McNally.
Campbell, J., Dunnette, M., Lawler, E., III, and Weick, K., Jr.
 1970   *Managerial Behavior, Performance, and Effectiveness*. New York: McGraw-
         Hill.
Campbell, J., Dunnette, M., Arvey, R., and Hellervik, L.
 1973   The development and evaluation of behaviorally based rating scales. *Journal
         of Applied Psychology* 57:15-22.
Campbell, J., McHenry, J., and Wise, L.
 1990   Modeling job performance in a population of jobs. *Personnel Psychology*
         43:313-333.
Carroll, S.
 1987   Business strategies and compensation systems. Pp. 343-355 in D. Balkin
         and L. Gomez, eds., *New Perspectives on Compensation*. Englewood Cliffs,
         N.J.: Prentice-Hall.
Carson, K., Sutton. C., and Corner, P.
 1990   Gender Effects in Performance Appraisal: A Meta Analysis. Unpublished
         manuscript, Arizona State University.

Cascio, W.
1987   *Costing Human Resources: The Financial Impact of Behavior in Organizations.* Boston: Kent.
Chandler, A.
1962   *Strategy and Structure: Chapters in the History of American Industrial Enterprise.* Cambridge, Mass.: MIT Press.
Christal, R.
1974   *The United States Air Force Occupational Research Project* (AFHRL-TR-73-75). Brooks Air Force Base, Tex.: Air Force Human Resources Laboratory.
Clark, C., and Primoff, E.
1979   Job elements and performance appraisal. *Management: A Magazine for Government Managers* 1:3-5.
Cleveland, J., Murphy, K., and Williams, R.
1989   Multiple uses of performance appraisal: Prevalence and correlates. *Journal of Applied Psychology* 74(1):130-135.
Cohen, R., and Greenberg, J.
1982   The justice concept in social psychology. Pp. 1-41 in J. Greenberg and R. Cohen, eds., *Equity and Justice in Social Behavior.* New York: Academic Press.
Conference Board
1977   Appraising managerial performance: current practices and future directions. *Conference Board Report No. 723.* New York: Conference Board.
1984   Pay and performance: the interaction of compensation and performance appraisal. *Conference Research Bulletin No. 155.* New York: Conference Board.
1990   Variable pay: new performance rewards. *Conference Board Research Bulletin No. 246.* New York: Conference Board.
Cook, F.
1981   When long-term incentives are not long-term incentives. *Proceedings of the American Compensation Association's Regional Conferences.* Scottsdale, Ariz.: American Compensation Association.
Cooper, W.
1981   Ubiquitous halo. *Psychological Bulletin* 90:218-244.
Cornelius, E., Hakel, M., and Sackett, P.
1979   A methodological approach to job classification for performance appraisal purposes. *Personnel Psychology* 32:283-297.
Cronbach, L.
1990   *Essentials of Psychological Testing.* New York: Harper and Row.
Deci, E.
1975   *Intrinsic Motivation.* New York: Plenum.
DeCotiis, T. A.
1977   An analysis of the external validity and applied relevance of three rating formats. *Organizational Behavior and Human Performance* 19:247-267.
Deming, E.
1986   *Out of the Crisis.* Cambridge, Mass.: Massachusetts Institute of Technology Center for Advanced Engineering.

DeNisi, A., Cafferty, T., and Meglino, B.
  1984   A cognitive model of the performance appraisal process: a model and research propositions. *Organizational Behavior and Human Performance* 21(3):358-367.

Dipboye, R., and de Pontbriand, R.
  1981   Correlates of employee reactions to performance appraisals and appraisal systems. *Journal of Applied Psychology* 66:248-251.

DiPrete, T.
  1989   *The Bureaucratic Labor Market: The Case of the Federal Civil Service.* New York: Plenum.

Doeringer, P., and Piore, M.
  1971   *Internal Labor Markets and Manpower Analysis.* Lexington, Mass.: Lexington Books.

Dornbusch, S., and Scott, W.
  1975   *Evaluation and the Exercise of Authority.* San Francisco: Jossey-Bass.

Doz, Y., and Pralahad, C.
  1981   Headquarters influence and strategic control in MNCs. *Sloan Management Review* Fall:15-29.

Dyer, L., and Schwab, D.
  1982   Personnel/human resource management research. Pp. 87-120 in T. Kochan, D. Mitchell, and L. Dyer, eds., *Industrial Relations Research in the 1970s: Review and Appraisal.* Madison, Wis.: Industrial Relations Research Association.

Dyer, L., and Theriault, R.
  1976   The determinants of pay satisfaction. *Journal of Applied Psychology* 61(5):596-604.

Dyer, L., Schwab, D., and Theriault, R.
  1976   Managerial perceptions regarding salary increase criteria. *Personnel Psychology* 29:233-242.

Edell, J., and Staelin, R.
  1983   The information processing of pictures in print advertisements. *Journal of Consumer Research* 10(June):45-61.

Ehrenberg, R., and Milkovich, G.
  1987   Compensation and firm performance. Pp. 87-122 in M. Kleiner, R. Block, M. Roomkin, and S. Salsberg, eds., *Human Resources and the Performance of the Firm.* Madison, Wis.: Industrial Relations Research Association.

Ellig, B.
  1982   *Executive Compensation: A Total Pay Perspective.* New York: McGraw-Hill.

England, P., and Dunn, D.
  1988   Evaluating work and comparable worth. *Annual Review of Sociology* 14:227-248.

Evans, P.
  1989   Organizational development in the transnational enterprise. Pp. 1-38 in R. Woodman and W. Passmore, eds., *Organizational Change and Development.* Greenwich, Conn.: JAI Press.

Fay, C., and Latham, G.
1982 Effects of training and rating scales on rating errors. *Personnel Psychology* 35:105-116.

Feild, H., and Holley, W.
1982 The relationship of performance appraisal system characteristics to verdicts in selected employment discrimination cases. *Academy of Management Journal* 25(2):392-406.

Feldman, J.
1981 Beyond attribution theory: cognitive processes in performance appraisal. *Journal of Applied Psychology* 66:127-148.
1986 Instrumentation and training for performance appraisal: a perceptual-cognitive viewpoint. In K. Rowland and G. Ferris, eds., *Research in Personnel and Human Resources Management.* Greenwich, Conn.: JAI Press.

Flanagan, J.
1954 The critical incident technique. *Psychological Bulletin* 51(4):327-358.

Flanders, L., and Utterback, D.
1985 The management excellence inventory: a tool for management development. *Public Management Forum* May-June:403-410.

Folger, R., and Konovsky, M.
1989 Effects of procedural and distributive justice on reactions to pay raise decisions. *Academy of Management Journal* 32(1):115-130.

Ford, J., Kraiger, K., and Schectman, S.
1986 Study of race effects in objective indices and subjective evaluations of performance: a meta-analysis of performance criteria. *Psychological Bulletin* 99:330-337.

Fossum, J., and Fitch, M.
1985 The effects of individual and contextual attributes on the size of recommended salary increases. *Personnel Psychology* 38:587-603.

Freeman, R., and Medoff, J.
1984 *What Do Unions Do?* New York: Basic Books.

Gaertner, K., and Gaertner, G.
1984 Performance evaluation and merit pay results in the Environmental Protection Agency and the Mine Safety and Health Administration. Pp. 87-112 in P. Ingraham and C. Ban, eds., *Legislating Bureaucratic Change.* Albany, N.Y.: SUNY Press.

Galbraith, J.
1977 *Organization Design.* Reading, Mass.: Addison-Wesley.

Galbraith, J., and Kazanjian, R.
1986 Organizing to implement strategies of diversity and globalization. *Human Resource Management* 25(1):37-54.

Gawthrop, L.
1984 *Public Sector Management Systems and Ethics.* Bloomington, Ind.: Indiana University Press.

Gerber, A.
   1988   Historical background: classification and compensation in the Federal Ser-
           vice. Unpublished staff paper, U.S. Office of Personnel Management.
Gerhart, B., and Milkovich, G.
   1990   Organizational differences in managerial compensation and financial perfor-
           mance. *Academy of Management Journal.*
Gomez-Mejia, L., Page, R., and Tornow, W.
   1982   A comparison of the practical utility of traditional, statistical, and hybrid
           job evaluation approaches. *Academy of Management Journal* 25(4)790-809.
Graham-Moore, B., and Ross, T.
   1983   *Productivity Gainsharing: How Employer Incentive Programs Can Improve
           Business Performance.* Englewood Cliffs, N.J.: Prentice-Hall.
Green, B., Wigdor, A., and Shavelson, R., eds.
   1991   *Measuring Performance in the Workplace.* Committee on Performance
           of Military Personnel, Commission on Behavioral and Social Sciences
           and Education, National Research Council. Washington, D.C.: National
           Academy Press.
Greenberg, J.
   1986a   Determinants of perceived fairness of performance evaluations. *Journal of
           Applied Psychology* 71:340-342.
   1986b   Organizational performance appraisal procedures: what makes them fair?
           Pp. 25-41 in R. Lewicki, B. Sheppard, and M. Bazerman, eds., *Research on
           Negotiation in Organizations.* Greenwich, Conn.: JAI Press.
   1987   A taxonomy of organizational justice theories. *The Academy of Management
           Review* 12(1):9-22.
   1990   Organizational justice: yesterday, today, and tomorrow. *Journal of Manage-
           ment* 16(2):399-432.
Greenberg, J., and Levanthal, G.
   1976   Equity and the use of overreward to motivate performance. *Journal of
           Personality and Social Psychology* 34:179-190.
Greene, C.
   1978   Causal connections among managers' merit pay, job satisfaction, and per-
           formance. *Journal of Applied Psychology* 58:95-100.
Greller, M., and Herold, D.
   1975   Sources of feedback. A preliminary investigation. *Organizational Behavior
           and Human Performance* 13:144-256.
Guion, R.
   1983   Comments on Hunter. Pp. 267-175 in F. Landy, S. Zedeck, and J. Cleveland,
           eds., *Performance Measurement and Theory.* Hillsdale, N.J.: Erlbaum.
Guzzo, R., and Bondy, J.
   1983   *A Guide to Worker Productivity Experiments in the United States.* Elmsford,
           N.Y.: Pergamon Press.
Guzzo, R., Jette, R., and Katzell, R.
   1985   The effects of psychologically-based intervention programs on worker pro-
           ductivity. *Personnel Psychology* 38:275-293.

Hackman, J., and Oldham, G.
   1976   Motivation through the design of work. *Organizational Behavior and Human
           Performance* 16:250-279.
   1980   *Work Redesign.* Reading, Mass.: Addison-Wesley.
Hackman, R., Lawler, E., and Porter, L.
   1977   *Perspectives on Behavior in Organizations.* New York: McGraw-Hill.
Halaby, C.
   1986   Worker attachment and workplace authority. *American Sociological Review*
           51:634-649.
Hammer, T.
   1988   New developments in profit sharing, gainsharing and employee ownership.
           In J. Campbell, ed., *Individual and Group Productivity in Organizations.*
           San Francisco: Jossey-Bass.
Hannan, M., and Freeman, J.
   1984   Structural inertia and organizational change. *American Sociological Review*
           49:149-164.
Harrigan, K.
   1988   Joint ventures and competitive strategy. *Strategic Management Journal*
           9:149-158.
Harris, M., and Schaubroeck, J.
   1988   A meta-analysis of self-supervisor, self-peer, and peer-supervisor ratings.
           Personnel Psychology 41:43-62.
Hartigan, J., and Wigdor, A., eds.
   1989   *Fairness in Employment Testing: Validity Generalization, Minority Issues,
           and the General Aptitude Test Battery.* Committee on the General Aptitude
           Test Battery, Commission on Behavioral and Social Sciences and Education,
           National Research Council. Washington, D.C.: National Academy Press.
Havemann, J.
   1990   Overhaul of federal pay urged. *The Washington Post*, March 22, 1990.
HayGroup, Inc.
   1989   *The Hay Report: Compensation and Benefits Strategies for 1990 and Beyond.*
           Philadelphia: HayGroup, Inc.
Heclo, H.
   1978   Issue networks and the executive establishment. Pp. 87-124 in A. King,
           ed., *The New American Political System.* Washington, D.C.: American
           Enterprise Institute.
Hemphill, J. K.
   1959   Job descriptions for executives. *Harvard Business Review* 37:55-67.
Heneman, H., III
   1985   Pay satisfaction. Pp. 113-115 in K. Rowland and G. Ferris, eds., *Research
           in Personnel and Human Resources Management Volume 3.* Greenwich,
           Conn.: JAI Press.
Heneman, R.
   1984   *Pay for Performance: Exploring the Merit-Pay System.* New York: Work
           in America Institute.

1990   Merit pay research. Pp. 115-139 in K. Rowland and G. Ferris, eds., *Research in Personnel and Human Resources Management Volume 8.* Greenwich, Conn.: JAI Press.

Heron, A.
1956   The effects of real-life motivation on questionnaire response. *Journal of Applied Psychology* 40:65-68.

Hewitt Associates
1985   *An Overview of Productivity Based Incentives.* Lincolnshire, Ill.: Hewitt Associates.
1989   *Compensation Trends and Practices.* Lincolnshire, Ill: Hewitt Associates.

Hills, F., Scott, K., and Markham, S.
1988   Pay System Structure as a Moderator of Pay-Performance Relationship and Employee Pay Increase Satisfaction. Paper presented at the National Academy of Management Meetings, Anaheim, Calif.

Hills, F., Scott, K., Markham, S. and Vest, M.
1987   Merit pay: just or unjust desserts. *Personnel Administrator* 32(1):53-59.

Holzbach, R.
1978   Comparisons of self- and superior ratings of managerial performance. *Journal of Applied Psychology* 63:579-588.

Hundal, P.
1969   Knowledge of performance as an incentive in repetitive industrial work. *Journal of Applied Psychology* 53:224-226.

Hunter, J.
1983   A causal analysis of cognitive ability, job knowledge, job performance, and supervisor ratings. Pp. 257-266 in F. Landy, S. Zedeck, and J. Cleveland, eds., *Performance Measurement and Theory.* Hillsdale, N.J.: Erlbaum.

Hunter, J., and Hunter, R.
1984   Validity and utility of alternate predictors of job performance. *Psychological Bulletin* 96:72-98.

Ilgen, D.
1990   Pay for performance: Motivational Issues. Working paper prepared for the Committee on Performance Appraisal for Merit Pay. National Research Council, Washington, D.C.

Ilgen, D., and Favero, J.
1985   Limits in generalization from psychological research to performance appraisal processes. *Academy of Management Review* 10:311-321.

Ilgen, D., and Feldman, J.
1983   Performance appraisal: a process focus. In L. Cummings and B. Straw, eds., *Research in Organizational Behavior (Vol. 5).* Greenwich, Conn.: JAI Press.

Ilgen, D., and Knowlton, W., Jr.
1981   Performance attributional effects on feedback from superiors. *Organizational Behavior and Human Performance* 25:441-456.

Ilgen, D., Barnes-Farrell, J., and McKellin, D.
1989   Performance Rating Accuracy. Paper presented at the 21st International Congress of Applied Psychology, Jerusalem.

Ilgen, D., Fisher, C., and Taylor, S.
  1979   Consequences of individual feedback on behavior in organizations. *Journal of Applied Psychology* 64:347-371.
Ingraham, P.
  1987   Building bridges or burning them? The president, the appointees and the bureaucracy. *Public Administration Review* September/October:425-435.
  1989   The design of civil service reform: lessons in politics and rationality. *Policy Studies Journal* Winter.
Ingraham, P., and Barrilleaux, C.
  1983   Motivating managers for retrenchment. *Public Administration Review* 43: 393-402.
Ingraham, P., and Rosenbloom, D.
  1990   The State of Merit in the Federal Government. An Occasional Paper of the National Commission on the Public Service, Washington, D.C.
Jacobs, R., Kafry, S., and Zedeck, S.
  1980   Expectations of behaviorally anchored rating scales. *Personnel Psychology* 33:595-640.
Jaques, E.
  1961   *Equitable Payment.* New York: Wiley.
Jenkins, J.
  1946   Validity for what? *Journal of Consulting Psychology* 10:93-98.
Kahn, L., and Sherer, P.
  1990   Contingent pay and managerial performance. *Industrial and Labor Relations Review* 43(3):107-120.
Kalleberg, A., and Lincoln, J.
  1988   The structure of earning inequality in the United States and Japan. *American Journal of Sociology* 94(Supplement):S121-S153.
Kanfer, R.
  1990   Motivational theory and industrial and organizational psychology. In M. Dunnette, ed., *Handbook of Industrial and Organizational Psychology.* Palo Alto, Calif.: Consulting Psychologists Press.
Katz, R.
  1974   Skills of an effective administrator. *Harvard Business Review* Sept-Oct:90-102.
Kaufman, H.
  1954   The growth of the federal personnel system. P. 106 in the American Assembly, *The Federal Government Service.* New York: Columbia University.
  1978   Reflections on administrative reorganization. Pp. 214-233 in F. Lane, ed., *Current Issues in Public Administration.* New York: St. Martin's Press.
Kavanagh, M., MacKinney, A., and Wolins, L.
  1971   Issues in managerial performance: multitrait-multimethod analyses of ratings. *Psychological Bulletin* 75:34-49.
Kerr, J.
  1985   Diversification strategies and managerial rewards: an empirical study. *Academy of Management Journal* 28(1):155-179.

Kiechel, W., III
    1989   When subordinates evaluate the boss. *Fortune* 119(13):201.
Kingstrom, P., and Bass, A.
    1981   A critical analysis of studies comparing behaviorally anchored rating scales
            (BARS) and other rating formats. *Personnel Psychology* 34:263-289.
Kopelman, R.
    1976   Organizational control system responsiveness, expectancy theory constructs,
            and work motivation: some interrelations and causal connections. *Personnel
            Psychology* 29:205-220.
    1986   Objective feedback. In E. Locke, ed., *Generalizing From Laboratory to
            Field Settings*. Lexington, Mass.: Lexington Books.
Kraiger, K., and Ford, J.
    1985   A meta-analysis of ratee race effects in performance ratings. *Journal of
            Applied Psychology* 70(1):56-65.
Kraut, A., Pedigo, P., McKenna, D., and Dunnette, M.
    1989   The role of the manager: what's really important in different management
            jobs. *The Academy of Management Executive* 3(4):286-293.
Krzystofiak, F., Newman, J., and Krefting, L.
    1982   Pay meaning, satisfaction, and size of a meaningful pay increase. *Psycho-
            logical Reports* 51:660-662.
Lamb, R., ed.
    1984   *Competitive Strategic Management*. Englewood Cliffs, N.J.: Prentice-Hall.
Landy, F., and Farr, J.
    1980   Performance rating. *Psychological Bulletin* 87(1):72-107.
    1983   *The Measurement of Work Performance*. New York: Academic Press.
Landy, F., Barnes-Farrell, J., and Cleveland, J.
    1980   Perceived fairness and accuracy of performance evaluation: a follow-up.
            Journal of Applied Psychology 65:355-356.
Landy, F., Barnes, J., and Murphy, K.
    1978   Correlates of perceived fairness and accuracy of performance evaluation.
            Journal of Applied Psychology 63:751-754.
Landy, F., Farr, J., and Jacobs, R.
    1982   Utility concepts in performance measurement. *Organizational Behavior and
            Human Performance* 30:15-40.
Latham, G.
    1988   Human Resource Training and Development. *Annual Review of Psychology*
            39:545-582.
Latham, G., and Wexley, K.
    1977   Behavioral observation scales. *Personnel Psychology* 30:255-268.
    1981   *Increasing Productivity Through Performance Appraisal*. Reading, Mass:
            Addison-Wesley.
Latham, G., Fay, C., and Saari, L.
    1979   The development of behavioral observation scales for appraising the perfor-
            mance of foremen. *Personnel Psychology* 32:299-311.
Lawler, E., III
    1971   *Pay and Organizational Effectiveness: A Psychological View*. New York:
            McGraw-Hill.

1973 *Motivation in Work Organizations.* Monterey, Calif.: Brooks/Cole.
1981 *Pay and Organization Development.* Reading, Mass.: Addison-Wesley.

Lay, C., and Jackson, D.
1969 Analysis of the generality of trait-inferential relationships. *Journal of Personality and Social Psychology* 12:12-21.

Levanthal, G., Karuza, J., and Fry, W.
1980 Beyond fairness: a theory of allocation preferences. Pp. 167-218 in G. Mikula, ed., *Justice and Social Interaction.* New York: Springer-Verlag.

Livernash, R.
1957 The internal wage structure. Pp. 143-172 in G. Taylor and F. Pierson, eds., *New Concepts in Wage Determination.* New York: McGraw-Hill.

Locke, E.
1968 Toward a theory of task motivation and incentives. *Organizational Behavior and Human Performance* 3:157-189.

Locke, E., Cartledge, N., and Knerr, C.
1970 Studies of the relationship between satisfaction, goal setting, and performance. *Organizational Behavior and Human Performance* 5:135-158.

Locke, E., Shaw, K., Saari, L., and Latham, G.
1981 Goal setting and task performance, 1969-1980. *Psychological Bulletin* 40:125-152.

Longenecker, C.
1989 Truth or consequences: politics and performance appraisals. *Business Horizons* November:1-7.

Longenecker, C., and Gioia, D.
1988 Neglected at the top: executives talk about executive appraisal. *Sloan Management Review* Winter:41-47.

Longenecker, C., Sims, H., and Gioia, D.
1987 Behind the mask: the politics of employee appraisal. *Academy of Management Executive* 1:183-193.

Mahoney, T.
1979 *Compensation and Reward Perspectives.* Homewood, Ill.: Richard D. Irwin.

March, J.
1981 Decisions in organizations and theories of choice. Pp. 205-244 in A. Van de Ven and W. Joyce, eds., *Perspective on Organization Design and Behavior.* New York: Wiley.

March, J., and March, J.
1978 Performance sampling in social matches. *Administrative Science Quarterly* 23:434-453.

March, J., and Simon, H.
1958 *Organizations.* New York: Wiley.

McCormick, E.
1976 Job and task analysis. In M. Dunnette, ed., *Handbook of Industrial and Organizational Psychology.* Chicago: Rand McNally.
1979 *Job Analysis: Methods and Applications.* New York: Amacon.

McCormick, E., Jeanneret, P., and Mecham, R.
1972 A study of job characteristics and job dimensions as based on the position analysis questionnaire (PAQ). *Journal of Applied Psychology* 56:247-267.

McEvoy, G., and Cascio, W.
  1988   Cumulative evidence of the relationship between employee age and job
         performance. *Journal of Applied Psychology* 74:11-17.
McIntyre, R., Smith, D., and Hassett, C.
  1984   Accuracy of performance ratings as affected by rater training and perceived
         purpose of rating. *Journal of Applied Psychology* 69:147-156.
Merit Systems Protection Board
  1988   *Toward Effective Performance Management in the Federal Government.*
         Washington, D.C.: U.S. Government Printing Office.
  1989   *Government Documents and Agency Reports: Personnel Management Sim-
         plification Efforts in the Federal Government.* Washington, D.C.: U.S.
         Government Printing Office.
  1990   *Working for America: A Federal Employee Survey.* Washington, D.C.: U.S.
         Government Printing Office.
Metzger, B.
  1978   *Profit Sharing in 38 Large Companies.* Evanston, Ill.: Profit Sharing
         Research Foundation.
Meyer, H.
  1980   Self-appraisal of job performance. *Personnel Psychology* 33:291-295.
Meyer, H., Kay, E., and French, J.
  1965   Split roles in performance appraisal. *Harvard Business Review* 43:123-129.
Meyer, J., and Rowan, B.
  1977   Institutional organizations: formal structures as myth and ceremony. *Ameri-
         can Journal of Sociology* 83:340-363.
Miceli, M., and Lane, M.
  1990   Antecedents of pay satisfaction: a review and extension. In K. Rowland and
         G. Ferris, eds., *Research in Personnel and Human Resources Management
         (Vol. 9).* Greenwich, Conn.: JAI Press.
Miles, R., and Snow, C.
  1978   *Organizational Strategy, Structure, and Process.* New York: McGraw-Hill.
  1983   Designing strategic human resource systems. *Organization Dynamics.*
Milkovich, G.
  1986   Gainsharing in managing and compensating human resources. Presented at
         Conference on Participation and Gainsharing Systems. Johnson Foundation
         Wingspread International Conference Center.
Milkovich, G., and Newman, J.
  1990   *Compensation.* Boston: Richard Irwin.
Mintzberg, H.
  1973   *The Nature of Managerial Work.* New York: Harper and Row.
  1975   The manager's job: folklore and fact. *Harvard Business Review* July-
         August:49-61.
Mitchell, D.
  1985   Shifting norms in wage determination. *Brookings Papers on Economic
         Activites 2.* Washington, D.C.: Brookings Institution.
Mitchell, D., and Broderick, R.
  1991   Flexible pay systems in the American context: history, policy, research, and

implications. In D. Lewin, D. Lipski, and D. Sockell, eds., *Advances in Industrial and Labor Relations*. Greenwich, Conn.: JAI Press.

Mitchell, D., Lewin, D., and Lawler, E.E. III
1990   Alternative pay systems, firm performance, and productivity. Pp. 15-94 in A. Blinder, ed., *Paying for Productivity*. Washington, D.C.: Brookings Institution.

Mohrman, A., and Lawler, E.
1983   Motivation and performance appraisal behavior. In F. Landy, S. Zedeck, and J. Cleveland, eds., *Performance Measurement and Theory*. Hillsdale, N.J.: Erlbaum.

Mowday, R.
1987   Equity theory predictions of behavior in organization. Pp. 89-110 in R. Stears and L. Porter, eds., *Motivation and Work Behavior (4th Edition)*. New York: McGraw-Hill.

Murphy, K.
1982   Difficulties in the statistical control of halo. *Journal of Applied Psychology* 67:161-164.

Murphy, K., and Cleveland, J.
1991   *Performance Appraisal: An Organizational Perspective*. Boston: Allyn and Bacon.

Murphy, K., and Constans, J.
1988   Psychological issues in scale format research: behavioral anchors as a source of bias rating. In R. Cardy, S. Peiffer, and J. Newman, eds., *Advances in Information Processing in Organizations (Vol. 3)*. Greenwich, Conn.: JAI Press.

Murphy, K., and Jako, B.
1989   Under what conditions are observed intercorrelations greater than or smaller than true intercorrelations. *Journal of Applied Psychology* 74:827-830.

Murphy, K., Balzer, W., Kellam, K., and Armstrong, J.
1984   Effects of the purpose of rating on accuracy in observing teacher behavior and evaluating teaching performance. *Journal of Educational Psychology* 76:45-54.

Murphy, K., Herr, B., Lockhart, M., and Maguire, E.
1986   Evaluating the performance of paper people. *Journal of Applied Psychology* 72:573-579.

Murphy, K., Martin, C., and Garcia, M.
1982   Do behavioral observation scales measure observation? *Journal of Applied Psychology* 67:562-167.

Napier, N., and Latham, G.
1986   Outcome expectancies of people who conduct performance appraisals. *Personnel Psychology* 39(4):827-837.

Nathan, B., and Alexander, R.
1988   A comparison of criteria for test validation: a meta-analytic investigation. *Personnel Psychology* 41:517-535.

Nathan, B., and Lord, R.
1983   Cognitive categorization and dimensional schemata: a process application

to the study of halo in performance ratings. *Journal of Applied Psychology* 68:102-114.

Nathan, R.
1983   *The Administrative Presidency.* New York: Wiley.

National Academy of Public Administration
1983   *Revitalizing Federal Management: Managers and Their Overburdened Systems.* Washington, D.C.: National Academy of Public Administration.

National Commission on the Public Service
1990   *Leadership for America: Rebuilding the Public Service.* Report of the National Commission on the Public Service. Lexington, Mass.: Lexington Books.

National Research Council
1990   *Recruitment, Retention, and Utilization of Federal Scientists and Engineers.* Office of Scientific and Engineering Personnel, National Research Council. Washington, D.C.: National Academy Press.

Newland, C.
1983   A mid-term appraisal of the Reagan presidency: limited government and public administration. *Public Administration Review* January/February:16-23.

Nigro, L.
1982   CSRA performance appraisals and merit pay: growing uncertainty in the federal workforce. *Public Administration Review* July/August:371-375.

Nunnally, J.
1967   *Psychometric Theory, Second Edition.* New York: McGraw-Hill.

O'Dell, C.
1981   *Gainsharing, Involvement, Incentives, and Productivity.* New York: American Management Association.
1987   *People, Performance and Pay.* Houston, Tex.: American Productivity Center.

Padgett, M.
1988   Performance Appraisal in Context: Motivational Influences on Performance Ratings. Unpublished Ph.D. dissertation, Department of Psychology, Michigan State University.

Pearce, J., and Perry, J.
1983   Federal merit pay: a longitudinal analysis. *Public Administration Review* 43:315-325.

Pearce, J., and Porter, L.
1986   Employee responses to formal performance appraisal feedback. *Journal of Applied Psychology* 71(2):211-218.

Pearce, J., Stevenson, W., and Perry, J.
1985   Managerial compensation based on organizational performance: a time series analysis of the effects of merit pay. *Academy of Management Journal* 28:261-278.

Perry, J., and Petrakis, B.
1987   Can Merit Pay Improve Performance in Government? Paper presented at the annual research conference of the Association for Public Policy Analysis and Management, October, 1987.

Perry, J., and Porter, L.
  1982   Factors affecting the context for motivation in public organizations. *Academy of Management Review* 7(1):89-98.
Perry, J., and Rainey, H.
  1988   The public-private distinction in organization theory: a critique and research strategy. *The Academy of Management Review* 13(2):182-201.
Perry, J., and Wise, L.
  1990   The motivational bases of public service. *Public Administration Review* 50:367-373.
Perry, J., Petrakis, B., and Miller, T.
  1989   Federal merit pay, round II: an analysis of the performance management and recognition system. *Public Administration Review* January/February:29-37.
Personnel Psychology
  1990   Special issue on the Army Selection and Classification Project (Project A). Vol. 43.
Pfeffer, J., and Baron, J.
  1988   Taking the workers back out: recent trends in the structuring of employment. Pp. 257-303 in B. Staw and L. Cummings, eds., *Research in Organizational Behavior, Volume 10*. Greenwich, Conn: JAI Press.
Pfiffner, J.
  1988   *Hitting the Ground Running: The Strategic Presidency*. Chicago: Dorsey Press.
Pinder, C.
  1984   *Work Motivation*. Glenview, Ill.: Scott Foresman.
Pitts, R.
  1976   Diversification strategies and organizational policies of large, diversified firms. *Journal of Economics and Business* 8:181-188.
Porter, M.
  1985   *Competitive Advantage*. New York: Free Press.
Pritchard, R., and Curts, M.
  1973   The influence of goal setting and financial incentives on task performance. *Organizational Behavior and Human Performance* 10:175-183.
Professional Managers Association
  1989   Legislation introduced to reform PMRS. *PMA Update* August:1-5.
Profit Sharing Council of America
  1984   *Profit Sharing: Philosophy, Practices, and Benefits to Society*. Evanston, Ill: Profit Sharing Council.
Rainey, H.
  1990   Public management: recent developments and current prospects. Pp. 157-184 in N. Lynn and A. Wildavsky, eds., *Public Administration: The State of the Discipline*. Chatham, N.J.: Chatham House.
Reilly, C., and Balzer, W.
  1988   Effect of Purpose on Observation and Evaluation of Teaching Performance. Unpublished manuscript, Bowling Green University.
Roethlisberger, F., and Dickson, W.
  1939   *Management and the Worker*. Cambridge, Mass.: Harvard University Press.

Rosen, C.
1986   *Employee Ownership in America.* Lexington, Mass.: Lexington Books.

Rynes, S., and Barber, A.
1990   Applicant attraction strategies: an organizational perspective. *The Academy of Management Review* 15(2):286-310.

Salancik, G.
1977   Commitment is too easy! *Organizational Dynamics* 6(1):62-80.

Salschieder, J.
1981   Divising pay strategies for diversified companies. *Compensation Review* Second Quarter:15-24.

Salter, M.
1973   Tailor incentive compensation to strategy. *Harvard Business Review* 51:181-188.

Schendel, D., and Hofer, C., eds.
1979   *Strategic Management: A New View of Business Policy and Planning.* Boston: Little, Brown.

Schmidt, F., and Hunter, J.
1977   Development of a general solution to the problem of validity generalization. *Journal of Applied Psychology* 62:529-540.

Schmitt, N., Gooding, R., Noe, R., and Kirsch, M.
1984   Meta-analyses of validity studies published between 1964 and 1982 and the investigation of study characteristics. *Personnel Psychology* 37:407-422.

Scholtes, P.
1987   *An Elaboration on Deming's Teachings on Performance Appraisal.* Madison, Wis.: Joiner Associates.

Schuster, M.
1984a   The Scanlon Plan: a longitudinal analysis. *Industrial and Labor Relations Review* 36:415-430.
1984b   *Union-Management Cooperation: Structure, Process, and Impact.* Kalamazoo, Mich.: W. E. Upjohn Institute for Employment Research.

Schwab, D., and Olsen, C.
1990   Merit pay practices: implications for pay-performance relationships. *Industrial and Labor Relations Review* 43:237-255.

Scott, W.
1981   *Organizations: Rational, Natural, and Open Systems.* Englewood Cliffs, N.J.: Prentice-Hall.

Sharon, A., and Bartlett, C.
1969   Effect of instructional conditions in producing leniency on two types of rating scales. *Personnel Psychology* 22:252-263.

Shore, L., and Thornton, G.
1986   Effects of gender on self- and supervisory ratings. *Academy of Management Journal* 29:115-129.

Skrowonek, S.
1982   *Building a New American State: The Expansion of National Administrative Capacities, 1877-1920.* New York: Cambridge University Press.

Smith, E.
  1982   Strategic business planning and human resources: part I. *Personnel Journal*
          August:606-609.
Smith, P., and Kendell, L.
  1963   Retranslation of expectations: an approach to the construction of unambigu-
          ous anchors for rating scales. *Journal of Applied Psychology* 7:149-155.
Spenner, K.
  1990   The Measurement of Skill: Strategies and Dilemma with Special Reference
          to the *Dictionary of Occupational Titles*. Paper presented at a conference,
          "Changing Occupational Skill Requirements: Gathering and Assessing the
          Evidence," Taubman Center for Public Policy, Brown University.
Sticker, L., Jacobs, C., and Kogan, N.
  1974   Trait interrelations in implicit personality theories and questionnaire data.
          Journal of Personality and Social Psychology 30:198-207.
Stone, K.
  1974   The origins of job structure in the steel industry. *Review of Radical Political
          Economics* 6(Summer):113-173.
Taylor, E., and Wherry, R.
  1951   A study of leniency in two rating systems. *Personnel Psychology* 4:39-47.
Taylor, F.
  1911   *The Principles of Scientific Management*. New York: Harper and Row.
Terborg, J., and Miller, H.
  1978   Motivation, behavior, and performance: a closer examination of goal setting
          and monetary incentives. *Journal of Applied Psychology* 63:29-39.
Thornton, G.
  1980   Psychometric properties of self-appraisals of job performance. *Personnel
          Psychology* 33:263-271.
Thornton, G., and Zorich, S.
  1980   Training to improve observer accuracy. *Journal of Applied Psychology*
          65:351-354.
Tolbert, P., and Zucker, L.
  1983   Institutional sources of change in the formal structure of organizations: the
          diffusion of civil service reform. *Administrative Science Quarterly* 28:22-39.
TPF&C/Towers Perrin
  1990   *Achieving Results Through Sharing: Group Incentive Program Survey Re-
          port*. New York: TPF&C/Towers Perrin.
U.S. Civil Service Commission
  1974   *Biography of an Ideal*. Washington, D.C.: U.S. Government Printing Office.
U.S. General Accounting Office
  1981   *Productivity Sharing Programs: Can They Contribute to Productivity Im-
          provement?* Washington, D.C.: U.S. Government Printing Office.
  1984   *A Two Year Appraisal of Merit Pay in Three Agencies*. Washington, D.C.:
          U.S. Government Printing Office.
  1987   *Status of Personnel Research and Demonstration Programs*. Washington,
          D.C.: U.S. Government Printing Office.
  1988   *The Senior Executive Service: Executives' Perspectives on Their Federal
          Service*. Washington, D.C.: U.S. Government Printing Office.

U.S. Office of Personnel Management
   1981   *Merit Pay Systems Design*. Washington, D.C.: U.S. Office of Personnel
           Management.
   1988a   *Performance Management and Recognition System: FY 1986 Performance
           Cycle*. Washington, D.C.: U.S. Office of Personnel Management.
   1988b   *Turnover in the Navy Demonstration Laboratories, 1980-1985*. Washington,
           D.C.: U.S. Office of Personnel Management.
Vancil, R., and Buddrus, L.
   1979   *Decentralization: Managerial Ambiguity by Design*. Homewood, Ill.: Dow-
           Jones/Irwin.
Van Riper, P.
   1958   *History of the United States Civil Service*. Evanston, Ill.: Row, Peterson.
Vaughn, Robert
   1989   The United States Merit Systems Protection Board and the Office of Special
           Counsel. *Policy Studies Journal* Winter.
Vroom, V.
   1964   *Work and Motivation*. New York: Wiley.
Wagner, J., Rubin, P. and Callahan, T.
   1988   Incentive payment and nonmanagerial productivity: an interrupted time
           series analysis of magnitude and trend. *Organization Behavior and Human
           Decision Processes* 42:47-74.
Wainer, H., and Braun, H., eds.
   1988   *Test Validity*. Hillsdale, N.J.: Erlbaum.
Waldo, D., ed.
   1971   *Public Management in a Time of Turbulence*. New York: Chandler.
Walker, L., Lind, E., and Thibaut, J.
   1979   The relation between procedural justice and distributive justice. *Virginia
           Law Review* 65:1410-1420.
Wallace, M.
   1990   *Rewards and Renewal: America's Search for Competitive Advantage Through
           Alternative Pay Strategies*. Scottsdale, Ariz.: American Compensation
           Association.
Walton, R.
   1979   *Work Innovations in the United States*. Boston: Division of Research,
           Harvard Business Review.
   1984   *From Control to Commitment: Transforming Workforce Management in the
           United States*. Boston: Divison of Research, Harvard Business Review.
Weiner, N.
   1980   Determinants of the behavioral consequences of pay satisfaction: a compar-
           ison of two models. *Personnel Psychology* 33:741-757.
Weitzman, M.
   1984   *The Share Economy: Conquering Stagflation*. Cambridge, Mass.: Harvard
           University Press.
Whyte, W.
   1955   *Money and Motivation*. New York: Harper and Row.

William Mercer, Inc.
1983   *Employer Attitudes Toward Compensation Change and Corporate Values.* New York: William M. Mercer, Inc.

Williams, K., Wickert, P., and Peters, R.
1985   Appraisal salience: effects of instructions to subjectively organize information. In *Proceedings of the Southern Management Association Meetings*, Orlando, Fla.

Wilmerding, L.
1935   *Government by Merit.* New York: McGraw-Hill.

Wyatt, S.
1934   Incentives in repetitive work: a practical experiment in a factory. *Industrial Health Research Board Report No. 69.* London: H.M. Stationery Office.

Wyatt Company
1987   *The 1987 Wyatt Performance Management Survey.* Chicago: Wyatt Company.
1989a   *The 1989 Survey of Locality Pay Practices in Large U.S. Corporations.* Philadelphia: Wyatt Company.
1989b   Results of the 1989 Wyatt survey: getting your hands around performance management. *The Wyatt Communicator* Fourth Quarter:4-18.

Zammuto, R., London, M., and Rowland, K.
1981   Organization and rater differences in performance appraisal. *Personnel Psychology* 35:643-658.

Zedeck, S., and Cascio, W.
1982   Performance appraisal decisions as a function of rater training and purpose of appraisal. *Journal of Applied Psychology* 67(6):752-758.

Appendixes

A

Survey Descriptions

A brief description of each survey used in the committee's review of private-sector performance appraisal, merit pay, and variable pay plan practices is presented below. Each description includes a complete survey reference.

The surveys are nearly all proprietary; they are not based on scientific sampling methods and report no sampling frame, error rates, or confidence intervals.

The American Compensation Association

1987 Report on the 1987 Survey of Salary Management Practices. Scottsdale, Ariz.: The American Compensation Association.

No. of Organizations: 1,395
Type of Organizations: 33% manufacturing; 40% services; 27% utilities/other
Size (employees): 31% < 1,000; 69% ≥ 1,000
Respondents: Top personnel officers
Response rate: 24%

Bretz, R., and Milkovich, G.

1989 Performance appraisal in large organizations: practice and research applications. Working Paper #89-17. Center for Advanced Human Resource Studies Cornell University, Ithaca, New York.

No. of Organizations: 63
Type of Organizations: Manufacturing
Size (employees): Mean: Exempt = 20,816; Nonexempt = 31,407
Respondents: Top personnel and compensation executives
Response rate: 70%

191

The Bureau of National Affairs
    1974   Management performance appraisal programs. Personnel Policies
            Forum Survey No. 104. Washington, D.C.: The Bureau of National
            Affairs.
No. of Organizations: 139
Type of Organizations: 50% manufacturing; 25% nonmanufacturing; 25%
                              nonprofit/government
Size (employees): 40% < 1,000; 60% ≥ 1,000
Respondents: Top personnel officers
Response rate: 60%

The Bureau of National Affairs
    1981   Wage and salary administration. Personnel Policies Forum Survey
            No. 131. Washington, D.C.: The Bureau of National Affairs.
No. of Organizations: 183
Type of Organizations: 49% manufacturing; 31% nonmanufacturing; 20%
                              nonprofit/government
Size (employees): 46% < 1,000; 54% ≥ 1,000
Respondents: Top personnel officers
Response rate: 60%

The Bureau of National Affairs
    1984   Productivity Improvement Programs. Personnel Policies Forum
            Survey No. 138. Washington, D.C.: The Bureau of National
            Affairs.
No. of Organizations: 195
Type of Organizations: 45% manufacturing; 27% nonmanufacturing; 28%
                              nonprofit/government
Size (employees): 53% < 1,000; 47% ≥ 1,000
Respondents: Top personnel officers
Response rate: 65%

(The Personnel Policies Forum surveys vary somewhat in their geographic
coverage, but typically try to cover major geographic regions; in the latest
survey we used, the responding 31 percent of the responding organizations
were headquartered in the South, 27 percent in the North Central states, 23
percent in the West, and 19 percent in the Northeast.)

The Conference Board
    1976   Compensating employees: lessons of the 1970s. Conference Board
            Report No. 707. New York: The Conference Board.
No. of Organizations: 493
Type of Organizations: 54% manufacturing; 46% services/retail & wholesale

Size (employees): 23% < 1,000; 77% > 1,000
Respondents: Top compensation executives
Response rate: Not reported

The Conference Board
> 1977 Appraising managerial performance: current practices and future directions. Conference Board Report No. 723. New York: The Conference Board.

No. of Organizations: 293
Type of Organizations: 41% manufacturing; 59% services/retail & wholesale
Size (employees): 29% < 1,000; 71% > 1,000
Respondents: Top personnel executives
Response rate: Not reported

The Conference Board
> 1984 Pay and performance: the interaction of compensation and performance appraisal. Conference Research Bulletin No. 155. New York: The Conference Board.

No. of Organizations: 557
Type of Organizations: 54% manufacturing; 46% services
Size (employees): Median: 9,600 manufacturing; 2,130 services
Respondents: Top compensation executives
Response rate: Not reported

The Conference Board
> 1990 Variable pay: new performance rewards. Conference Board Research Bulletin No. 246. New York: The Conference Board.

No. of Organizations: 435
Type of Organizations: 43% manufacturing; 57% services/retail & wholesale
Size (sales): Only companies with sales of > $100 million
Respondents: Top compensation executives
Response rate: 16%

HayGroup, Inc.
> 1989 Compensation and benefits strategies for 1990 and beyond. *The Hay Report.* Philadelphia: HayGroup, Inc.

No. of Organizations: 1,098
Type of Organizations: 78.1% industrial; 21.9% financial
Size (employees): Not reported
Respondents: Top compensation managers
Response rate: Not reported
(This report is a compilation of several HayGroup surveys; we used the results from The Hay Compensation Report, 1989.)

Hewitt Associates

    1989   Compensation Trends and Practices Survey, 1989. Lincolnshire, Ill:
           Hewitt Associates.

No. of Organizations: 705
Type of Organizations: 33% manufacturing; 67% services
Size (employees): 33% < 1,000; 67% ≥ 1,000
Respondents: Compensation managers
Response rate: Not reported

Committee on Performance Appraisal for Merit Pay, National Research Council

    1990   The committee solicited additional information on performance ap-
           praisal from 28 Conference Board member firms. The respondents
           represented all major industrial sectors and are generally considered
           leading firms in human resource management. A draft summary of
           the responses of these firms is available through the committee's
           staff files.

O'Dell, C.

    1987   People, Performance, and Pay: A Full Report on the American
           Productivity Center/American Compensation Association National
           Survey of Non-Traditional Reward and Human Resource Practices.
           Houston: American Productivity Center.

No. of Organizations: 1,598 (some multiple units of firm)
Type of Organizations: 46% goods; 46% services; 8% government
Size (employees): Not reported
Respondents: 83% personnel; 17% other managers
Response rate: 36%

TPF&C/Towers Perrin

    1990   Achieving Results Through Sharing: Group Incentive Program
           Survey Report. New York: TPF&C/Towers Perrin.

No. of Organizations: 144 companies (177 variable plans)
Type of Organizations: 77% manufacturing; 23% services and retail/wholesale
Size (employees): Median = 2,600; Range = 26 to 300,000
         (sales): Median = $500 million
Respondents: Variable plan designers
Response rate: Not reported

U.S. General Accounting Office

    1981   Productivity Improvement Programs: Can They Contribute to Pro-
           ductivity Improvement? AMFD-81-22. Washington, D.C.: U.S.
           Government Printing Office.

No. of Organizations: 54
Type of Organizations: 93% manufacturing; 7% services and retail/wholesale
Size (employees): Range from 100 to 100,000
Respondents: Reported only as "officials" of firms
Response rate: 56%

Wallace, M.
   1990   Rewards and Renewal: America's Search for Competitive Advantage Through Alternative Pay Strategies. Scottsdale, Ariz.: The American Compensation Association.

No. of Organizations: 46
Type of Organizations: 83% manufacturing; 17% services/utilities
Size (employees): Mean = 19,362; Range = 55 to 90,000
Respondents: Wallace conducted case studies; interviewed key executives, managers, and employees
Response rate: Not applicable

The Wyatt Company
   1989   Results of the 1989 Wyatt survey: getting your hands around performance management. Pp. 4-18 in *The Wyatt Communicator* Fourth Quarter, 1989.

No. of Organizations: 3,052
Type of Organizations: 30% manufacturing; 40% services; 5% utilities/transportation/oil; 6% retail/wholesale; 19% government/nonprofit/other
Size (employees): 65% < 1,000; 35% $\geq$ 1,000 (25% > 10,000)
Respondents: 93% senior and middle personnel managers
Response rate: Not reported
This survey has a broad geographic representation with 24 percent in
the Northeast, 20 percent in the Southeast; 21 percent in the Great Lakes; and
15 percent in the Pacific states (north and south).

The Wyatt Company
   1989   The 1989 Survey of Locality Pay Practices in Large U.S. Corporations. Philadelphia: The Wyatt Company.

No. of Organizations: 80
Type Organizations: 44% manufacturing; 19% services; 37% utilities/other
Size (employees): 67% $\leq$ 50,000; 33% > 50,000
Respondents: Top compensation managers
Response rate: Not reported

The Wyatt Company

    1987   The 1987 Wyatt Performance Management Survey. Chicago: The
           Wyatt Company.

No. of Organizations: 805

Type Organizations: 35% manufacturing; 40% services; 25% other

Size (employees): 20% ≤ 1,000; 33% 1,000–5,000; 20% > 5,000

Respondents: Personnel managers

Response rate: Not reported

B

Biographical Sketches

George T. Milkovich (Chair) is M.P. Catherwood professor in human resource management at the Center for Advanced Human Resource Studies in the School of Industrial and Labor Relations, Cornell University. He has authored over 100 publications dealing with a wide range of issues related to managing human resources. He serves as a consultant to major international corporations, consulting firms, and government agencies. Prior to obtaining a Ph.D. at the University of Minnesota, he was employed by Exxon and Honeywell in human resource management positions. He has also served on the board of editors of eight research journals. He has coauthored several books, including two leading textbooks: *Compensation* (third edition) and *Human Resource Management* (sixth edition).

James N. Baron is professor of organizational behavior, Business School Trust faculty fellow for 1990–1991 in the Graduate School of Business, and professor of sociology at Stanford University. He teaches and does research in the areas of complex organizations, human resource management, labor market and employment policy, and social inequality. His research has appeared in such journals as the *American Sociological Review,* the *American Journal of Sociology, Administrative Science Quarterly,* and *American Economic Review.* He has conducted studies of gender segregation and pay equity for the National Research Council. He has a B.A. from Reed College, an M.S. from the University of Wisconsin, and a Ph.D. from the University of California at Santa Barbara, all in sociology.

197

Michael Beer is professor of business administration at the Harvard Business School, where he teaches and does research in the area of human resource management, organizational effectiveness, and organizational change. He has a Ph.D. in psychology from Ohio State University. His most recent book, *The Critical Path to Corporate Renewal*, reports on a study of corporations attempting to revitalize themselves. He serves on the editorial boards of several journals, is a consultant to a number of Fortune 500 companies, and has served on the board of governors of the Academy of Management. Prior to joining the faculty at Harvard in 1975, Beer was director of organizational research and development at Corning Glass Works, where he led the company's efforts to innovate in the organization and management of human resources.

Renae F. Broderick is currently a senior research associate at the Center for Advanced Human Resources Studies in the School of Industrial and Labor Relations at Cornell University. Previously she was a senior compensation consultant for The Wyatt Company, an assistant professor at the Anderson Graduate School of Management, University of California at Los Angeles, and on the corporate personnel policy and planning staff at General Motors Corporation. Her work experience has been in compensation and personnel planning, and her research interests center on the strategic use of compensation and other personnel systems in organizations and on international personnel issues. She has a B.A. in psychology from Macalester College, an M.A. from the University of Minnesota, and a Ph.D. from Cornell, in human resources/industrial relations.

Charles C. Brown is professor of economics at the University of Michigan and program director at the Institute for Social Research. His research interests include a range of empirical issues regarding the workings of labor markets. In the past few years, he has been studying firms' choice of method of pay, the relationship between soldiers' performance and their propensity to reenlist in the Army, and differences in compensation and employment policies between large and small employers. His work has appeared in the *American Economic Review*, *Journal of Political Economy*, *Quarterly Journal of Economics*, *Journal of Human Resources*, and *Industrial and Labor Relations Review*. His book called *Employers Large and Small* (with James Medoff and Jay Hamilton) has recently been published by Harvard University Press. He has a Ph.D. in economics from Harvard University.

Thelma Crivens is assistant professor in the School of Industrial and Labor Relations at Cornell University. She received a master's degree in industrial and labor relations from Michigan State University and a law degree from George Washington University. Crivens teaches labor law relating to the federal and private sectors and employment discrimination. Her areas of research are in labor law and employment discrimination.

Charles E. Fiero is co-chairman of MLR Enterprises, Inc., a communications holding company with investments in newspapers and magazines. Prior to the formation of MLR Enterprises, he was chairman of the Hay Group, a worldwide management consulting company specializing in compensation and human resource management. Fiero's professional background is in finance, having spent 25 years with the Chase Manhattan Bank, most recently as executive vice president.

Daniel R. Ilgen is the John A. Hannah professor of organizational behavior in the departments of psychology and of management at Michigan State University. His research has addressed issues of leadership, motivation, and the process of appraising performance. With respect to the latter, his primary concerns are with factors that affect the acquisition, memory, and retrieval of information about the performance of others. He has served as the president of the Society of Industrial and Organizational Psychology, a division of the American Psychological Association. He has served, or is serving, on a number of editorial boards, including the *Academy of Management Review*, the *Journal of Applied Psychology*, *Motivation and Emotion*, and *Organizational Behavior and Human Decision Processes*. He received a B.S. degree from Iowa State University and M.A. and Ph.D. degrees in psychology from the University of Illinois.

Patricia W. Ingraham is associate professor and director of the Master's Program in Public Policy and Administration at the State University of New York at Binghamton. She is coeditor of *Legislating Bureaucratic Change: The Civil Service Reform Act of 1978* and *The American Public Service: An Agenda for Excellence*, and has published extensively on the American federal bureaucracy. She has an M.A. from Michigan State University and a Ph.D. from the State University of New York at Binghamton.

Anne S. Mavor is associate study director of the Committee on Performance Appraisal for Merit Pay. Trained as an experimental psychologist, her current interests include performance measurement, information processing, and decision making. Prior to joining the National Research Council she spent several years as a consultant in the behavioral and social sciences working in the areas of information system design, training, and program evaluation.

William A. Morrill is a research executive at Mathtech, Inc., with more than 20 years of prior service in the federal government in both senior career and appointive positions. He has focused on the public policy issues underlying this report from leadership positions in the Council for Excellence in Government and the National Academy of Public Administration. He has and continues to serve the National Research Council in a variety of roles, currently as a member of the Committee on National Statistics and a recent appointee to the Commission on Behavioral and Social Sciences and Education.

Kevin R. Murphy is professor of psychology at the Colorado State University. He is a fellow of the American Psychological Association and of the Society for Industrial and Organizational Psychology and is a member of the editorial boards of the *Journal of Applied Psychology, Personnel Psychology,* and *Human Performance.* He has published extensively in the areas of performance appraisal, human judgment and decision making, and psychological measurement and is coauthor (with Jeanette N. Cleveland) of *Performance Appraisal: An Organizational Perspective* and (with Charles O. Davidshofer) *Psychological Testing: Principles and Applications* and coeditor (with Frank E. Saal) of *Psychology in Organizations: Integrating Science and Practice.* He has a B.A. in psychology from Siena College, an M.S. from Rensselaer Polytechnic Institute, and a Ph.D. from Pennsylvania State Unviersity, both in industrial/organizational psychology.

James Perry is professor of public and environmental affairs in the School of Public and Environmental Affairs at Indiana University, Bloomington. He has a B.A. from the University of Chicago, and M.P.A. and Ph.D. degrees from the Maxwell School at Syracuse University, in public administration. He is past president of the Section on Personnel Administration and Labor Relations of the American Society for Public Administration and past chair of the Public Sector Division, Academy of Management. His research focuses on public management and public personnel issues. He has written numerous articles and books, including *Technological Innovation in American Local Government* (with K.L. Kraemer), *Labor-Management Relations and Public Agency Effectiveness* (with H.A. Angle), and *Public Management: Public and Private Perspectives* (with K.L. Kraemer).

Walter H. Read is the director of corporate compensation and benefits for the IBM Corporation. In his current position, he has worldwide responsibility for establishing the strategic direction and policy for compensation, benefits, international assignments, human resource information systems, and performance management systems. He is an alumnus of the Stanford Business School and is a past chairman of The Conference Board on Compensation.

Alexandra K. Wigdor, study director of the Committee on Performance Appraisal for Merit Pay, is director of the Division on Education, Training, and Employment in the social sciences commission of the National Research Council. Her previous work as an NRC staff officer has included a study of the General Aptitude Test Battery (1989), a series of studies of job performance in the military, and the 1982 study, coedited with Wendell R. Garner, *Ability Testing: Uses, Consequence, and Controversies.* Trained as a historian, her research interests now include human performance assessment, the legal and social dimensions of psychological testing, and the development of government policy on testing and selection.

Index

W